SELF AND SOCIAL CONTEXT

RAY HOLLAND

Department of Sociology and Psychology
Chelsea College, University of London

M

First published 1977 by
THE MACMILLAN PRESS LTD
London and Basingstoke
Associated companies in Delhi Dublin
Hong Kong Johannesburg Lagos Melbourne
New York Singapore and Tokyo

Typeset, printed and bound in Great Britain by
REDWOOD BURN LIMITED
Trowbridge & Esher

British Library Cataloguing in Publication Data

Holland, Ray
    Self and social context.
    1. Personality
    I. Title
    301.11'01   HM299
    ISBN 0-333-19811-5
    ISBN 0-333-19812-3 Pbk

To Sue, Zed and Zoe

Contents

Preface

This book is an attempt to follow a single theme entailing critical reading into the territories in and between several disciplines in the human sciences. A critique of personality theories, using psychoanalytic insights within a sociology of knowledge, develops into a criticism of role theories and the sociology of knowledge itself. This constant turning of disciplines and theories back on to themselves seeks reflexive clarification of the 'knowledge' produced in the belief that reflexivity is both a problem and a resource for the human sciences. I realise it is only a beginning, but after struggling with the problem for a long time I now think it has become more of a resource than a problem.

As I see it the division of labour in intellectual work has taken a pathological turn and the personal and material benefits of specialisation now cost too much in terms of neglected areas and misconceived issues. We need above all to understand the psychological and social forces at work in the processes of knowledge production.

Since recent work in the sociology of science, knowledge and ideologies generally lacks a psychological dimension, I hope the situated critical analyses undertaken here will offer some possible lines of development in this direction.

Ray Holland

Chelsea College,
University of London

Acknowledgements

Phil Sealy, through his seminar at the LSE, helped me to start on this line of work and gave unfailing support and advice no matter how I used it.

Colleagues in the Department of Humanities at Chelsea College, particularly Harold Silver, Colin Falck, Judith Ryder and Oliver Williams, shared their experience as we worked together. Similarly with later colleagues in the Department of Sociology and Psychology, especially Esther Saraga. The most practical lessons in the sociology of knowledge have been learned from fellow members of the AUT, the group which most clearly embodies and protects university standards. In this and other college work Frank Lesser's sense of collective responsibility has set a standard.

Aaron Esterson, George Gross and Paul Senft were greatly valued friends in the earlier days of *The Human Context* editorial board. So were the members of various study groups on psychoanalytic and political matters around this time.

I owe an immeasurable debt to my wife Sue, that rarity among psychoanalytic therapists who not only dares to face the social and political implications of her work but carries through these insights into a radical practice. Zed, our son, though barely speaking, knows better than we the dialectic of inspiration and challenge.

Hermine Ball and Shirley White literally worked overtime to type the manuscript giving encouragement as well as their skills.

In giving thanks for all this help I also take full responsibility for what I have turned it towards.

1
Introduction

One's first impression on looking at the field of personality theories is of a great range and variety of contending approaches. And yet on closer examination there are certain basic themes which arise in different theories; like the concept of a 'natural' or 'true' self which struggles to emerge against all the pressures and distorting influences of a social environment, or Freud's discoveries which appear in a number of different guises. Thus it is possible, and may be useful, to explore personality theories at the level of these themes in addition to whatever work may go on by way of specific empirical testing of particular theories. This approach is especially relevant in a study which, while respecting the necessary autonomy of the disciplines of psychology and sociology, is designed to raise questions about the relation between them and the possibilities and needs for inter-disciplinary study. Personality theories are attempts to construct knowledge of a particularly significant kind—knowledge of what it is to be a human being, with all that this entails in terms of a formative social context—and this makes it imperative to call upon a pre-dominantly sociological method of appraisal which derives from the sociology of knowledge, as well as a careful psychological assess-ment of the theories.

In at least one area, role theories, there is as much work in sociology as in psychology, and as well as providing a fruitful starting point for exploring the relation between the two, it is of sufficient breadth in its implications to pose the even bigger question of the relations between all the social and behavioural disciplines—what might be called for the moment, and with admitted postpone-ment of issues of definition, 'the human sciences'.

The main themes have various characteristics: in some cases a theme has been set going by one man, for example Freud; but in others it may be the kind of intellectual tradition which is not readily identi-fied with one man but rather with a group or succession of theorists, for example existentialism and phenomenology. In any case it will be necessary to look at each theme firstly for what it offers as a contribution to knowledge and then in a contrasted and much neglected perspective: it must be examined in the light of the reactions it has provoked in other theorists. Where these reactions are the substantive part of a new alternative theory it will be an important if not crucial test of the foundations of the new theory to ask whether its reaction is based on a clear understanding of the old theory. Where it is not then some alternative grounding must be sought for the new theory and if this is not found independently of its qualities of reactive misunderstanding then it must be rejected. More constructively, it may be possible to improve a number of theories by relating them more securely to their foundations in the currents of thought and ideas which their authors drew upon with insufficient understanding. Whether the balance of results is constructive or otherwise will not be decisive for the project since it can be argued from the range and quantity of personality theories that they embody superfluous false knowledge which must, more than anything, be cleared before new work can go ahead.

The basic method of this study will be to read closely the work of representative theorists paying special attention to the tone and style in order to detect deeper meanings than may be evident in the surface statements. The truism that in order to understand we must read the text conceals an immensely difficult project which is coming to recognition in the new structuralist approaches to Freud and Marx, in the growing emphasis within sociology on social reality as constructed in discourse, and in psychology when it grapples with the complexities of meaning and communicative behaviour.

1.1 UNDERSTANDING, VALUES AND MEANING

Although it is a useful methodological point when the scientist is reminded that he should attempt to keep his own values and preferences out of his work, or at least state them clearly so that others may make allowance, there is very little possibility of this being done by personality theorists. All concepts of the person involve the scientist's self and so evaluation is inescapable. A disinterested concept of the self is impossible for it would be contradictory. Outright claims to objectivity in this field turn out to be consciously, or more often unconsciously, disguised evaluative perspectives. So it will be necessary to apply sociological techniques of value analysis in order to reach a full understanding of the theories.

However, there is a problem at a much lower level than that of values: it is at the level of language and meaning. It comes with the first attempt to discover what a theorist is saying—the attempt to understand what he means by what he says. The very ambiguity of language presents difficulties, particularly where it is being used to describe insubstantial and even mystical aspects of human behaviour and existence.

Perhaps it will be useful to speak of three levels in terms of which reading must proceed. Firstly, the work must be analysed in terms of the writer's direct statements—the common property meanings of his assertions—for which nothing more than a good dictionary is needed. Secondly, it is necessary to try to understand the overt value positions taken up by particular theorists—a cross-cultural and historical problem since all concepts are socially and historically located. Thirdly, the implicit, unstated value positions must be uncovered. So often it is in the groundwork of assumptions on which a theory is built that the most radical evaluations are embedded and what is taken as a datum or starting point is sometimes well on the way towards a certain kind of theory. Particularly interesting are the cases where a theory contradicts itself by failure to realise its over-all implications—its assertions at another level of analysis.

It must be emphasised that use of a spatial metaphor of 'three levels' of analysis is an over-simplification. The 'levels' interpenetrate and there is no neutrality or purity in language that allows it to be used to convey *either* meaning or evaluation as desired. Even a dictionary approach to a theorist's direct statements will bring up common property meanings *and* evaluations.

Merleau-Ponty gives warning of another problem: that of a theorist's own private use of the common language. If he has anything to say other than the commonplace, he is bound to extend the language as he develops his theory. He may begin in a familiar language with readily understood meanings

. . . but these meanings sometimes combine to form new thought which recasts them all.[1]

It is for this reason that

. . . only the central theme of a philsosphy, once understood, endows the philosopher's writings with the value of adequate signs.[2]

It seems clear that communication, though not impossible, is problematic on several analytically distinct but not existentially separable levels; and it is only by facing these difficulties that understanding will be won. There is no safe refuge in a mere proclamation of objectivity, however well intended.

In summary, the programme for understanding begins with the words on the page but goes beyond the words to consider the backcloth of assumptions against which they are placed, to their redefinition as a consequence of particular use by a theorist who sees the world and himself from a given social and historical perspective, and to the central themes that inform his work.

I begin to understand a philosophy by feeling my way into its existential manner, by reproducing the tone and accent of the philosopher.[3]

1.2 MISUNDERSTANDING AND 'POSITIVE GENERALITY'

The difficulties of understanding complex ideas are very great, leaving plenty of room for reshaping and reinterpretation as an idea passes from one scholar to another, particularly if it crosses boundaries of culture, class and different historical periods. It is not therefore a great condemnation of a theorist to say that he has persistently misread another's work; indeed it should be expected. W. H. N. Hotopf's study of the literary critic and educationist I. A. Richards, shows that a man may misunderstand *his own work*, or fail to heed warnings against misreading even though he has issued the warnings himself.[4] The discovery of contradictions in the work of a man who is consciously struggling with problems of meaning and comprehension would suggest that there are many more contradictions or distortions in the work of less self-conscious writers. This is what I wish to bring out in the work of self theorists although I cannot pretend to the depth of analysis that Hotopf achieved. In this study I offer what seem to me striking examples of misunderstanding and, therefore, abuse of ideas by certain theorists or groups of theorists. It does not commit me to a conspiracy theory of society to say that groups of scholars share a common tendency to misread an idea or to attend to it selectively with preconceived assumptions. For there need be no conscious aim on their part if they simply share common cultural or occupational values.

My most general thesis on the basis of the evidence which follows this preliminary, is that American personality theorists, whilst feeding on ideas from other cultures, notably Europe, persistently misread, misunderstand and finally abuse these ideas. They do it unconsciously so as to make the idea fit their own basic cultural assumptions which emphasise optimistic, self-reliant, healthy, religious (but not obsessively so) individualism. The damage is greatest when the idea is at the opposite pole from American values, as in the case of existentialism with its exploration of anxiety, alienation and despair. I put it polemically so as to state my 'central theme' with maximum clarity: it seems to me that American personality theorists (and perhaps even the general body of American social scientists, but that is a larger problem, beyond the scope of this study) in looking round for ideas, come across bodies of work which so obviously contain valuable insights and crucial concepts that they cannot be ignored. But at the very moment of taking up what is valuable they unconsciously change it by selection, emphasis and attenuation. They cannot see or face the reality which is shown to them because it contradicts their *concepts of themselves*. They retreat to a more positive view: but to show that they have incorporated the other ideas they generalise the analysis so as to place the threatening concepts in a more positive over-all context.

> Some theories of becoming are based largely upon the behaviour of sick and anxious people or upon the antics of captive and desperate rats. Fewer theories have derived from the study of healthy human beings, those who strive not so much to preserve life as to make it worth living.[5]

This double knock at the clinical picture of man and at the behaviourists' treatment of their rats, capped by an assertion that life really is worth living, is just one example of the technique. I call it 'the retreat into positive generality'.

Of course it is a crude thesis to suggest that this is true of all American theorists and it would be a gross over-simplification and polarisation to answer their so-called positive generality with the mirror image of negative generality. However, I hold that there is a difference between consciously stating a generalisation which attempts to capture the central theme of a group of theories and which will be qualified in detailed examination, and a relatively unconscious lapse into the kind of superficial generality which is exemplified above.

The tone of positive generality appears not only in particular theories but also in textbooks which present a range of material without attempting any deep criticism.

> We have attempted to present each theory in a positive light, dwelling upon those features of the theory that seem to us most useful and suggestive. Although we have included a brief critique of each theory it has not been our primary intention to evaluate these theories.[6]

Nevertheless there is an evaluation in the choice of particular theories for inclusion in what the publishers called, with a touch of promotional enthusiasm, 'the first objective and comprehensive review of the major theories of personality'. Limitations of space forced criteria upon the authors who chose to exclude McDougall's Hormic Theory and Role Theory. The first of these was excluded because its influence was considered to be 'less systematically developed' than the theories included, even though role theory 'contains a leading idea of considerable value and importance'.

I suggest that role theory was expendable to psychologists writing primarily for psychology students, because it is an area in which the centre of gravity is neither exclusively psychological nor exclusively sociological. In a non-trivial sense it is interdisciplinary, and yet in spite of its value and promise it was dropped. This raises another important general theme in personality theories.

1.3 THE INTERDISCIPLINARY VOID

Although certain phenomena, in this case the contribution of role training and performance to the structure of personality are inherently interdisciplinary, there tends to be relatively little research or theory which is fully grounded in both sociology and psychology, not to mention other disciplines such as philosophy and anthropology which might contribute essential considerations for a rigorous and yet sufficiently complex role theory. If this is correct then it is worth asking why there is a void of this kind between disciplines. It calls for a rather high level analysis of how disciplines came to define their present boundaries and yet it is well within the sphere of a sociological study of the division of labour in intellectual work. It may be, as Devons and Gluckman[7] suggest, that it is difficult to learn enough about more than one discipline to be able to handle their resources and techniques with real competence. Devons and Gluckman describe ways of using the knowledge produced in a separate but relevant discipline in such a way that the work of one discipline can go ahead without it being necessary to raise deeper questions within another. For example, an accurate though superficial knowledge of personality structure may provide a workable and useful model for the purposes of a sociological study. This is feasible and it may be that it is a vital factor in the rapid progress of science. Ravetz[8] has certainly shown that the production of 'standardised facts' useful to workers in other specialities and other disciplines, without any need for them to know the deeper mysteries involved in their original discovery, allows the scientific process to go on more economically. However, there is a distinction between using an assumption about the subject matter of another discipline as one taken-for-granted element in a study, and addressing directly the interaction of subject matters of two disciplines, as in a thorough examination of 'role'. Thus in this strong definition of interdisciplinary work—where it is not just a case of one providing techniques or roughly accurate working models for another—there will be problems for which the researcher can find no strong disciplinary support. Interdisciplinary work may then necessitate the acceptance of a marginal role with all the implications of identity confusion and anomie. Possibly this is why Devons and Gluckman say that

> ... the different social and human sciences may be different realms, in whose borderlands trespass is dangerous save for the genius.[9]

This is an unfortunate way of putting it since the person who now ventures into such areas must somehow escape the implication that he lays claim to qualities of genius. Would it not be better to acknowledge that the little work so far done on the role[10] of the scientist indicates that occupation of dual roles or the occupation of hybrid roles[11] is apparently one of the most fruitful and productive of all positions within the social organisation of science. In this way the genius becomes less a figure of supreme individual powers and more, though not completely, the creature of particular situations. The more just balance of individual powers and social determination appears more plausible than an evocation of genius, and allows ordinary mortals to move into these more fertile areas. Eventually there must be a comparative study of the development of academic disciplines; however, there is a more modest task which might indicate something of the relations between disciplines within the human sciences. It will be to examine the phenomenon and conceptualisation of role playing to see how its treatment by sociologists and psychologists throws light on the relation between the disciplines. By good fortune there is a psychological theory of personality—personal construct theory[12]—which attaches great importance to role, and this will be used as a way in to some broader questions about sociological and related role theories, and their place in the human sciences.

The justification for speaking of an interdisciplinary void may at this stage be taken as the frequent polarisation of role into a normative or conformist concept (sociology) and an individual or autonomous concept (psychology). This is not to say that the concepts necessarily have these characteristics but that they are seen to have them by psychologists who refer to sociological theories and sociologists who refer to psychological theories. Often it is nothing more than an error of reification which mistakes the intentionally limited concept of the psychologist for an inadequate model of the person in social context, whereas the sociologists' focus upon the social structural aspects of role is seen as a denial of autonomy. Many confusions in the nomothetic versus idiographic controversy rest on this error.

A further reason for paying attention to certain interdisciplinary problems at this time can be found in the patterns of development of the disciplines. In sociology there is a new field of work, ethnomethodology, which is seen by its protagonists as fundamentally challenging the sociological orthodoxy of positivism. It places the process of self-creation by negotiation of reality at the centre of investigation and proposes a reinterpretation of role theories to take account of the 'deep structure' of rules which order the surface 'prescriptions for behaviour'. It embraces a phenomenological concern for the experiencing, symbol-using self, and offers a more humanistic sociology.

The parallel in psychology is the group of personality theorists who have asserted the priority of the self, or the whole person against the positivism (behaviourism) of orthodox psychology in the name of a humanistic psychology.

Both groups have seen themselves as dissidents arguing for the humanism that has been missed in the orthodox (and that is a term of sharp criticism) social and behavioural sciences, and both have sought a foundation for their aims in philosophies which they have scarcely understood—from Marxism, phenomenology and existentialism to Eastern mystical beliefs. Yet there is no sign of these groups meeting each other in spite of their common and powerful assertion of the priority of the person in the human sciences.

1.4 REACTIVE CHARACTERISTICS OF THEORIES

It follows from the fact that self-theories are value-laden that the introduction of a new theory is more like the launching of a new social movement than the discovery of some technique or process in the natural sciences. There is more than a simple analogy here: personality theories imply sociopolitical theories just as sociopolitical theories imply certain models of man. This is why so much of the work is polemical; as much concerned to reject earlier models as to establish new ones. And when an earlier model is rejected it is not usually in the mood of calm revision, it is with a sense of righteousness at having found a truer view of man, his nature, and even his destiny. There is a religiosity in self-theories, whether or not their authors are explicitly religious: a grotesque example of this is Maslow's use of 'greater frequency of mystical experiences' as a criterion of maturity or self-actualisation.

There is nothing more revelatory of a self-theory than the ideas, cultural values or schools of thought it chooses to react against. Not only does a theory define itself in relation to well-known landmarks when it rejects a given position, it also shows, in the manner and style of its reaction, its own implicit assumptions. A further point is that the earlier view often contains insights that are so well established as to be nearly incontrovertible or ideas that would be useful for a new theory if only they could be detached from their context. The effect is a relationship of extreme ambivalence between a theorist and his sources and perhaps this accounts for much of the misreading and misrepresentation that shows up so well the limiting assumptions that are built in to the new work.

Given that the focus and manner of reaction are revelatory of the nature of self-theories, there follows an attempt to place the theories of Mead, Sullivan, Erikson, Allport, Jourard, Maslow, Rogers and

Kelly in relation to the ideas they reject, and in relation to the ideas they borrow, but only after translation into a more 'positive generality'.

Self-theories show, in their structure and presentation, a reaction to *Freud* but a need for many of his concepts; a reaction to *behaviourism* but a need for scientific methods and even scientific respectability; and a reaction to *existentialism* but a need for phenomenology as a method for the elucidation of intersubjective experience.

The first group of theorists—Mead, Sullivan and Erikson—will be used to demonstrate the reaction to Freud by an attempt to set off a social definition of the self against Freud's alleged individualism.

The other theorists, Allport, Jourard, Maslow, Rogers and Kelly will be used to demonstrate the reaction to behaviourism. There is a complication here because this group can be used equally well to demonstrate the reaction to Freud, but a reaction that does not go in the direction of a more social self. These theorists are primarily concerned with unique individuality. This being so, they defend the unique individual against Freud, and against the social-self theories. Nevertheless, their most direct conflict is with behaviourism and it is this battle that most unites them. A second complication, but an interesting one, is that some of these individualists show some interest in existentialism, finding themselves attracted to the stress on individual experience that is characteristic of this school of thought but repelled by the picture of an alienated and despairingly negative self. In general, then, these individualist theorists are primarily in reaction to behaviourism but secondarily in an approach/avoid conflict towards two other theories—Freud and existentialism. From Freud they need clinical methods which give such primacy to the individual case but they dislike the 'pathological' self-picture; from existentialism they need phenomenological methods which give primacy to individual experience but they cannot accept the distressingly vulnerable self-picture which emerges. The result is that they dabble with Freudian clinical concepts, borrowing at the same time a weakened phenomenology in the context of a neutered existentialism.

1.5 PSYCHOANALYTIC THEORY IN BRITAIN

While the American personality theorists developed their particular pattern of reaction to Freud, the main stream of Freudian work embodied in the person of Freud, together with some of his relatives and colleagues, moved to Britain. Here an autonomous area of self-theory has grown out of Freud through Klein, Winnicott and Fairbairn into what is known as object relations theory.[13] It provides an opportunity to examine another set of reactions to Freud in another sociocultural environment. By comparison with America there is a greater individualism in British self-theory without any strong theme of the social-self, and already this seems to indicate a possible sociocultural influence at work.

Another interesting aspect of the British situation is that it has produced in Laing, Esterson and Cooper[14] a further example of borrowing from the existentialist school but this time with a fuller acceptance of radical aspects of existentialism and of Marx's contribution. Exploration of this area will complete the picture of major contributions to self-theory.

1.6 FREUD, HUSSERL AND MARX

If the various processes of reaction to Freud, behaviourism, existentialism and Marx can be established as more often than not based on a misunderstanding of the source, it would seem logical to pursue a clearer understanding of the sources in anticipation of a sounder theory. Already this has begun: a clearer 'reading' of Marx has been undertaken by Althusser,[15] of Freud by Lacan[16] and of Husserl by phenomenological movements in France, Britain and the United States.[17]

The dangers of a return to the roots of a theory are obvious: that the originator may be elevated and idealised, his writings treated as doctrine and successors who attempt modifications as heretics. But this is only to acknowledge that just as there are valid and invalid reasons for rejecting a theory so are there valid and invalid reasons for embracing one, and what is needed is careful discrimination of the patterns of acceptance and rejection by close reading of the relevant texts.

1.7 A HUMAN SCIENCE OF SELF IN SOCIAL CONTEXT

Whether the project of careful reading, analysis and criticism embodied here will lead to an advance in knowledge remains to be seen. That one discipline, sociology, should be used to explicate another, psychology, and that a new interdisciplinary or trans-disciplinary field of work should thereby be established is a delicate undertaking. As well as the Devons and Gluckman viewpoint that trespass over disciplinary boundaries is usually folly, there are other words of caution from sources of a more philosophical kind. James Dagenais has warned against the notion of a philosophical synthesis of the results of various sciences.

It is at once clear that the role of philosopher as *reflecting upon the data of science* in order to answer the question about man is no longer a supportable option. The results of the scientific endeavour are already prescribed by the originating options of scientists.[18]

However, Dagenais distinguishes between philosophy and philo-sophical anthropology, the latter being dependent upon its capacity to clarify its own presuppositions. It is interesting that Dagenais comes by a different route to a conception that Winch with his Witt-gensteinian background arrived at some time ago. In denying that sociology can be a (natural) science Winch asserts that the subject matter of sociology requires *uncommitted* enquiry.

. . . philosophy is concerned with elucidating and comparing the ways in which the world is made intelligible in different intellectual disciplines: and how this leads on to the elucidation and com-parison of different forms of life. The uncommittedness of philosophy comes out here in the fact that it is equally concerned to elucidate its own account of things; the concern of philosophy with its own being is thus not an unhealthy Narcissistic aberration, but an essential part of what it is trying to do.[19]

This common ground between linguistic analysis and phenomenology has been noticed already and clarified to some extent.[20] At a crude level of comparison there is clear similarity between their approaches to social phenomena: they both refuse to take categories for appraisal of phenomena uncritically but would trace them back to their formative stages, the linguistic analyst to their function within a rule-governed system of language use or 'form of life', the phenomenologist to the ground of experience of which the cate-gorisation and conceptualisation are but a limited expression. Both have their limitations. Winch is eager to deny that sociology can be a natural science and so contrasts philosophy too sharply against science.

Science, unlike philosophy, is wrapped up in its own way of making things intelligible to the exclusion of all others. Or rather it applies its criteria unselfconsciously; for to be self-conscious about such matters *is* to be philosophical.[21]

Philosophy has never been so pure, or it would lack any kind of competing paradigms; and science has never been so unselfconscious or it would not have changed. Furthermore, to encourage sociologists to return always 'to the language itself' (to echo the phenomenologists' intention of returning 'to the things themselves') is to give too little recognition to those material social processes which determine language to some degree and, in the formation of ideologies, leave areas of language as epiphenomena needing more than a linguistic analysis.

On the other hand, Dagenais in his very thorough examination of the models of man embodied in a range of sociological and psychological theories would elucidate as the deeper foundation of these various theories the distinctive human capacity which constitutes them.

What founds both the human sciences and philosophy—and, I maintain, all approaches to the meaning of man—must be found in something which gives them all meaning. The special problem, then, is not to make one science of philosophy and the 'sciences' about man, but to found all of them in one primordial intentionality which makes sense of all of them while leaving them autonomous.[22]

Again

... all understanding of human being in the world, whether scientific or philosophical, is founded upon a pre-scientific and pre-philosophical experiencing of human being as self-and-other-in-the-world.[23]

This determination to take nothing for granted but to trace back even philosophy to its roots in human experience is a radical programme indeed and Dagenais claims only to have written the prolegomenon. What it may underestimate is the extent to which speech, language and philosophies are not referable to an underlying intentionality or experience but are the human activities in which intentionality and certain important qualities of symbolic experience are achieved in process of their articulation. This is to move a little way in the direction of Winch.

Another difficulty with a radical programme which accepts 'self/other' as its fundamental unit is that it promises little for *social* theory, which must address itself to collective experience and phenomena at a group level. It is a long way from recognition of the 'intersubjectivity' of our being to an appreciation and account of the complex social forms this may give rise to.

Nevertheless it is in the space defined by such philosophers as Winch and Dagenais that an effort at critical, experiential reading of available theories may be carried on, and the addition of critical resources from the sociology of knowledge which seeks to understand forms of knowledge by explaining to some degree the conditions of their production may sharpen the cutting edge of critical appreciation.

NOTES AND REFERENCES

1 M. Merleau-Ponty. *Phenomenology of Perception*, Routledge, London (1962), p 179
2 ibid., p. 179
3 ibid., p. 179
4 W. H. N. Hotopf. *Language, Thought and Comprehension*, Routledge, London (1965)
5 G. W. Allport. *Becoming*. Yale University Press, New Haven, Conn., and London (1955), p. 18
6 C. S. Hall and G. Lindzey. *Theories of Personality*, John Wiley, New York and Chichester (1957)
7 E. Devons and M. Gluckman. *Closed Systems and Open Minds* (ed. M. Gluckman), Oliver & Boyd, Edinburgh (1964)
8 J. R. Ravetz. *Scientific Knowledge and its Social Problems*. Clarendon, University Press, Oxford (1971)
9 E. Devons and M. Gluckman. *Closed Systems and Open Minds* (ed. M. Gluckman), Oliver & Boyd, Edinburgh (1964), p. 261
10 M. Mulkay. Some aspects of cultural growth in the natural sciences. *Soc. Res.*, **36**, 1 (1969), 22–52
11 J. Ben-David. Roles and innovations in medicine. *Am. J. Sociol.*, **65** (1960), 557–68
12 G. A. Kelly. *The Psychology of Personal Constructs*, Norton, New York (1955)

13 H. J. S. Guntrip. *Psychoanalytic Theory, Therapy and the Self*, Hogarth, London (1971)
14 R. D. Laing and A. Esterson. *Sanity, Madness and the Family*, Tavistock, London (1964)
   R. D. Laing and D. G. Cooper. *Reason and Violence*, Tavistock, London (1964)
15 L. Althusser and E. Balibar. *Reading 'Capital'*, New Left Books, London (1970)
16 A. Wilden. *The Language of the Self*, Johns Hopkins, Baltimore, Md. (1968)
17 The effort to understand and propagate phenomenological approaches has produced innumerable conferences and publications dominated by an exegesis of Husserl.
18 J. J. Dagenais. *Models of Man*, Nijhoff, The Hague (1972), p. 147
19 P. Winch. *The Idea of a Social Science*, Routledge, London (1958), p. 102
20 J. M. Hems. Husserl and/or Wittgenstein. *Int. Philos. Q.* **8** (1968), 547–78
21 P. Winch. *The Idea of a Social Science*, Routledge, London (1958), p. 102
22 J. J. Dagenais. *Models of Man*, Nijhoff, The Hague (1972), p. 153
23 ibid., p. XI

2
Reaction to Freud—Social-Self Theories

It is possible to establish certain polarities or oppositions for the purpose of placing theorists in relation to each other. One such opposition is between individual and social emphases in self-theories. If Freud is used as the embodiment of individual emphasis because of his concentration on the growth and persistence of certain structures of personality, it is possible to use G. H. Mead as an embodiment of social emphasis because of his essentially social definition of the self in terms of a 'generalised other'. It is not just a convenient opposition for purposes of exposition, the opposition is actually expressed in Mead's work.

> In the more or less fantastic psychology of the Freudian group, thinkers are dealing with the sexual life and with self-assertion in its violent form. . . . under the normal conditions . . . the individual is making his contribution to a common undertaking.[1]

This is a perfect example of the reaction to Freud's insights that places the threatening elements out of the way as abnormal, asserting at the same time a more positive generality—'the common undertaking'. More will be said about Mead's attitude to Freud but the limited purpose here is to establish a polarity so that two other social-self theorists can be placed on the same axis at intermediate points between Mead and Freud.

Sullivan, in defining his interpersonal psychiatry, which includes the concept of a self-system, speaks of a

> . . . very striking convergence of thought in the psychobiology of Meyer and the social psychology of Mead, which is concerned with the evolution of the self.[2]

Freud is linked with Meyer

> Both the Freudian discoveries and the formulae of Meyer centre their attention on the individual person, as the central unit of study.[3]

And so Sullivan stands at a point of convergence between the Meyer/Freud (individual) position and the Mead (social) position. But where, exactly, does Sullivan stand? Is he closer to Freud or to Mead? It appears that he is closer to Mead

> [Mead's work] showed very clearly that the unique individual person was a complex derivative of many others. It *did not quite* [my emphasis] serve for the purpose of psychiatry as here defined, because there was, you might say, no source of energy presented to account for shifts in roles, the energy expended in playing roles, and so on.[4]

The position so far then is this:

Freud	Sullivan	Mead
individual		social

The imaginary ground between Sullivan and Freud is occupied by E. H. Erikson. He is very close to Freud, using nearly every concept of the Master, but he places personality development more certainly and explicitly in social context by means of a role analysis. The concept of role is Mead's major contribution to social science (although he took it over from William James and Charles Cooley). But if Erikson has the concept of role in common with Mead he also moves far away from Mead's position by reason of his sharply different attitude to Freud. The contrast between Mead's near ridicule of Freud ('more or less fantastic') and Erikson's reverence, is clear enough.

So the social-self axis runs from Freud to Mead, with Erikson and Sullivan upon it.

Freud	Erikson	Sullivan	Mead
individual			social

I shall now go on to discuss in more detail the self-theories of Mead, Sullivan and Erikson, in turn, and in that order.

2.1 G. H. MEAD

There is a central theme in the work of G. H. Mead which influences the local meaning of his particular statements and which, as a fundamental attitude, sets limits to what he is able to see or accept in the work of other people. It is the philosophical theme of 'self-realisation' through an organic society, which runs through the work of J. J. Rousseau, T. H. Green, B. Bosanquet and R. MacIver. The apparent explanatory power of this Idealist theory is so great that its exponents often speak in quasi-religious terms. Bosanquet describes 'genuine' individuality as 'at once a distinct assertion of the self, and a transition from the private self into the great communion of reality'.[5] This 'expansion' of the self is very much like Mead's idea that in some circumstances

> ... a person does get outside of himself, and by doing so makes himself a member of a larger community ... This enlarged experience has a profound influence. It is the sort of experience which the neophyte has in conversion.[6]

There is no room in this kind of world-view for conflict, death instincts, despair or alienation: indeed one can sense the slight disgust with which Freud's work is put aside as dealing with 'sexual life and with self-assertion in its violent form'. At another point Mead discusses humour. He agrees that the 'I', or private aspect of self, can enjoy another's fall at the same time as the 'me', or social aspect of self, urges help for the fallen. He cannot say this without adding, 'There is nothing vicious about it'. I do not suggest for a moment that Mead is consciously moderating the Freudian picture but I think this is the effect of his interpretation which must be referred ultimately to his own self-concept.

Mead's account of the self is well known. I pick out the essential points

> What I particularly want to emphasize is the temporal and logical pre-existence of the social process to the self-conscious individual that arises within it ... his mind is the expression in his own conduct of this social situation, this great co-operative community process which is going on.[7]

There are two aspects of the self

> The 'I' is the response of the organism to the attitudes of the others; the 'me' is the organized set of attitudes of others which one himself assumes.[8]

The conversation of gestures involved in any kind of co-operative act (even co-operative acts between animals, such as copulation) makes possible the development of language. Only man has taken this step and so differentiates himself from other animals. Because we can hear our own voices, the self can be an object to itself. We can also anticipate the other's response; we can take over the other's attitude.

When the response of the other becomes an essential part in the experience or conduct of the individual; when taking the attitude of the other becomes an essential part in his behaviour—then the individual appears in his own experience as a self; and until this happens he does not appear as a self.[9]

But this myriad of interpersonal reflections has no unity until the attitudes of others are taken in as a generalised attitude:

The organized community or social group which gives to the individual his unity of self may be called 'the generalized other'.[10]

The parallel with Rousseau's 'general will', the basis of Idealist theories, is very striking. Other phrases confirm Mead's debt. He speaks of the social relations of all

. . . as an organized and unified whole.[11]
. . . common responses . . . give him what we term his principles
. . . [such a man] has character in the moral sense.[12]
We cannot have rights unless we have common attitudes.[13]

He even follows the Idealists to the point at which the general will is recognised as the highest form of rationality

. . . the other appears in our experience in so far as we do take up such an organized and generalized [rational] attitude.[14]

By self-realisation, a man 'belongs' to a society of all rational beings . . .[15] It becomes clear that this *social* definition of self is achieved in the context of such a generalised and even mystified conception of 'society' that it is unlikely to bring greater clarity to the concept of self. Nevertheless Mead's work has been influential in America for some time and there is at present a re-awakening interest. Peter Berger has suggested that Mead's concept of the self is similar to that of Heidegger, the existentialist.

In fact (and this ought to give us a long pause), Heidegger's *Man* bears uncanny resemblance to what Mead has called the generalized other.[16]

I am not sure what Berger intends us to so with the long pause but if he wants us to say that Mead's work contains an existential insight, we can only do this if we add that Mead's picture of the self, the society, and of the self/society relation is so benign that it lacks any trace of existential sensitivity. Certainly he provided the terms for an existential analysis, but in the context of such a different central theme that these terms must have carried, for him, not a scrap of existential meaning. It is only necessary to ask what Mead did with the three fundamental elements of his social theory—the self, the society, and the self/society relation?

From the self he removed all viciousness, violent self-assertion, fantasy and anxiety: from the society he generalised out the cultural or class-based fragmentations and conflicts (it became a 'great co-operative community process'): is it any wonder that when self met society a 'conversation' between the 'I' and the 'me' took place?

2.2 H. S. SULLIVAN

Sullivan's attitude to Freud was ambivalent. He seemed to avoid mentioning Freud. At the same time he found it necessary to make some acknowledgement when defining his own distinctive kind of interpersonal psychiatry.

> Needless to say, behind all this phase of psychiatry are the discoveries of Sigmund Freud.[17]

He acknowledges discoveries, not 'work', 'concepts' or 'theories' because this would involve him too closely. And there is another distancing passage

> The setting up of the psychiatric field as a study of interpersonal relations is certainly necessary if psychiatry is to be scientific; furthermore, by this simple expedient of so defining psychiatry, we weed out from the serious psychiatric problems a great number of pseudo-problems—which since they are pseudo-problems, are not susceptible of solution, attempts at their solution being, in fact, only ways of passing a lifetime pleasantly.[18]

This is more of a reaction to Freudianism than to Freud but it is very strong. It shows, furthermore, Sullivan's great desire for scientific respectability, which he soon emphasises

> Let me repeat that psychiatry as a science cannot be concerned with anything which is immutably private; it must be concerned

only with the human living which is in, or can be converted into, the public mode.[19]

Scientific psychiatry is obviously on guard against the unconscious, against the unrecoverable id contents, and against the Freudian personality structure, which rested on the unconscious as a source of energy. Strangely enough, what Sullivan needs is precisely a source of energy. When he said that Mead's concept of the self 'Did not quite serve' it was on the grounds that there was no source of energy presented to account for shifts in roles, etc. When Sullivan introduces energy under the term 'dynamisms', it seems to have much in common with the Freudian theory: 'dynamisms' serve basic needs through certain body zones with a special 'dynamism' for the self-system. Whatever the similiarities he will not call it an instinct, drive or libido theory; nor use even the term 'mental energy'.

> [Experience is] in final analysis experience of *tensions* and experience of *energy transformations*. I use these terms in exactly the same sense as I would in talking about physics; there is no need to add adjectives such as mental . . .[20]

So in purifying the concept of energy he needs, if he is to bring about a convergence of Mead and Meyer/Freud, Sullivan has generalised his analysis to the point at which experience is considered as a field of forces in exactly the same sense as the terms are used in physics. Needless to say, Sullivan does not manage to discuss experience or behaviour in purely physical terms: this is certainly the case when he tries to convey a sense of what he means by anxiety. Anxiety is likened to the group of experiences known as 'awe', 'horror' and 'loathing' and he is particularly concerned with accurate and full transmission of his meaning because anxiety is the special 'dynamism' that attaches to the development of a 'self-system'. This study is concerned primarily with 'the self' and will therefore concentrate on the self-system within Sullivan's work. Already it must be noted that there is a contradiction between his use of pure energy concepts and his phenomenological description of the kinds of feelings and experiences that make the energy available.

Before going deeply into the self-system it will be clearer if Sullivan's concept of personality, of which the self-system is only a special part, is outlined. For his general conception of personality Sullivan takes from Mead the idea of interpersonal situations in the context of which a self emerges as the complex derivative of the 'generalised other'.

... personality is the relatively enduring pattern of recurrent interpersonal situations which characterise a human life.[21]

Basically this is a field theory, which ties in perfectly with his concepts of tensions and energy transformations to form a model of the personality/society relation based on an analogy with the physical sciences. The source of this model can be seen in Sullivan's quotations from Bridgman (operational definitions) and Lewin (vectors and forces forming a life space). It is not surprising, therefore, to find him setting out his work in 'scientific' form:

My theorem is this: *The observed activity of the infant arising from the tension of needs induces tension in the mothering one, which tension is experienced as tenderness and as an impulsion to activities toward the relief of the infant's needs.*[22]

As Mabel Blake Cohen said in an introduction to *The Interpersonal Theory of Psychiatry*

The use of this type of generalisation avoids the pitfalls of instinct theory, yet has the merit of bringing a wide variety of individual responses together into a meaningful category.[23]

But a question mark must be left against this assertion since general categories can equally well obscure relevant differences. Such categories can be made 'meaningful' by definition but this is no guaranteee of usefulness or truth.

Within his central theme of 'scientific' generalising Sullivan describes the development of what he calls the 'self-system'. The self-system is

... the system involved in the maintenance of felt interpersonal security ...[24]

Satisfaction of basic needs (air, water, sugar, etc.) depends on a response to the child by 'mothering ones'. Such responses can be neither confidently foreseen nor controlled, which means that unbearable, unspecific, unmanageable *anxiety* is present. Anxiety becomes a secondary dynamism over and above any physico-chemical needs of the child. The self-system is

... an organisation of educational experience called into being by the necessity to avoid or to minimise incidents of anxiety.[25]

[It is] derived wholly from the interpersonal aspects of the necessary environment of the human being ...[26]

Being perceptually dissociative, the *security operations* of the self-system achieve some autonomy from reality, which therefore prevents them from being tested easily and possibly abandoned as irrelevant. Supportive therapy designed to reduce anxiety might allow the self-system to expand so as to correctly perceive, and therefore cease to be threatened by, a wider range of interpersonal experience, but the self-system is itself

... the principal stumbling block to favourable changes in personality ...[27]

[It is] an equilibrating factor in living, whether the living be fortunate or unfortunate.[28]

As Sullivan's theory is gradually unfolded it seems that Freud's concepts are being reintroduced under different, more general names: security operations work very much like defence mechanisms; Sullivan's dream theory sounds very familiar

... unsatisfied needs from the day ... are satisfied, in so far as may be, by covert operations, symbolic devices, which occur in sleep.[29]

And it seems that Sullivan is aware of this at some level because whenever he describes anything that might be associated with Freud he explicitly dissociates himself. The most revealing thing about these disclaimers is their *tone and choice of words:*

This dynamism [the self-system] is an explanatory conception; it is not a thing, a region, or what not, such as superegos, egos, ids, and so on.[30]

... the use of such terms [incorporation or introjection] in connection with the development of the self-system is a rather reckless oversimplification, if not also a great magic verbal gesture, the meaning of which cannot be made explicit.[31]

To turn Sullivan's own theory against him for a moment, against what is he carrying on security operations? From what is he trying to dissociate himself? And the answer is clear. He is securing himself against what to him is an unacceptable concept of human nature and, by implication, against a certain *concept of self*. Notice again the choice of words.

A great many years of preoccupation with this problem [malevolence in childhood] has eventuated in a theory which is calculated to get round the idea that man is essentially evil. One of the great social theories is, you know, that society is the only thing that prevents everybody from tearing everybody to bits, or that man is possessed of something wonderful called sadism.[32]

Sullivan's 'positive generality' can now be seen to have two facets: the first is a positive conception of man as 'not evil', as involved in nightmarish anxiety only as a 'not me'; the second is a set of 'scientific' generalisations which enable him to submerge in more general but less meaningful categories, the unacceptable picture of a partially malevolent, sadistic, aggressive human being that he associates with Freud, while incorporating into his work nearly every other insight of Freud.

2.3 E. H. ERIKSON

G. H. Mead's work was used to define a point of opposition to Freud. Sullivan occupied an intermediate position on the Mead/ Freud axis, and now Erikson's position is to be explored. It is worth noting that Mead's extreme reaction came first in time; Sullivan followed with his much greater use of Freudian discoveries even though he was at pains to distinguish his work from Freud's; and Erikson came last, moving very close to the original Freudian position. Not too much significance can be attributed to this apparent return to the original insight, but a related fact of some interest is that anthropological work seems to have been at its least in Mead, of moderate importance to Sullivan, and of great importance to Erikson.

Erikson's closeness to Freud is demonstrated both in his direct acknowledgements and in the whole range of Freudian concepts which he retains as part of his own theoretical structures. The justification for putting him on an axis that points toward Mead is that Erikson places personality development more certainly and more explicitly in social context, using a concept that belongs more to Mead than to any other theorist—the concept of 'role'.

Erikson's theory of personality development is centred on the Freudian concept of the 'ego'. It could be called an 'ego theory of the self'. It works on three levels

> A human being . . . is at all times an organism, an ego, and a member of a society and is involved in all three processes of organization.[33]

> We are speaking of three processes, the somatic process, the ego process, and the societal process.[34]

> . . . the meaning of an item which may be 'located' in one of the three processes is codetermined by its meaning in the other two.[35]

Freud himself was clear about the first two processes, which he called the 'constitutional' and the 'accidental'

> . . . the relation between the two [constitutional and accidental] . . . is a co-operative and not a mutually exclusive one. The constitutional factor must await experiences before it can make itself felt; the accidental factor must have a constitutional basis in order to come into operation. To cover the majority of cases we can picture what has been described as a 'complemental series' [this was 'aetiological series' in a 1915 footnote, revised for the 1920 edition] in which the diminishing intensity of one factor is balanced by the increasing intensity of the other . . .[36]

Childhood was seen to be the crucially important stage because in this stage the basic disposition of the person is laid down. In later life this basic disposition meets experience, and in the face of traumatic experience is likely to regress to a childhood pattern of behaviour.

> All the factors that impair sexual development show their effects by bringing about a regression . . .[37]

In these two short passages can be found the major part of Erikson's theory. The 'complemental series' is the basis of Erikson's 'stages of development'. Freud himself changed the term 'aetiological series' (emphasis on causation and pathology) to 'complemental series' (emphasis on transaction and social environment) and this was in line with his shift of interest from the id to the ego. In other words, Erikson's work is substantially a Freudian theory with a nearly identical use of the concepts of libido, stages of development and regression of fixation:

> Only those who specialize in the extreme intricacies of mental disturbances and of ordinary mental quirks can fully appreciate what clear and unifying light was thrown into these dark recesses by the theory of a libido, of a mobile sexual energy which contributes to the 'highest' as well as to the 'lowest' forms of human endeavour—and often to both at the same time.[38]
>
> ... Freud showed that sexuality develops in stages, a growth which he firmly linked with all epigenetic development.[39]
>
> ... the kind of compulsive neurotic whom we have just described was to Freud an individual who although overtly anti-anal, was unconsciously *fixated* on or partially *regressed* to a stage of infantile sexuality called the anal–sadistic stage. Similarly, other emotional afflictions prove to be fixations or regressions to other infantile zones and stages.[40]

The debt is clear, as Erikson is the first to acknowledge. But how, exactly, does Erikson differ from or go beyond Freud, and what is the value of his contribution?

He changes Freud's emphasis on psychosexual development by setting in balance against it a parallel process called psychosocial development.

> I am attempting to lay the ground for a detailed account of the dovetailing of psychosexual and psychosocial epigenesis, i.e. the two schedules according to which component parts, present throughout development, come to fruition in successive stages.[41]

This takes some weight off genitality as a criterion off maturity

> A system must have its Utopia. For psychoanalysis the Utopia is 'genitality'.[42]
>
> But does pregenitality exist only for genitality? It seems not. In fact, the very essence of pregenitality seems to be the absorption of libidinal interests in the early encounter of the maturing organism with a particular style of child care and in the transformation of its inborn forms of approach (agression) into the social modalities of the culture.[43]

Having achieved this redefinition of development into more social terms he carried through the epigenetic stages of pregenitality into adult life, making eight stages in all, which together form the 'life cycle'. Already there are implications of a central theme in all this. The psychosexual and psychosocial are said to 'dovetail'; aggression is said to be transformed into 'the social modalities of the culture'; the epigenetic stages are added to and rounded out into a 'life cycle'. The general tenor of Erikson's theory is fitting together, unifying and completing. Developmental stages are a series of *'potentialities for changing patterns of mutual regulation'*, which is a much more optimistic reading than Freud would have given to the meeting of an organism with a society.

It is worth looking at one stage of development in greater detail to see how Erikson arrives at his more positive outlook.

Freud's own exploration of the anal stage of development is a concrete phenomenological analysis of the experience of children as they pass through a phase in which they are being subjected to the necessary frustrations of social regulation by parents. There is no way out of the dilemma presented to the child by this conflict between the demands of its instinctual drives and the limits imposed on them by the socialising parents. Even though control of the anal functions may be achieved, it is only at psychic cost to the child in terms of repressed wishes which may be turned against the self. As with each of the other stages there is an obstacle to be overcome and a price to pay for doing it.

> ... we may perhaps be forced to become reconciled to the idea that it is quite impossible to adjust the claims of the sexual instinct to the demands of civilization; that in consequence of its cultural development renunciation and suffering, as well as the danger of extinction in the remotest future, cannot be avoided by the human race.[44]

Erikson's picture of the developing child is benign and positive compared with this. At the anal stage, as at all the others, Erikson sets up a *conceptual opposition*—autonomy versus shame and doubt—and this conceptual opposition *generalises* the dilemma. At the organismic level, muscular development makes possible retention and elimination. At the psychic level, firm reassuring control of the child 'will enable him to learn self-control, will protect him against 'meaninglessness and arbitrary experience of shame and of early doubt', and will help him develop a sense of autonomous choice. If denied this support there is a danger that he will try to gain control by compulsive, stubborn retention, or aggressive elimination. 'Shaming' at this stage may lead to shamelessness: doubt may lead to psychic fear of attack from behind. At the social level, anal training is related to law and order: the principle of law and order

. . . apportions to each his privileges and his limitations, his obligations and his rights. A sense of rightful dignity and lawful independence on the part of adults around him gives to the child of good will the confident expectation that the kind of autonomy fostered in childhood will not lead to undue doubt or shame in later life. Thus the sense of autonomy fostered in the child and modified as life progresses, serves (and is served by) the preservation in economic and political life of a sense of justice.[45]

By the time Erikson has carried through his analysis in these general terms, all trace of Freud's 'adversary' concept of the self has disappeared. Anality is seen not so much as the occasion of a forced choice between two equally costly alternatives, as with Freud, but as a process, the outcome of which will be a more or less integrated ego. One of the alternatives will allow an autonomous ego to pass on to the next stage with its libidinal interests transformed into the 'social modalities of the culture'. In a very subtle way Erikson has generalised away the fundamental conflict between the developing organism and society, into a conceptual opposition. At the social level of analysis Erikson's language is very much like that of G. H. Mead and the Idealists—the 'child of good will' realises himself in the orderly society where there is 'a sense of justice'.

Consideration of adolescence as a stage of development will bring up Erikson's best known concept, 'identity', and will show again how he moderates Freud. The adolescent stage is crucial for the developing ego because it is not merely the period in which genitality is achieved; it is the pivotal point on which a whole life turns:

It is at the end of adolescence, then, that identity . . . must find a certain integration as a relatively conflict free psycho-social arrangement—or remain defective or conflict-laden.[46]

Conflict can be avoided, it seems, provided integration is strong enough. The ego can

. . . learn to consolidate the most important conflict free achievements in line with work opportunities.[47]

He is aware that society may not provide 'work opportunities' but he sees this as a problem only for minority groups such as American negroes. What if all the minority groups were added up? Would it not amount to a sizeable proportion of the population? What if the groups who are deprived of education and of work opportunities on a social class basis were added to the minorities? Would this not be a majority of the population? How, then, can Erikson justify his relatively conflict-free model of the personality, except perhaps as his idealisation of what might be? Freud's more terrifying concept of the self is, for all its apparent pessimism, the more liberating concept because it provides a ground for radical criticism of a society. The paradox in Erikson's work is that he arrives at his holistic models of the self and society on the basis of what appears, from his use of words, to be a radical criticism—such words as 'ideologies', 'exploitation', etc.—but the conflicts he looks at are all resolved by his central theme which is *integration:* 'identity', which is 'the organisation of experience in the individual ego', is an integrative concept of the most general kind. Personality development is said to be a life-long process of 'self realisation coupled with mutual recognition', another integrative idea. He has managed to rescue Freud's concept of the ego only by changing and confusing it. With Freud it was necessarily in a situation of conflict and anxiety; at the mercy of the id and the superego but unable to aggress, it turned the aggressive drives inwards as a self-destructive force.

> Thus it may be suspected that the individual dies of his internal conflicts. [48]

In turning away from this dark picture of the self, Erikson, too, has retreated into 'positive generality'.

At the beginning of this study I said that central themes influence local meanings: this seems to be the case with Erikson. I also suggested that central themes derive from fundamental attitudes of their authors, particularly in relation to their concepts of themselves. Is it possible to get some clue as to Erikson's self-concept or fundamental attitude to see if this will account for the structure and style of his work?

> I came to psychology from art, which may explain, if not justify the fact that at times the reader will find me painting contexts and backgrounds where he would rather have me point to facts and

concepts. I have had to make a virtue out of a constitutional necessity by basing what I have to say on representative description rather than on theoretical argument.[49]

It is clear from Erikson's 'representative description' of the material he selects that he is an artist; witness the astonishingly beautiful analogy between the oral anxiety of the Yurok people and the uncertainty of the salmon run on which they depend as a culture; and also between a Yurok person's mouth and jaws, and the jaw-like trap that is built across the river to catch the salmon. But Erikson the artist integrates and unifies his picture, and in the end it is, like many fine works of art, good, but not quite true.

2.4 A THEORY BY INVERSION—S. M. JOURARD

The most pure form of reaction to a theory is that which inverts the theory without disturbing its structure and produces a mirror image in which all the original elements are present but seen in a different way. Such is the case with Sidney Jourard's theory of the 'transparent' self, which bases itself substantially on Freud whilst inverting every vicissitude and distortion of communication entailed by Freud's theory into an opportunity for winning back our existence by 'disclosing' ourselves to each other. The theorists who dealt with threatening aspects of Freud's work by assimilating them to a more positive and general context of some kind might be described as defensively rationalising the threat. Jourard does not so much rationalise as *deny* Freud, producing in reaction the most effulgent and superficial kind of utopian existentialism.

In his early work Jourard uses the strategy of proposing that psychologists should concern themselves with the 'healthy personality', as though to imply that Freud's model of personality structure applies only or predominantly to the sick.[50] As in the many other instances where this technique of gaining distance from Freud is used,[51] it is not argued or demonstrated but simply asserted as a kind of common sense. He acknowledges that Freud belongs in 'history's hall of fame',[52] that he gave his patients the opportunity to 'be' in free association, and that this process of *self-disclosure* is a factor in effective therapy. He would then go beyond Freud by making self-disclosure the primary factor determining health, extending even to physical health through psychosomatic processes.

... this talking about oneself to another person is what I call self-disclosure. It would appear, without assuming anything, that self-disclosure is a factor in the process of effective counselling or psychotherapy. Would it be too arbitrary an assumption to propose that people become clients *because they have not disclosed themselves in some optimum degree to the people in their life?*[53]

He attributes the non-disclosure to role-playing, which is placed in sharp contrast with real self-being.

Roles for people in Victorian days were even more restrictive than today, and Freud discovered that when people struggled to avoid being and knowing themselves, they got sick.

... Groddeck shows the contrast between the *public self—* pretentious role playing—and the warded off but highly dynamic *id*—which I here very loosely translate as 'real self'.

Roles are inescapable. They must be played or else the social system will not work. A role by definition is a repertoire of behaviour patterns which must be rattled off in appropriate contexts, and all behaviour which is irrelevant to the role must be suppressed.[54]

It is evident that there is a kind of splitting process going on in which self is separated from role, role is then equated with *pretentious* role playing against which the *real* self struggles, and finally a caricature or parody of both the concept and the phenomenon of role is embodied in the words 'rattled off in appropriate contexts'. And although he speaks of the very loose translation of id as real self, the fact that it is done at all shows a willingness to overlook all the socially formative processes which might give something 'real' and valuable to the self. The socially formative processes, which are a continuous transformation of social structure into socialised selves, are either overlooked, leading to the evocation of desirable human qualities from the id or 'natural' aspects of the person; or the social is made synonymous with whatever distorts and limits personal growth. The result is an impoverishment of both the psychological concept of self and the sociological concept of social structure. Most particularly the concept of socialisation, which belongs to social psychology conceived as a non-trivial interdisciplinary study, is lost, since its complexity and significance are reduced to that of a one-way process of suppression of real selves.

Jourard's failure to grasp the complexity of social processes shows itself at other points. When he refers to social structures it is in such vague terms as 'social systems that tend to prevent authentic existence',[55] or as 'the status quo', 'the Establishment', 'institutions'. The critical mood of these references is not supported by any power of discrimination which might give precision, and therefore a cutting edge, to the assertions. In fact there is such a loose and anecdotal form that names can be thrown in for effect, in awkward contexts and without any substantial discussion or bibliographical acknowledgement. It was the case with his reaction to Freud and it is so again in relation to Marx.

> . . . most of us live in a conceptual world, unrefreshed by new perceptual experiences of the beings we have named. This can get to be a stagnant world, one that sensitive men feel to be suffocating and boring. And because the social world in which we live resists change—for reasons Marx made abundantly clear—we are shaped and socialized, such that our imaginative consciousness becomes crippled.[56]

As a consequence of his superficial analysis of the problem, Jourard's recommendations for remedying it are unrealistic. For example, he calls for the creation of respectable 'check-out places, where people could go, preferably before they get sick, to be whatever they want to be, with private cells and communal rooms, a minimal routine and spartan meals. The healing effects of such retreat, self-exploration and self-disclosure would reduce the need for psychotherapeutic and psychiatric treatment such that

> Sales of drugs would diminish, and the directors of pharmaceutical firms would send lobbies to Washington to persuade legislators the houses were subversive and un-American.[57]

Although Jourard says that such places would probably only be healing for middle-class people he does not follow through to any of the implications of his own statement; that it would only solve the problems of the minority already least deprived; that the 'respectability' of the retreats to middle-class users would not make them acceptable to working-class people, who would anyway be unable to afford them; that in general middle-class people can already find private help and treatment for their neurotic illnesses whilst working-class people, more frequently diagnosed as 'schizophrenic', must rely on the predominantly pharmaceutical treatments available in the large psychiatric institutions (thus ruling out any need for drug firms to lobby the legislators).

It is not too strong to say that Jourard's solutions are *fantastic*: they presuppose that class differences have already disappeared (if 'check-out' places for all were possible), or that there could be such a change in attitudes that social relationships would be transformed.

> If, beginning with the president's office in Washington, a serious dedication to human awakening was awakened, with appropriate budget appended, a fantastic revolution would have thereby been commenced.[58]

This is the most incredibly revealing passage in all of Jourard's work. The idea that a president, whose personality is subject to extremely fine sifting processes which make up the power system, could be 'awakened' to the extent that he would seek to change the power structure—and by implication that the interests embedded in that structure would let him—must be high fantasy. Notice also the language in which it is couched: the repetition of 'awakening', 'awakened', as though to bring it about by the power of words; the sudden lapse into the most bureaucratic of phrases, 'with appropriate budget appended', with the realisation that wishes must command resources; and then the ambiguity of 'fantastic revolution'— meaning perhaps a far-reaching revolution, perhaps a fantasy about revolution or a wish that the people involved could admit their fantasies (their ids, their real selves), and so be revolutionised. Jourard's own self, disclosed in the form of his writing much more clearly than in the throw-away autobiographical chapter in which he seeks explicitly to disclose himself, seems to consist of an over-whelming wish to improve men in their social relationships, but such inadequate concepts of the self or of social structures that he cannot produce either effective criticism or suggestions for realistic alternatives. He is a man which a profound wish, but nothing to say; and that is why his language is repeatedly invaded by phrases which are dictated by the obstacles he encounters in disclosing his wishes. In the light of this the form of his empirical work may now perhaps be better understood.

Jourard's empirical work is based on a conviction that self-disclosure and body contact are of great importance, both as foci of research which might transform psychology and as means of 'getting in touch' to counteract the alienating forces of modern society.

If I did not think self-disclosure was the most important thing in the world to study, I would not have carried on with the work as far as we carried it.[59]

In relation to the discipline of psychology

... eighty years of scientific research in psychology, as it reposes on the library shelves, may not embody an authentic image of man. In fact it may be a museum of the lies told by suspicious subjects to experimenters they did not trust. I therefore proposed that we do all of psychology over again.[60]

As a countervailing force

... in a society which fosters the alienation of person from person, I can think of no more direct way to get in touch than by touching.[61]

The strong feelings then struggle to emerge from the grip of a method of investigation which does, in the worst sense, attempt to 'do all of psychology over again'. Basically it consists of asking people to say how much they tell each other about themselves or how much they touch each other. Certain regularities and typical patterns are mapped for various categories of people—kinsmen, students, nurses, age grades, national groups—and the degree of self-disclosure is varied experimentally to show consequences of the change. The 'dyadic effect' by which disclosure begets disclosure is discovered and emphasised presumably because it provides a kind of 'evidence' to support Jourard's method. Of this method he said that when he found his client-centred and modified psychoanalytic techniques did not work with provincial people he tried to offer intelligent, well-intentioned help in the context of sharing his experiences. At first he was anxious about the change as well as about the possibility that therapists might unwittingly serve as counter-revolutionary agents for the status quo. But after a while

I found that the outcomes of our counseling or therapeutic trans-actions were much more mutually satisfying. Moreover, I didn't have the feeling I was functioning as an unwitting agent of social control.[62]

Since the argument is about 'unwitting' social control it is clearly insubstantial to say 'I didn't have the feeling' etc. However, the absence of concepts of the social, mentioned earlier, will again account for Jourard's complete failure to answer his own point, just as an absence of any sense of the available sociological evidence enables him to 'discover' the phenomenon of communication, the dyadic basis of relatively equal status interchanges, the different patterns of disclosure between different categories of people. This is the unfortunate sense in which he attempts to do psychology over again: he selects one aspect of a sociopsychological phenomenon (in the past it might have been, say, instinct, meaning, cognitive dissonance, achievement), gives it an overriding importance such that it might revolutionise both psychology and our societies, and then researches it laboriously showing little more than the fact that there is such a phenomenon which can be measured. The phenomenon is, however, so reduced by 'unwitting' extraction from its social and psychological context that the results of research are extremely disappointing. And yet the form of this research is self-consciously orthodox, even to the point of saying

> We did the kinds of things one does to reduce error in measurement, such as test for reliability, ensure that the content of the questionnaire was representative of a person's experience, simplify the instructions, and explore some of the dimensions of validity.[63]

He then admits that his questionnaires could be a record of 'thousands of lies', but takes comfort in the fact that 'at least the subjects lied with some consistency'. There is in this no sensitivity to these qualities of human action which rest on control of information, making it almost certain that the respondents 'lied', that is, selectively disclosed themselves. Neither is there any awareness of the social processes which create norms of self-disclosure; nor of the degree to which power structures operate through control of information and communication. Nor, finally, to the phenomenon of lying, quite consistently—indeed with pathological consistency—to oneself. No wonder Freud was sent upstairs to 'history's hall of fame'.

Once again the language of Jourard's papers tells everything: they begin with a cry from the heart, which is quickly strangled in simplistic surveys or experiments so typical of the questionnaire studies of American undergraduates which litter the pages of older psychology journals that he does literally seem to be doing all of psychology over again, speaking the jargon of crude measurement. Lastly the 'feeling' breaks through again and the call goes out to 'get in touch' and save the world.

As a type of process in the creation of theories by reaction to existing theories, Jourard defines for us the case in which a man of great capacity for human feeling interrogates his experience and attempts to translate one mode of this experience into a theory of self. However, the repressed part of his text can be seen through the surface of this transparent self—it is Freud, the uncompromising, bitter, even cynical, but patient questioner who is so much more often put away than answered.

REFERENCES

1 G. H. Mead. *Mind, Self and Society*, University of Chicago Press, Chicago (1934), p. 211
2 H. S. Sullivan. *Interpersonal Theory of Psychiatry*, Tavistock, London (1955), p. 17
3 ibid., p. 16
4 ibid., p. 17
5 B. Bosanquet. *Philosophical Theory of the State*, Macmillan, London and Basingstoke (1899), p. 117
6 G. H. Mead. *Mind, Self and Society*. University of Chicago Press, Chicago (1934), p. 219
7 ibid., pp. 186–8
8 ibid., p. 175
9 ibid., p. 195
10 ibid., p. 154
11 ibid., p. 157
12 ibid., p. 162
13 ibid., p. 164
14 ibid., p. 195
15 ibid., p. 200
16 P. Berger. *Invitation to Sociology*, Pelican, Harmondsworth, Middx (1966), p. 168
17 H. S. Sullivan. *Interpersonal Theory of Psychiatry*, Tavistock, London (1955), p. 16
18 ibid., p. 19
19 ibid., p. 20
20 ibid., p. 35
21 ibid., p. 110
22 ibid., p. 39
23 ibid., p. xv of Introduction by M. B. Cohen

24 ibid., p. 109
25 ibid., p. 165
26 ibid., p. 190
27 ibid., p. 169
28 ibid., p. 373
29 ibid., p. 330
30 ibid., p. 167
31 ibid., p. 166
32 ibid., p. 213
33 E. H. Erikson. *Childhood and Society*, Pelican, Harmondsworth, Middx (1965), p. 31
34 ibid., p. 32
35 ibid., p. 33
36 S. Freud. *Standard Edition*, Vol. VII (ed. J. Strachey), Hogarth, London (1953), p. 239
37 ibid., p. 240
38 E. H. Erikson. *Childhood and Society*, Pelican, Harmondsworth, Middx (1965), p. 57
39 ibid., p. 59
40 ibid., p. 55
41 Identity and the life cycle. *Psychol. Issues*, **1**, 1 (1959), 121
42 *Childhood and Society*, Pelican, Harmondsworth, Middx (1965), p. 86
43 ibid., p. 88
44 S. Freud. *Standard Edition*, Vol. XI (ed. J. Strachey), Hogarth, London (1957), p. 190
45 E. H. Erikson. *Childhood and Society*, Pelican, Harmondsworth, Middx (1965), p. 15
46 Identity and the life cycle, *Psychol. Issues*, **1**, 1 (1959), 120–1
47 *Childhood and Society*, Pelican, Harmondsworth, Middx (1965), p. 112
48 S. Freud. *An Outline of Psychoanalysis*, Hogarth, London (1949), p. 8
49 E. H. Erikson. *Childhood and Society*, Pelican, Harmondsworth, Middx (1965), p. 15
50 S. M. Jourard. *Personal Adjustment. An approach through the study of healthy personality*, Macmillan, New York and London (1958)
51 G. W. Allport. *Pattern and Growth in Personality*, Holt, Rinehart & Winston, New York (1961), p. 148

52 S. M. Jourard. *The Transparent Self*, Van Nostrand, New York and Wokingham, Berks. (1964), p. 21
53 ibid., p. 21
54 ibid., p. 22
55 *Self-Disclosure*, Wiley, New York and Chichester (1971), p. 188
56 *Disclosing Man to Himself*, Van Nostrand, New York and Wokingham, Berks. (1968), p. 176
57 ibid., p. 203
58 ibid., p. 196
59 S. M. Jourard. *Self-Disclosure*, Wiley, New York and Chichester (1971), p. 187
60 S. M. Jourard. *The Transparent Self*, Van Nostrand, New York and Wokingham, Berks. (1964), p. 19
61 S. M. Jourard. Out of touch. *New Society*, 9 Nov. (1967), p. 662
62 S. M. Jourard. *Self-Disclosure*, Wiley, New York and Chichester (1971), p. 16
63 ibid., p. 102

3
The Reaction to Behaviourism and Refusal of Alternatives

3.1 G. W. ALLPORT

Personality theorists who opposed themselves to Freud because of what they regarded as his psychological bias could take up the aim of creating a more social definition of self, and find in this a clear goal which made relevant a body of knowledge and an area of research to occupy them for many years. In retrospect this work can be seen to have reinforced a dichotomy between person and society and to have brought about some reworking and attenuation of the original contributions by Freud; nevertheless, as a theme it unified one of the neo-Freudian groups, leading to a certain amount of genuinely interdisciplinary research between anthropology and psychoanalysis.

A rather different pattern is discernible in other cases where the flight from a particular identification is much more obvious whilst the existence of a clear alternative is not assured. Such unrelieved role-conflict must call for sustained and powerful strategies if a self is to be held together and I offer as an example of this G. W. Allport. His most likely, and therefore most threatening, identification is in the role of American psychologist. It is threatening because he sees American psychology as governed by 'associationist and reactive hypotheses',[1] or by 'the creeds of positivism and behaviorism'.[2] Language of this provocative kind contradicts the extremely conciliatory and humble attitude professed in the same essay.

As I have said elsewhere, some of my colleagues treat personality as a quasi-closed system. I respect their work and know that eventually their contributions will fit into the larger frame. I feel no personal animosity towards the associates with whom I have ventured to disagree. But what I dislike in our profession is the strong aura of arrogance found in presently fashionable dogmas. To my mind humility is a virtue appropriate for social and psychological scientists to cultivate.[3]

If the indirectness of the style is translated, Allport is saying that the (nameless) others are arrogant and dogmatic; and yet he cannot reject them—they will all 'fit into the larger frame'—nor will he admit to disliking them. The contradictions and denials in this are so great that I feel they must be taken into account in attempting to explain and understand the creation of a body of knowledge which runs to over one hundred and forty items in forty-six years.[4] There is evidence[5] that at one time he was the second most influential theorist in American clinical and abnormal psychology, and it is my impression that his work is very frequently cited in general psychology courses designed for early years at university, extramural courses, college of education courses and in schools: in short it is a large and influential body of knowledge.

How is it then that this work has gained acceptance and honours for its author? What role has he taken up and why does he react to behaviourism with such vigour? Do his arguments damage behaviourism to a significant extent? Fortunately there is among his many papers and books a short autobiography which, with exemplary consistency and sincerity, he has offered to us as insight into the relations between himself and his work.

Merleau-Ponty's statement that the 'central theme' of a philosophy gives meaning to its particular uses, finds an echo in Allport's conception of the 'personal idea'.

> Bergson held that every philosophic life pivots on a single 'personal idea', even though the attempt to express this idea never fully succeeds. This dictum, savoring as it does of idealism and romanticism, is alien to the Lockean image of man that dominates Anglo-American psychology. And yet I confess I am attracted to this proposition. It seems to state in a broad way a testable hypothesis.[6]

And Allport is quite willing to express his personal idea as clearly as he can.

> I suppose it has to do with the search for a theoretical system— for one that will allow for truth wherever found, one that will encompass the totality of human experience, and do full justice to the nature of man.[7]

He goes on to say that the idea is given better expression by the fact that his former PhD students presented him with two volumes of their work, inscribed 'From his students—in appreciation of his respect for their individuality'. So it is clear enough, not least to its author, that his central theme is a concern for the whole man in his unique individuality; and it is a scientific idea calling for a 'theoretical system' and 'testable hypotheses'. Thus Allport's work has taken on the quality of a *perpetual reminder*. Whenever any psychologist has sought to detect similarities between people or to establish a common dimension Allport has weighed in with a statement that the unique qualities of the separate person must not be neglected. Whenever a psychologist has dealt with one aspect of a person Allport has been eager to stress that this is only one part of the picture; that a unique integration of qualities defines the person. And although he acknowledges that abstraction is a productive scientific technique he is always ready with an emphatic, moralistic warning to any psychologist who practises it

. . . he has no right to forget what he has decided to neglect.[8]

All this is clear enough for it is on the surface of Allport's work. It is interesting mainly because the discipline of psychology has found it possible to admit, and indeed to embrace, its own 'honourable opposition'. It has created the role of critic for one who will remain within the rules of a complex, knowledge-producing game; a critic who feels no animosity to those he disagrees with, who sees his own work as a supplement and not an alternative to whatever he criticises, who will express his spiritual ideas in the terminology of science; who will, above all, allow the huge enterprise of psychology as a natural science to proceed carrying its philosophical and meta-physical problems in the separate compartment reserved for personality and personalistic psychology, a reminder that at its inception psychology needed to differentiate itself from philosophy and hold firmly to the growing natural sciences. It is not that separation of these large themes results in such concentration upon them as would lead to new discoveries; rather that they become both separated and trivialised or mystified.

Humility and some mysticism, I felt, were indispensable for me . . .[9]

What is not clear, though in my view much more interesting, is the way in which Allport sustains his role, occasionally running close to danger when more radical questions are touched upon. For example, he says

> No problem is more challenging than the degree and manner to which the structure of a person's thought reflects his own personal life history. Given a certain start in life and a certain environmental impetus, must a life evolve a certain cognitive content and style?[10]

Immediately the question is dropped; the next sentence reads

> The following autobiographical essay does not of course answer this question.[11]

I disagree and will try to show how rich the humble, carefully chosen words are for insight into Allport's work, but first it is worth noting how he frames the above question before setting it aside. 'Given a certain start in life and a certain environmental impetus' implies a considerable importance for events of childhood, and yet he regularly criticises Freud for this assertion; 'must a life evolve a certain cognitive content and style?', splits cognition from the more emotional processes which may affect a person's choice of emphasis in the study of personality and the ways in which their cognitions interact with emotionally charged attitudes. There is a further implicit split between 'content and style' which again contradicts his own holistic principles, until the question falls apart, unanswerable, and unanswered, because of the way it is put. What then is the point of the question? I think it is a gesture of humility which is not carried through to self-criticism but serves merely to show that he has taken certain possibilities into account and thereby escaped their limitations. In effect, humility saves him both from self-criticism and from the need to carry through and destroy if necessary what he feels to be worth criticising: it creates the generally positive stance which is the Allport self.

Textual evidence has already shown that Allport's repeated calls for humility, and denial of personal animosity are at war with strong feelings

> . . . what I dislike in our profession is the strong aura of arrogance found in presently fashionable dogmas.[12]

Furthermore, he believes that if psychologists embraced behaviourism and positivism

Our methods would be restricted, our theories one-sided, and our students would be intimidated by a tyrannical and temporary scientism.[13]

And possibly the greatest contradiction in all in this self-styled 'polemical' work is that the targets are rarely specified and criticised in detail. They usually remain the broadest categories such as learning theory, dimensionalism, over-emphasis on unconscious processes, projection tests and simplified drive theories of motivation.[14] Consequently the criticisms have little effect and often reveal such a limited appreciation of the criticised areas that people working in them are probably further convinced of the rightness of their approach.

Another noticeable quality of Allport's writing is that he spends much time constructing his own role as the lone critic keeping up a steady defence against a majority who swing with popular sentiment. The opposition are labelled 'fashionable explanatory principles',[15] 'popular formulae',[16] 'presently fashionable dogmas',[17] whilst he goes on, Jesus-like, protecting a precious truth. All this from a man whose personal idea about unique individuality is probably the most *popular* idea of all in a society founded on the premise of individual freedom, and whose personal position and influence are fully established.

If the notion of a Jesus-figure seems exaggerated, consider Allport's characterisation of the ill-defined others as 'prevailing psychological idols',[18] 'the creeds of positivism and behaviorism'[19] 'a dimensional debauch'.[20] The source of this religiosity, which interestingly he projects into others, speaking always in the language of science, might be found in the autobiography where he describes his mother as bringing to her sons

... an eager sense of philosophical questing and the importance of searching for ultimate religious answers.[21]

With these words Allport once again casts a glance at the possibility of deeper analysis but does not pursue it; he says that 'family relationships are of highest explanatory importance' but the autobiographer

... does not know how to separate primary formative influences in his heredity and early environment from those that are of minor or negligible significance.[22]

Allport should speak for himself and not cast aside so lightly the whole psychoanalytic tradition. His reason for rejecting Freud is so clinically significant at such an elementary level that the slightest degree of insight would throw his own personal idea into severe doubt. He mentions in a joking tone, 'Yes, my single encounter with Freud was traumatic'. His account of the meeting I must quote in full.

With a callow forwardness characteristic of age twenty-two, I wrote to Freud announcing that I was in Vienna and implied that no doubt he would be glad to make my acquaintance. I received a kind reply in his own handwriting inviting me to come to his office at a certain time. Soon after I had entered the famous red burlap room with pictures of dreams on the wall, he summoned me to his inner office. He did not speak to me but sat in expectant silence, for me to state my mission. I was not prepared for silence and had to think fast to find a suitable conversational gambit. I told him of an episode on the tram car on my way to his office. A small boy about four years of age had displayed a conspicuous dirt phobia. He kept saying to his mother, 'I don't want to sit there . . . don't let that dirty man sit beside me'. To him everything was *schmutzig*. His mother was a well-starched *Hausfrau*, so dominant and purposive looking that I thought the cause and effect apparent.

When I finished my story Freud fixed his kindly therapeutic eyes upon me and said, 'And was that little boy you?' Flabbergasted and feeling a bit guilty, I contrived to change the subject. While Freud's misunderstanding of my motivation was amusing, it also started a deep train of thought. I realized that he was accustomed to neurotic defenses and that my manifest motivation (a sort of rude curiosity and youthful ambition) escaped him. For therapeutic progress he would have to cut through my defences, but it so happened that therapeutic progress was not here an issue.

This experience taught me that depth psychology, for all its merits, may plunge too deep, and that psychologists would do well to give full recognition to manifest motives before probing the unconscious. Although I never regarded myself as anti-Freudian, I have been critical of psychoanalytic excesses.[23]

How incredibly ingenuous is this report. Allport, the young, keen scholar from a 'wholesome' background,[24] going to see the sexually dirty (this was 1922) Freud,[25] flustered into a free association so precise in its reference that it might have been used as an example of the power of psychoanalytic theory, and then denying its relevance continuously ever since. It is the purest case I know of reaction to a theory which cannot be ignored (he did go to see Freud) but which cannot be admitted into the self-concept without drastic censorship. Thus Allport surrounds Freud with a positive generality—firstly by admitting the force of drives primarily in infancy:

Although drives cannot account for all later motivation, they are with us all our life, and in infancy they completely dominate the motivational scene. [26]

Secondly, by contrasting health and sickness

Some theories of becoming are based largely upon the antics of captive and desperate rats. Fewer theories have derived from the study of healthy human beings, those who strive not so much to preserve life as to make it worth living. [27]

To try to limit the importance of Freud to childhood is quite beside the point since it is precisely the connection between childhood and adulthood which is contained in the theory. Furthermore, for many decades, before the development of child analysis the clinical evidence had been gathered retrospectively from adults. [28]

The consequences of this kind of working over and reshaping of theories may be estimated by the credit given to Allport in a major textbook.

Perhaps no other psychologist has had so influential a role in restoring and purifying the ego concept as Allport. [29]

Again, after all these years, the sense that Freud's theory needs to be cleaned up, or 'purified'.

In moving away from Freud Allport notes that some Freudians have spoken of the autonomy of the ego and he links this with his concept of the functional autonomy of motives—the concept that motives may be transformed from an original base into a new quality typical of the motives of the 'mature, healthy, normal' person. In a sense he makes room for some motives to be strong prime movers fuelled by conscious will or, as he calls it, 'propriate striving'. This attempt to counterbalance Freud and the drive theorists takes him close to the existentialists, a position which he treats with almost as great ambivalence as he shows towards Freud. In his 1937 book

Allport makes no reference to existentialism but gradually he notices a correspondence between his own concept of propriate striving and the existentialists' insistence that a man, by reason of his ability to choose, is responsible for the direction of his life whatever that direction is. One implication of Sartre's work, for example, is that to explain one's behaviour as determined by unconscious motives is a kind of bad faith. The difficulty is that existentialists such as Sartre are godless, radical and determined to open themselves to the more desolate aspects of human experience, so that Allport is faced with the problem of filtering out the unwelcome elements. He does it by explaining them as socioculturally influenced.

> When life is a hard struggle for existence, and when, as in war-torn Europe, there appears to be 'no exit' (Sartre), then personalities do in fact grow tense and develop a heavier sense of duty than of hope. In America, on the contrary, where the search for a rich, full life suffers fewer impediments, we expect to find a more open, gregarious, trusting type of personality. This expectation is reflected in the prevailing optimism of American psycho-therapy . . . [30]

It is tantalising to see Allport move to the very brink of self-criticism and then draw back. At other times he touches on the same issue, saying at one point that he expected German psychologists to understand better his morphogenic methods. He goes just a little further in relation to South Africa.

> . . . my own psychological bias had perhaps led me to under-estimate the forces of history and of traditional social structure more strikingly evident in South Africa. [31]

Thus at the crucial point of contact between Allport's 'individual' and the sociocultural environment he avoids any encounter strong enough to undermine the 'personal idea[1] which informs his work. This in spite of the fact that he is regarded as a *social* psychologist.

Having sealed off the threatening aspects of existentialism by sociocultural explanation, which is not carried through substantially enough to include his own theory, Allport is able in his later work to refer extensively to the particular group of American personality theorists known as existentialists, notably Rogers and Maslow. But since these theorists have by now produced their own special kind of benign existentialism they do not pose a threat. In another section the production of this special kind of existentialism will be examined in some detail.

Finally the most accurate description of Allport's theory is prompted by his tendency to register every development in personality theory no matter how distant it may be from his own and to take out of it some item which he finds acceptable. For example, he notes

> a Hindu formulation of the essential nature of man ... more synoptic and complete than any one school of Western thought.[32]

Giving it one page Allport passes on, saying that he included it 'as a bare token of adequacy'. Thus Allport's theory is a *collection* of elements taken from their context by the strategy of positive generality, controlled firmly by his personal idea or central theme. Considered as a process in the production of knowledge it can be seen that knowledge does not arise solely as a result of the creation of new ideas: in many cases 'new knowledge' is a *response* to what are thought to be the dominant ideas in a field, and the quality of the response may be controlled by the self-concept of a theorist (together with its socioculturally influenced components) acting as a paradigm and limiting rather severely what is allowed into serious consideration.

REFERENCES

1 G. W. Allport. *The Person in Psychology*, Beacon Press, Boston, Mass. (1968), p. 376
2 ibid., p. 376
3 ibid., p. 405
4 ibid., bibliography
5 C. S. Hall and G. Lindzey. *Theories of Personality*, Wiley, New York and Chichester (1957), p. 290
6 G. W. Allport. *The Person in Psychology*, Beacon Press, Boston, Mass. (1968), p. 376
7 ibid., p. 406
8 ibid., p. 405
9 ibid., p. 382
10 ibid., p. 376
11 ibid., p. 376
12 ibid., p. 406

13 ibid., p. 406
14 ibid., p. 405
15 ibid., p. 405
16 ibid., p. 405
17 ibid., p. 406
18 ibid., p. 404
19 ibid., p. 406
20 ibid., p. 99
21 ibid., p. 379
22 ibid., p. 378
23 ibid., p. 383
24 ibid., p. 379
25 G. W. Allport. *Pattern and Growth in Personality*, Holt, Rinehart & Winston, New York (1961), p. 148
26 ibid., p. 191
27 G. W. Allport. *Becoming*, Yale University Press, New Haven, Conn., and London (1955), p. 18
28 A. Freud. *Normality and Pathology in Childhood*, Penguin, Harmondsworth, Middx (1973), p. 13
29 G. W. Allport. *Theories of Personality*, Wiley, New York and Chichester (1957), p. 289
30 G. W. Allport. *Becoming*, Yale University Press, New Haven, Conn., and London (1955), p. 81
31 G. W. Allport. *The Person in Psychology*, Beacon Press, Boston, Mass., (1968), p. 401
32 G. W. Allport. *Pattern and Growth in Personality*. Holt, Rinehart & Winston, New York (1961), p. 565

4
A Kind of Existentialism

4.1 G. A. KELLY

Some time ago I was asked by Don Bannister, who knew that I had begun to work on the sociology of knowledge in relation to personality theories, to write something on George Kelly for a wide-ranging symposium he intended to publish. At this time I had not studied Kelly very closely although I had looked at Rogers, Maslow and Allport, being greatly interested in their patterns of reaction to Freud, behaviourism and existentialism. In relation particularly to existentialism it seemed to me that just as the neo-Freudians had 'socialised' Freud so as to create a more bland, optimistic, acceptable and marketable kind of knowledge based on his work, so had the more individualist psychologists imported another great European source of knowledge—phenomenology and existentialism—but in such a selective way that much of its force and originality had been left somewhere in mid-Atlantic or in the customs posts for knowledge which surround societies, determining what can be let in and at what price to the importer.

In working on Kelly I was struck by his intense crusading individualism which seemed to lack any knowledge of *social* facts, or of philosophical predecessors whose work he tried to reinvent in simplified form. His quite genuine 'innocence' and willingness to look freshly at human personality seemed, however, to exemplify the phenomenological method of existentialism even though he repudiated existentialism by virtue of his extremely superficial and biased view of it. This contradiction added support to my own working hypothesis that American culture formed a particularly interesting case of the operation of cultural norms in relation to both the importation and the independent creation of knowledge. On the one hand certain kinds of knowledge were excluded by the self-concepts of the American theorists but on the other hand they were forced by the nature of the subject matter to invent its rough equivalent. I therefore characterised Kelly as a 'reluctant existentialist'.[1]

Another group, sharing much with Kelly, were in contrast, willing to call themselves existentialists, but only on certain conditions: that they be allowed their own very special interpretation of the phenomenological and existentialist sources. In so doing they create an American variant of existentialism which shows with stark clarity the transformation processes involved in taking up a 'foreign' body of knowledge and provides at the same time a critique of the variant as it now stands—an American kind of existentialism. I shall look first at Abraham Maslow and Carl Rogers, who are usually regarded as leading spokesmen for the third force or humanistic group of psychologists, and then say a little more about George Kelly before summarising and criticising the characteristics and influence of this field of knowledge.

4.2 A. H. MASLOW

In order to simplify reference I shall concentrate on the set of papers chosen by Abraham Maslow in 1969 for publication under the title *The Farther Reaches of Human Nature*.[2] Although his death in 1970 prevented him from carrying through an intention to rewrite and update the material, adding a preface and epilogue, it seems to represent his mature thought in a reasonably fair way. There is no evidence that he planned to retract or alter his views substantially and I assume his revised manuscript would have read like the main body of his work: a constant and fairly repetitive reflection on a few main themes.

Like so many self-theorists, Maslow began with a reaction to behaviourism. The birth of a child changed him as a psychologist.

> It made the behaviourism I had been so enthusiastic about look so foolish that I could not stomach it any more. It was impossible. (p. 167)

The positivistic 'scientific', value-free mechanomorphic psychology (p. 3) consists of non-theories; a denial (in the psychoanalytic sense) of the problems (p. 336). And yet even here Maslow equivocates and shows an inability to firmly reject anything, matched as will become apparent by a reciprocal inability to unconditionally accept other work, with the possible exception of Carl Rogers'. Behaviourism is therefore allowed a place in a superordinate scheme which integrates it along with Freudianism into a 'third force', humanistic psychology, which is again surpassed by a fourth, transcendent psychology (p. 4), thus avoiding the pathologies of dichotomous thinking (p. 167). Yet a further contradiction is generated by this view of dichotomous thinking as pathological, which stands so uneasily alongside Maslow's own predilection for setting out tables and lists of human motives, values and pathologies in dichotomous terms (e.g. p. 333). He appears to resolve this dilemma by including in his list of 'fully human' attributes the ability to transcend dichotomies (p. 333) but the fact that he puts this ability into his list of 'B values', the fully human qualities Maslow wishes to emphasise, means that it is excluded from the list of 'D values' which correspond to the more elemental needs of a human being for protection and identity, etc. In other words there is still a dichotomy of B values and D values. How does he resolve that?

He resolves it by choosing to regard the D values and the B values as a continuum. Having overcome possible deficits at the level of biology and identity the human being can go on to embrace the goals and rewards of 'being' more fully human. This reveals a typical Maslow technique for joining together or transcending the polarised opposites which he either discovers or creates by his own terminology. It is so pervasive a strategy that I am inclined to call it his central theme—*the integration of differences and oppositions*. Not only does he put the D values and the B values on a continuum, he also attempts to integrate the human and the biological—wo/man and nature—by arguing that there is a given 'instinctoid' tendency for the human being to self-actualise, that is to go beyond the satisfaction of the more basic needs to seek satisfaction of the higher needs (another dichotomy) which relate to the more spiritual and transcendental human experiences. He then uses this same argument—an instinctoid tendency flowing over from the biological to the human—to assert that the higher values are not simply chance elaborations or elusive, scientifically untestable fancies, but biologically given tendencies which seek to realise themselves. Deprivation can occur at all levels; at the level of the desire for truth and mystical experiences as well as at the lower levels of need, at the level of 'metamotives' as well as at the level of motives.

Lack of metamotive gratifications, or of those values, produces what I have described as general and specific metapathologies. I would maintain these are deficiency diseases on the same continuum with scurvy, pellagra, love-hunger, etc. (p. 23)

Thus all aspects of human existence are integrated and a single medical model of deficiency leading to disease may be applied everywhere. What benefits accrue to Maslow from this extreme simplification? Mostly, I think, the benefits of scientific credibility: for when challenged about the religiosity of his psychology of transcendence he can point to loosely relevant biological evidence or biological investigation techniques. For example, he feels a need to justify his recommendation that psychologists should study the most 'moral ethical or saintly people' (p. 7), and says

> I propose for discussion and eventually for research the use of selected good specimens (superior specimens) as biological assays for studying the best capability that the human species has. (p. 5)

The fact that criteria of goodness are not as readily available in the human sphere as they are in the biological casts a shadow of doubt across his mind but he rapidly dispels it by the conclusion that philosophers have failed to agree because they have included bad specimens in their deliberations instead of concentrating on the good, an incredibly self-confirming pattern of argument. As biological evidence for a conviction that his chosen group, the 'self-actualisers', really are good he cites Olds' study of self-stimulation by rats with implanted electrodes—the rats stimulate pleasure rather than pain (p. 11). Kamiya is also said to have shown that human subjects can to some extent control their EEG patterns and this means it is possible to 'teach people how to feel happy and serene' (p. 12). The fact that some people take pleasures of a perverse kind is disposed of by dichotomising healthy and unheathly pleasures. He then moves quickly to the conclusion that self-regulation will have the most desirable consequences; it is anti-authoritarian and brings into serious consideration the Taoist viewpoint (p. 14).

The speed of this movement from implanted electrodes to Taoism is breathtaking. In each case examples are dwelt upon only long enough to extract a hint or suggestion that can be turned towards his central theme. He arrives at Taoism, probably feels a little naked scientifically and draws back, without the courage to accept or reject, only to integrate.

> . . . normative zeal is not incompatible with scientific objectivity, but can be integrated with it, eventuating in a higher form of objectivity, i.e., the Taoistic. (p 365)

It seems that Maslow projects, or goes in search of, dichotomies and then pulls the extremes closer together by word-play: this he calls transcendence. In the process he picks up just what he needs from the extremes and jettisons any unwelcome implications.

Having anchored the 'highest' human strivings in the biological, partly as a way of keeping a foothold in science, he is faced with the problem of what biological qualities come in to the human being. Already he has suggested that self-regulative tendencies will produce desirable results and he adds to this the idea that there is available a *real self* which only needs to be released or facilitated by cultural or social non-interference. The 'real self' which struggles to actualise itself, is of course mostly a projection into 'nature' of Maslow's preferred human characteristics. The fact that it is a projection can be seen by the contradictory evidence he presents for its existence. He claims that just because it exists in his good specimens it is 'species wide' and 'supracultural' (p. 341), even though his good specimens are relatively few. He assumes that all are striving even though few make it (p. 26). The majority are held back by cultures which do not facilitate actualisation (by non-interference) (p. 153) and, indeed, the majority of cultures, historically, do not actualise the human potential. To that extent normality is no guide;

... normalcy would be rather the kind of sickness or crippling or stunting that we share with everybody else and therefore don't notice. (p. 27)

Passing over for the moment the radical social critique implicit in this view we are thrown back again onto the criterion group—the self-actualisers—and particularly the transcendent ones who enjoy mystical experiences. But even Maslow becomes less than sure about these categories of people

... those who were clearly healthy, but with little or no experiences (sic) of transcendence, and those in whom transcendent experiencing was important and even central. As examples of the former kind of health, I may cite Mrs Eleanor Roosevelt, and, probably Truman and Eisenhower. As examples of the latter, I can use Aldous Huxley, and probably Schweitzer, Buber and Einstein.

It is unfortunate that I can no longer be theoretically neat at this level. I find not only self-actualizing persons who transcend, but also *non*-healthy people, non-self-actualizers, who have important transcendent experience. (p. 293)

However, little setbacks like this do not lead Maslow to question the basis of his theory but rather to 'transcend' its inadequacies by inventing a fresh, more inclusive, but of necessity increasingly general, criterion—the retreat into positive generality I identified earlier. For example, after applying the health/sickness criterion over the continuum of human experience, and seeing deviants as groping ineffectually in the common human direction of self-actualisation towards transcendence, he attempts to assimilate these differences to the concept of 'full humanness', against which deviations may be seen as diminutions of humanness (p. 296). A progression along the path of reaction to behaviourism can now be seen: his own 'peak experience' at the birth of a child turns him away from behaviourism towards more holistic concerns which lead him through a variety of fields in search of views and evidence which are compatible or supportive, and gradually to the limits of human transcendental experience as more and more inclusive categories have to be found in order to integrate the differences and oppositions which intrude upon and threaten his various 'integrations'.

However, there are two things he cannot move beyond very easily: the first is his identification with existentialism resulting from the primary position he accords to B (being) values; the second is his identification with Freud whose practice he wishes to retain in a very substantial way. Existentialism does not delay him all that long. A dichotomy allows him to reject 'nay-saying existentialism' (p. 335). Sartre is said to deny biology (p. 193) and so his kind of arbitrary existentialism may be flatly rejected (p. 33) along with Genet's 'crummy' books (p. 179). Although in yet another contradiction reminiscent of Allport and Kelly he embraces these existentialists' concerns. Sartre's autodidact, the tragi-comic figure who is reading his way through the public library in alphabetical order, has a parallel in Maslow's work

> There is a story by O. Henry about a man who decided that since the encyclopedia encompassed all knowledge, he wouldn't bother going to school, but would simply memorize the encyclopedia. He started with the As, worked his way on through the Bs, Cs and so on. Now *that's* a sick rationality. (p. 95)

I seriously doubt whether Maslow's rejection is based on a reading of Sartre rather than a stereotype. Furthermore Maslow speaks elsewhere (p. 352) of a person's consciousness of 'ultimate existential smallness', again close to Sartre.

Freud, who is much more of an internalised and vocational necessity to Maslow, calls for rather stronger defensive operations, although no more so than was apparent in the cases of Mead, Allport, Sullivan and Jourard. He restates the aims of psychoanalysis in more 'biological' terms by suggesting that it tries

... to help one to become conscious of one's animal urges, needs, tensions, depressions, tastes, anxieties. So also for Horney's distinction between a real self and a pseudo-self. Is this also not a subjective discrimination of what one truly is? And what *is* one truly if not first and foremost one's own body, one's own constitution, one's own functioning, one's own specieshood? (I have very much enjoyed, *qua theorist*, this pretty integration of Freud, Goldstein, Sheldon, Horney, Cattell, Frankl, May, Rogers, Murray, etc., etc., etc. Perhaps even Skinner could be coaxed into this diverse company since I suggest that his list of 'intrinsic reinforcers' for his human subjects might very well look much like the 'hierarchy of instinctoid basic needs and metaneeds' that I have proposed! (p. 33)

Amidst this quite incredible desire to integrate all things it is clear that Freud is to be allowed in only through the neo-Freudians whose main effort has been directed towards moderating his work to fit American cultural values. And thus it is a 'cleansing and a correction of what Freud was groping towards' (p. 356). What a resounding cry this is for the American personality theorist! The reaction to Freud.

The great discoveries Freud made we can now add to. His one big mistake, which we are correcting now, is that he thought of the unconscious merely as undesirable evil. (p. 180)

A little earlier it was apparent that Maslow's views on normalcy implied a radical social critique. How does he manage questions at the social level? In general he marshals integrative concepts such as Ruth Benedict's 'synergy' (Ruth Benedict and Wertheimer were Maslow's venerated teachers and his prototype self-actualisers). Synergy describes situations in which social goals and practices are consonant with individual self-interest (p. 210), another implicit polarisation which Maslow works out in a typically contradictory way. The liberal ideal of an absence of great social pressure (p. 153) struggles against the necessity for leadership (p. 232) (by good specimens) and the necessity of expelling those who behave in a dystopian way. Since his own range of experience is narrow (p. 197) he ignores sociological predecessors (p. 217), fails to address problems of power in relation to education (p. 76) or the major variable of social class except as a deficiency for some people. His remedy for education is that it should be modelled on art and creativity training, though not modern art, and he seems unconscious of the likely industrial backlash. In fact his innocence of the ideological aspects of industrial organisation is nearly unbelievable. For example

I've been amazed to be plucked at in the last couple of years by big industries of which I know nothing. (p. 84)

He does not realise that the more sophisticated managers now call for character training in terms quite as mystifying and contradictory as his own.[3] So he recommends 'Eupsychian management' for creative personnel (p. 246). His advice on choosing creative personnel conflicts with companies' experience that the types he recommends are thought of as troublemakers (p. 97), yet the contradiction is seen as merely curious. He seriously thinks that by good management it will be possible to allow people to self-actualise, to receive 'metapay' in the form of opportunities to realise their metavalues; that differences of ordinary pay will no longer matter and that money can be 'desymbolised' so that it no longer attaches to 'success, respectworthiness or loveworthiness' (p. 308). Such revolutionary proposals should not be seen as surprising since Maslow is post-Marxian, and even capable of integrating Marx and Hegel by placing their materialist and spiritual ideas on another continuum. The omnipotence of his integrating capacities in relation to theories is matched by a similar belief that the human being is a 'self-evolver' (p. 10) capable of thinking himself into new conditions of existence, an extremely naive, apolitical and ahistorical view. Indeed there is a *studied* naivety about Maslow's position: he cheerfully ignores a reminder from a philosophical colleague that he has simply overlooked two thousand years of human struggle with a problem, and gets on with fashioning his own scheme (pp. 28, 66, 134).

As I see it this studied innocence is an attempt to rediscover the 'phenomenological reduction', available for half a century in Europe from Husserl the originator of the human experiential approach,[4]

somebody Maslow simply does not mention. Again the European sources stand ignored or filtered out in the process of transition, while Maslow goes hunting round Taoism, Zen and Suzuki for a not too radical infusion of phenomenological sensitivity. Recall Allport's flirtation with the mystical religions.

Contradictions are woven in every direction as Maslow sets up dichotomy after dichotomy, an irresponsibility about the creation of false oppositions which is not mitigated by the mystifying (as well as sometimes mystical) ways in which he produces integrations. He does not seem to be aware that false polarisations, which of necessity distort that to which they loosely refer, result in false integrations. I have shown how it relates to various theorists but it occurs also in relation to whole disciplines.

A total cultural determinism is still the official orthodox doctrine of many or most of the sociologists and anthropologists. This doctrine not only denies intrinsic higher motivations, but comes perilously close sometimes to denying 'human nature' itself. The economists, not only in the West but also in the East, are essentially materialistic. (p. 337)

The strain of attempting to integrate all things, to place all human experience on a single scale of humanness, a Platonic essence, with a common origin in biology and a common end in transcendence means that some of the elements have to be forced or reworked into distorted form before they will fit. All is gathered in, but at a cost to understanding and with quite misleading consequences. He manages to clear out all threatening material and to create a benign nature, a happy unconsciousness, a beautiful ultimate reality and is encouraged in this by the hundreds of thousands of people who like to hear it this way (p. xvi). So why study his work in this deeply critical way? In Maslow's own words

> . . . the study of the 'innards' of the personality is one necessary base for the understanding of what a person can communicate to the world, and what the world is able to communicate to him. (p. 161)

4.3 C. R. ROGERS

There are many similarities between the writings of Carl Rogers and Abraham Maslow, as they both acknowledge by reference to the other's work. Where they differ at the most general level of expression is in their respective degrees of cautiousness and control. Maslow's extensive lists of qualities and characteristics of the self-actualising person read like free association transcripts or an attempt to bring into existence by repetitive exhortation the desirable human attributes. The power of this word-play is almost unbounded, drawing in the most far-reaching social and philosophical problems, the most diverse theorists and bodies of knowledge, for integration by means of ever-widening superordinate categories. Rogers has his writing much more under control: it is repetitive, though remarkably unified by continued dwelling on the central theme of a positive real self which strives for actualisation and can be facilitated in this by certain kinds of interpersonal relationships. Although he addresses certain wider social and philosophical problems it is usually with greater caution than Maslow displays. In a sense Rogers' is more intensely specialised than Maslow, making less explicit use of Freud and focusing on relatively conscious aspects of communication, relatedness and the possibility of getting in touch with one's deeper, organismic feelings.

If it were accepted that the present lines of demarcation between disciplines and specialities are drawn on some objectively advantageous basis, Rogers' greater specialisation could be seen as a strength; but where the adequacy of interdisciplinary and transdisciplinary knowledge is in question, and the division of labour in intellectual work is regarded as having possible unintended harmful consequences for the creation of knowledge, the very specialisation may be seen as a retreat from wider problems. As in the previous examples chosen for study it will be taken that in the field of personality theories the self-concept of the theorist may set limits on the forms of knowledge produced. On the reflexive principle that personality theorists must at least be open to investigation in the light of their own theory the following starting point suggests itself.

Most of the ways of behaving which are adopted by the organism, are those which are consistent with the concept of self.[5]

What then is Rogers' self-concept and how does it relate to his behaviour of producing a personality theory?

The first surprise is that, for a theorist whose whole work turns on the desirability of communicating feelings and the real self, there is only a relatively small amount of material which reveals Rogers' own self. The autobiographical material is useful but not very personal or deeply self-reflective; it yields to interpretation rather than giving more directly. The only area in which Rogers does set out more fully his concerns is in relation to his role as therapist or group facilitator, and then it is not that he reveals his own self, but rather that he insists on the need to use and risk the self in therapy and then shows from transcripts and subsequent communications what process has taken place in clients. This may be seen, however, as an aspect of his specialisation. He is not interested in content but in process. The facilitative process will be set in motion when the therapist is in touch with his own feelings and able to communicate them if he chooses, when the client feels himself to be accepted as he is, whatever he is, and the therapist exercises and communicates empathic understanding.[6] Thus the 'goal' of therapy is the creation of a facilitative interpersonal relationship and the valued consequence is that the client may then go out to change existing relationships in the direction of this model. Process is a quite sufficient goal for Rogers in view of his deep conviction that the actualising tendency in human beings is, on balance, positive: if the process can be set going the outcome is, within reason, assured.

Does the autobiographical material throw any light on the genesis of this particular theory? Rogers describes his early family life as marked by close ties, often of a subtly controlling kind, within a family where he was the fourth of six children. The family did not mix and was dominated by religious and ethical standards stressing the value of hard work.

So I was a pretty solitary boy, who read incessantly, and went all through high school with only two dates.[7]

His parents bought a farm, partly as a hobby and partly to keep their children away from the possibly harmful influence of suburban life. So in spite of the family's material prosperity it appears to have provided an environment lacking any opportunity for an expressive, sensual or self-determining kind of experience; quite a serious deprivation for a sensitive person.

There were two kinds of consolation available which Rogers himself says had an important influence on his later work: a passionate interest in observing and breeding gorgeous nightflying moths, and a practical, experimental interest in scientifically designed animal feeding methods. The manner of expression shows that the moths provided a socially acceptable and compensatory activity for the 'natural' beauty of human existence and relationships suppressed by the extremely 'puritanical' mode of family life. It seems also to have served as a way of creating a differentiated identity within a 'controlling' family, for Rogers 'became an authority' on this subject. Animal feeding experiments formed a contrasting, highly useful area of interest in line with the family style and it was an extension of this work that defined Rogers' initial college subject. In a sense the family's controlling influence continued to suppress the life of feeling, although not for long because over two years he gradually changed his vocation to the ministry and his subject to history. A six-month trip to China in 1922 (the year Allport went to see Freud) taught him respect for different points of view and allowed him to become emancipated from the religion of his family. He fell in love with and married a girl known since childhood.

Having transferred to the very liberal Union Theological Seminary he joined some other independently inclined students in pressing for a freely questioning seminar by means of which he, and others, moved away from religion.

My beliefs had already changed tremendously, and might continue to change. It seemed to me it would be a horrible thing to *have* to profess a set of beliefs, in order to remain in one's profession. I wanted to find a field in which I could be sure my freedom of thought would not be limited.[8]

The basic pattern of Rogers' self-development is therefore extremely consistent and plain to see; a gradual process of permitted and supported emancipation from family, professional and social pressures towards the situation where he can exercise freely his own wishes and choices. Thus client-centred therapy is modelled precisely on the man himself: its goal is a continuous process of movement away from the expectations and values of others toward self-determining, self-respecting (actualising) choice. There is a great and genuine strength in this therapeutic stance because it implies that Rogers is truly present in the consultation as the embodiment of a model of therapy and as a person looking for the kind of awareness in another that he has himself achieved. There are, however, certain questions that must be faced.

Rogers' range of social experience is very limited. He moved from the confines of his family into college, then to a fellowship in child guidance, and out into a job with the Society for Prevention of Cruelty to Children. He seems to have been remarkably fortunate in finding some reasonable opportunity to exercise his developing interests, and although the job entailed professional isolation and was poorly paid

> I think I have always had a feeling that if I was given some opportunity to do the thing I was most interested in doing, everything else would somehow take care of itself.[9]

There is a clear direction here of retreat from external and religious principles into the self. He was then 'completely immersed' in providing a psychological service for delinquent and underprivileged children. The theme of retreat is a constant one.

> My wife and I have found isolated hideaways in Mexico and in the Caribbean where no one knows I am a psychologist; where painting, swimming, snorkeling, and capturing some of the scenery in color photography are my major activities. Yet in these spots, where no more than two to four hours a day goes for professional work, I have made most of whatever advances I have made in the last few years. I prize the privilege of being alone.[10]

It seems that nothing external or social has ever seriously interfered with this privileged retreat into a beautiful natural environment or with the psychological goal of remaining *in process* of self-discovery. He says himself that on transfer to the university world he was lucky enough to be made a full professor thus avoiding the vicissitudes of anxious competition for preferment. But does process never have an outcome, a result, an achieved goal? My impression is that Rogers tries hard to avoid arriving at anything which might embody a prescription, a guide, a criterion or a principle—after all he spent a large part of his life slowly getting rid of such things.

> *Life, at its best, is a flowing, changing process in which nothing is fixed.*[11]

But contradiction is not far away: even process therapy begins to crystallise into typical patterns and typical stages[12] so that Rogers is able to write about them at some length. The contradiction is that when setting out and publishing these 'significant learnings' he says

> I do not know whether they would hold true for you. I have no desire to present them as a guide for anyone else.[13]

Clearly this is just a little over the boundary between extreme liberalism and naivety.

It is to be expected that the optimal situation for the operation of Rogers' extremely individualistic conception of human action is one-to-one therapy where there is, so to speak, a moratorium on social pressures. It is of some interest to see what happens when Rogers is pulled towards wider social contexts, for example in a consultative capacity. In ascending levels of generality these contexts are: groups, particularly encounter groups of which he has become a leading exponent; institutions, particularly of the educational kind where he has supervised some extensive interventions; and international relations, on which he passes occasional comments.

Groups are treated exactly according to the model of personal therapy, using identical facilitative techniques with a similar faith in the outcome.

. . . I have gradually developed a great deal of trust in the group process. This is undoubtedly similar to the trust I came to have in the process of therapy in the individual, when it was facilitated rather than directed. To me the group is like an organism, having a sense of its own direction even though it could not define that direction intellectually.

. . . a group recognizes unhealthy elements in its process, focuses on them, clears them up or eliminates them, and moves on towards becoming a healthier group. This is my way of saying that I have seen the 'wisdom of the organism' exhibited at every level from cell to group.[14]

It will be necessary to look more penetratingly at Rogers' most fundamental assumption—that the organism has a predominantly positive actualising tendency—but for the moment it is sufficient to notice that the group context does not reverse in any way the retreat into self/organism which characterises his client-centred therapy.

At the level of the institution Rogers has been called in to supervise the reorganisation of an education system. Being given the necessary top administrative support he introduced group methods throughout the women's college, eight high schools and fifty elementary schools of a Catholic school system, with beneficial results in the form of classroom innovations, improved communication, the removal of some serious interpersonal frictions and increased participation and self-direction. He reports another example of an attempt to cope with the immense problems of the Louisville inner-city schools and hopes that it will provide exciting possibilities for experiment and change. He sees the project as tackling the problem at its roots. There is nothing to indicate awareness of a new level of problem in institutions: it is assumed that the roots of the problem are to be found in the kinds of personal relationships which exist and that facilitation of 'healing' group processes will set in motion changes which after a period of turmoil will be beneficial.

Now it seems quite plausible that within certain limits greatly beneficial changes do result; in the case of some individuals the changes may be profound. However, the degree of organisational change is likely to be small, and confined to problems of adaptation to changing conditions in order to preserve basic goals, since the group process can only be introduced with the approval of the authorities responsible for organisations. In short, power relationships in the social structure are not touched by Rogers' approach and yet the *roots* of many difficulties must lie here.

When the much higher level of international relations is considered the strain of applying a model derived from personal therapy becomes even more apparent. Rogers' suggestion, based on his belief that diplomatic exchanges involve a kind of false self, is that diplomatic delegations should be accompanied by several citizens of equivalent calibre who would meet together as persons with a neutral facilitator. The understanding reached in this informal, personal context would be fed back to the delegations, possibly opening the way to 'realistic' negotiation.[15] Rogers offers it as 'a fantasy' but presumably it is the best he can do. It shows that for him what is 'real', and so 'realistic' is personal encounter on the client-centred model. He seems to refuse to recognise that collectivities interact according to necessarily distinct ground rules, no less complicated than those which apply to persons but structured in a quite different way. A diplomatic interchange will have its ritual level, its power level, its practical level covering detailed arrangements for the ceremonial and to some extent its personal level as ambassadors, aides and agents get to know each other. It may seem rather hard on Rogers to criticise the person specialist for inadequate fantasies in the social structural sphere. It is hard, but necessary in order to raise the more general problem in the sociology of knowledge of what effects subject specialisation may have on the forms of knowledge produced. It is also essential for improving conceptualisations of the person that the relation between organismic variables and social variables be very fully explored, to which purpose Rogers provides a beautiful example of a person-centred theory which moves exclusively in the organismic direction for its principles of explanation at the great cost of losing all credibility when 'applied' to social phenomena, whether these be groups, institutions or societies.

It may be, as the ethologists argue, that there is something to learn from the social organisation of animal groups or from studies of creatures nearly related to human beings. I must say frankly that I have not been impressed by the social relevance of findings by serious students in this field and that I have been appalled at the irresponsible looseness of argument contained in the more popular literature on this area.[16] However, Rogers never appeals to the evidence on this question; he simply evokes wonder and admiration for natural processes in a way that suggests an irrational faith arising from the earlier consolations provided by his study of nature—the gorgeous, night-flying moths. Another parable he relates is that of seeing a piece of seaweed attached to a rock take the full force of ocean waves. The phallic weed disappeared and seemed certain to have been smashed or dislodged but it rose again as the waters subsided, standing as a symbol of natural resilience.

Further evidence of the irrationality of Rogers' adherence to an organismic model is the way in which he 'splits' the organismic and the social, projecting exclusively good qualities onto the organismic level. He finds it immensely satisfying to behold the orderly processes in nature; one of his 'significant learnings' is that 'the facts are friendly'.[17] On the social side of the split are all those unfriendly, limiting and distorting influences, the expectations of others[18] and the social pressures to conform, against which Rogers prefers to trust his organismic feelings.

> Neither the Bible nor the prophets—neither Freud nor research—
> neither the revelations of God nor man—can take precedence over
> my own direct experience![19]

The force of his reaction to Freud and the religious limitations of his family are evident in the text. There is also a very clear indication of the direction in which he is moving as a result of that reaction. The Bible may be considered as both the religious authority of his nearly fundamentalist parents and the virtually unquestionable social values which constrained his earlier life: he casts off this, and the prophets—

his parents. He then rejects Freud, the great secular authority on personality and bringer of the news that human nature is destructive, together with those other dehumanising agents the researchers. It must be remembered that at one time Rogers practised Freudian therapy at the Institute for Child Guidance whilst doing doctoral work of a 'highly statistical and Thorndikean'[20] kind at Teachers College. The latter I take to be the researchers he wishes to reject because he later welcomed other researchers who could provide confirmatory evidence for his theory. Finally he rejects both God and men. This rejection of men seems paradoxical against his belief in the positive qualities of self-actualisation but it is the expression of a profound ambiguity in Rogers' work. 'Men' normally impose on a person evaluations; they do not offer 'unconditional positive regard', and this results in the creation of a self with *introjected* values which may be at variance with the person's organismic valuing. There is now apparent a peculiar resonance between rejecting the introjected values coming in from society, rejecting Rogers' parents' values, and rejecting Freud whose values he had at one time introjected. The limiting consequence of this dynamic is that Rogers' theory becomes totally non-social: personal and interpersonal, yes, but asocial; a reification of social interaction into the mysteries of personal encounter. Encounter which in therapy is not even encounter with another but with the organismic self.

The relationship to Freud is quite as ambivalent as any so far discovered. On the one hand he acknowledges Freud and on the other tries to put as much distance between the two theories as he possibly can.

> By and large the psychoanalytically oriented Freudian group has developed, out of its rich clinical experience, a point of view which is almost diametrically opposed to the hypotheses regarding the capacities and tendencies of the human organism formulated [by Rogers].[21]

Careful examination of Rogers' conceptualisation of self-development shows that it is consistent with Freud over major areas—the conscious and preconscious self, the 'defensive' processes. Much of what he objects to in Freud seems to be based on a misunderstanding or misreading. For example, Rogers contrasts the unconditional positive regard of client-centred counsellors with the 'evaluative' stance of the Freudians. He reports an early formative experience of first admiring a particular interview technique and then being appalled by it.

I hunted it up again and re-read it. I was appalled. Now it seemed to me to be a clever legalistic type of questioning by the interviewer which convicted this parent of her unconscious motives, and wrung from her an admission of her guilt.[22]

A parody of Freud!

When considering the question of transference Rogers shows very carefully that client-centred counsellors deal with it by demonstrating such consistent unconditional positive regard that the client cannot realistically attribute transference feelings to the counsellor but must acknowledge them as coming from the self. This seems an oblique answer. Surely the aim of the Freudian therapist is identical —to show *eventually and at the right time* that the feelings projected by the client into the therapist came not from the therapist but from the self in its earlier experience. The difference is that the Freudian analyst is prepared to hold the transference feelings, and possible acting out behaviours, long enough for the client to re-experience and go beyond them.

The result of Rogers' ambivalence is then the elaboration of a substantially Freudian theory in terms which provide a bland translation of the Freudian processes. Where Freud faced both the destructive forces of the organism (although we must not, like Rogers, neglect the life forces of Eros), and the penalties as well as the advantages of social control, Rogers splits the personal and the social. He makes the organism positive and social controls merely a hindrance to the emergent processes of the organism. In other words he fails to discriminate the qualities of social control that may exist and in so doing retreats from the social into the personal.

The rest of Rogers' work never departs from the basic pattern already set out. It does not help his case that he sees in the organism a 'socialised' nature:[23] it is only a weak attempt to integrate the organismic/social split in his conceptualisation. He does not explain how social conditions come to be so generally bad when the positive actualising tendency in human organisms has had so long to achieve its ends. He shows that encounter groups have great appeal for relatively prosperous people but does not pursue explanations of why they are less popular in ghetto areas[24] and governmental situations.[25] I think it is because these facts are *not friendly* to his self-concept.

In relation to existentialism he shows exactly the kind of superficial knowledge and opportunist use of the ideas as Maslow and Allport. The encounter group is described as having an existential implication in that it is concerned with 'the here and now of human feelings and of living one's life'.[26] An important theme for him is 'the existential quality of satisfying living'.[27] He has gained insights from Kierkegaard,[28] mentions Sartre's concept of reflexive awareness,[29] although it is not indexed, and refers to Martin Buber frequently, but says 'I am not a student of existential philosophy'.[30] In other words it is much like his occasional references to Oriental philosophies which, in common with Allport's and Maslow's, seem designed to add a dash of spice to the ideas without taking on any serious implications. It is the same attitude which throws in an isolated reference to Popper's 'open society' as consonant with client-centred approaches, without acknowledging the controversial nature of the concept and the ideological uses to which it has been put. The incompatibility of many of these elements, picked up to provide general support, is never faced.

It would be wrong, in relation to a theorist whose model of man conceives the person as continuously open to experience and ready for change, to ignore certain changes in Rogers' ideas. As he says, these have not altered its basic direction but are worth noticing.

When presenting his work, by invitation, in the context of the American Psychological Association's encyclopaedic volumes entitled *Psychology: A Study of a Science*, Rogers notes his changed attitude to theories and research.

> The thought that we were making a start on a theoretical system would for me have been a most distasteful notion even as little as a dozen years ago. . . . I like to think that the theoretical systems and far-reaching web of research which have developed, have grown in an organic fashion.[31]

It is strikingly clear that choice of the organism as a model of process and source of values can be extended without limit to provide a criterion of good science, and yet none of the research goes deeply enough to test the basic theory, present from the outset, that the organism outweighs the formative influence of the social environment in creating the human being.

Although Rogers repeats his autobiography of 1955 in the American Psychological Association's 1959 publications there is a very significant omission: although he mentions his adolescent interest in scientific agriculture he does not repeat the story of his fascination with the gorgeous night-flying moths, that deep and abiding inspiration which as a central theme permeates every aspect of Rogers theory accounting both for its genuine though limited strengths and its disabling evasion of any strong encounter with the human *social* being.

4.4   THEORIES IN LIMBO

Maslow and Rogers have been chosen to speak for an American kind of existentialism because they are widely acknowledged as two of its leading exponents. There are other theorists and therapists associated with existentialism but I leave them aside because of the overriding need for relatively deep analysis of some few cases which show knowledge in process of creation. It is hypothesised that other American existentialists generally show more in common with the position here defined than departure from it.

Kelly provides a foil to the existentialists in that he stumbles unwittingly into existentialist practices even against his distaste for all that he associates with the term. All three, Maslow, Rogers and Kelly, clearly know so little of what is available in this field that some explanation is needed for their 'directed ignorance', and I suggest there is ample evidence of the rejection of unread, misread, misunderstood sources—both Freud and existentialism—under control of their self-concepts. This is also to say under *social* control since self-concepts relate strongly, though not totally, to social contexts within which they arise.

Maslow and Rogers borrow some of the terminology of existentialism but not its substance; Kelly recreates some of the substance but rejects the terminology. Either way it produces an insubstantial body of knowledge, which is neither rooted in its predecessors nor capable of dealing with human experience and action. Having lost its earthly grip it cannot, as a science, ascend to heaven: it remains in the limbo of fantasy.

REFERENCES

1 R. A. Holland. George Kelly: constructive innocent and reluctant existentialist. In *Perspectives in Personal Construct Theory* (ed. D. Bannister), Academic Press, New York and London (1970)

2 A. Maslow. *The Farther Reaches of Human Nature*, Pelican, Harmondsworth, Middx (1973)

3 S. P. Chambers. Education and industry, *Nature, Lond.* **203** (1964), 227–30

4 E. Husserl. Philosophy as rigorous science (trans. Q. Lauer). In *Phenomenology and the Crisis of Philosophy*, Harper & Row, New York and London (1965)

5 C. R. Rogers. *Client-Centered Therapy*, Houghton-Mifflin, Boston, Mass. (1951), p. 507

6 C. R. Rogers. *On Becoming a Person*, Constable, London (1961), p. 61

7 ibid., p. 5

8 ibid., p. 8

9 ibid., p. 10

10 ibid., p. 15

11 ibid., p. 27

12 ibid., p. 125

13 ibid., p. 13

14 C. R. Rogers. *Encounter Groups*, Penguin, Harmondsworth, Middx (1969)

15 ibid., p. 142

16 A. Storr. *Human Aggression*, Penguin, Harmondsworth, Middx (1968). Reviewed in *Human Context*, 11, 1 (1970)

17 C. R. Rogers. *On Becoming a Person*, Constable, London (1961), p. 25

18 ibid., p. 103

19 ibid., p. 24

20 C. R. Rogers. *Psychology: A Study of a Science*, vol. 3 (ed. S. Koch), McGraw-Hill, New York and Maidenhead, Berks. (1959), p. 186

21 ibid., p. 248

22 C. R. Rogers. *On Becoming a Person*, Constable, London (1961), p. 11

23 C. R. Rogers. *Client-Centered Therapy*, Houghton-Mifflin, (1951), pp. 488 and 524

24 C. R. Rogers. *Encounter Groups*, Penguin, Harmondsworth, Middx (1969), p. 18
25 ibid., p. 141
26 ibid., p. 168
27 C. R. Rogers. *On Becoming a Person*, Constable, London (1961), p. 163
28 ibid., p. 110
29 ibid., p. 147
30 ibid., p. 199
31 C. R. Rogers. *Psychology: A Study of a Science*, vol. 3 (ed. S. Koch), McGraw-Hill, New York and Maidenhead, Berks. (1959), p. 186

5
Role Theory and the Human Sciences

No other single concept would seem to offer more possibilities for exploration of the relation between persons and societies, or between the disciplines which typically deal with personal and social phenomena—namely psychology and sociology—than the concept of role. It is not that long-standing and widespread use of the concept, extending even into other related disciplines such as anthropology and philosophy, has turned up results which can be summarised or integrated: instead the picture which emerges is full of curiosities. Debates arise about the impoverished view of man which is said to be implicit in role analysis (Dahrendorf, 1968; Wrong, 1961). Paradoxically, in view of the interdisciplinary possibilities of the concept and its potentially integrative qualities as 'mediator' between the social and the personal, it gives rise to separate specialisms.

> Ironically, the very divisions role theory sets out to mend in its unified theory of mind, self and society have rebounded in other forms. In America, its aspects of person have readily succumbed to specialization so that the exploration of the self was assimilated to psychological pursuits, the role structure to sociology, and in practice, its social behaviourism to the rather narrow exigencies of small group research.[1]

There is acknowledgement of the very considerable importance of the concept.

> The concept of role is the central concept in the social sciences.[2]

But disappointment with the results followed by repeated attempts to rescue the concept and clarify it

> ... neither the conceptual and terminological confusion (evident in role theory), nor the imprecise nature of the concept as it is empirically understood (a point stressed by many philosophers) should deter us from attempting to formulate theories and working hypotheses in this 'strategic area' of social analysis.[3]

However, in all this there is very little concern with the extent to which the state of role theory *can be accounted for in psychological and sociological terms*. That is to say, there is no attempt to explore the possibility that psychologists' and sociologists' own roles may influence their definitions and uses of the concept of role. Or to put it another way, that the division of labour in intellectual work, for example the professionalisation of psychology and sociology, might have consequences for the kinds of knowledge produced. Here then is a new approach.

Just as personality or self-theories can be examined for the ways in which theorists manage to cope with the inescapable *self*-description and definition involved in human sciences so may role theories be analysed. In both cases the person producing the theory is included within the subject matter he attempts to understand. The usual term for this kind of approach is 'reflexive', a word which has begun to appear in the human sciences in particular uses but which has long been implicit in social theory: Hegel, Marx, Freud and Husserl all call in a sense for man to comprehend himself by understanding the conditions under which knowledge and false knowledge arise. In recent attempts to use reflexivity as an important principle there is little work which addresses itself to the relations between disciplines. Predominantly the aim is to remake a particular discipline on a more reflexive model. For example at the macro level Alvin Gouldner has proposed a reflexive sociology—a sociology which accounts for its own existence. At the micro level ethnomethodologists are using reflexivity to account for particular qualities of language use (with acknowledgements to Chomsky) and, by analogy, for particular qualities of social action seen as resting on a 'deep structure' (again Chomsky) which may be elucidated by ethnomethodological techniques.

Some newer kinds of existential and humanistic psychology are insisting on the necessity for reflexivity, often as reaction to what are seen as the dehumanising tendencies of positivism and behaviourism. All these are good impulses in that they seek to bring into the centre of human sciences what is most distinctively human, that is, man's capacity to reflect upon himself. What is needed is not just the exhortation to attend to this neglected or submerged quality of man but a detailed and documented account of some of the ways in which man's power of self-reflection (by creation of knowledge of the human) has been diverted, distorted or driven into error. At this early stage just one or two simple but thorough case studies of what has gone wrong will be more useful than general exhortations which are embarrassingly frequent in psychology and sociology, to begin our disciplines all over again and get it right this time because the key to it all has been discovered.

I therefore propose to look at some examples of the formulation and uses of role theory, paying particular attention to the relations between disciplines in the human sciences. To some extent it will be necessary to dwell upon error and to emphasise misunderstanding but to this purpose: that the human sciences may be enabled to accept and integrate their history, moving on to new beginnings which rest upon recognition of inadequacies, and not, as is frequently the case, on a denial of the past, giving rise to exaggerated optimism for a new approach.

A theory which displays exactly the above qualities—a new supposedly radical approach standing in ambivalent relation to its antecedents—is available in George Kelly's personal construct theory. It began as a role theory (although this is not widely appreciated) and, being a psychological theory which makes ambitious claims to wide social relevance, it carries interdisciplinary implications. All this makes it an unusual but particularly apposite starting point for the present project. It will provide leads into other theories and other critiques.

5.1 PERSONAL CONSTRUCT THEORY AND ROLE

From time to time there emerges in the human sciences some new theoretical approach which claims, with due modesty, to provide such a fresh insight into certain phenomena that it will revitalise a whole discipline. Frequently in the human sciences it is a new concept of man—an attempt to emphasise a previously neglected aspect of human action or experience and an attempt to work out some consequences of the new viewpoint.

In psychology George Kelly has offered us personal construct theory, the concept of man as a scientist, continuously testing hypotheses; Don Bannister, together with his colleagues, has taken up the theory, developing and testing it, frequently in the most demanding circumstances such as its application to schizophrenic thought, behaviour and therapy. By now the achievement is manifest and, subject to one or two reservations about the structure of the theory, I want to make it clear that I admire the work and take delight in the growing body of research to which it gives rise. Having said that I would then ask that they be patient, as ever, while I examine a quality of the theory which is not so much a weakness of the theory itself but a weakness of the human sciences: the lack of integration between disciplines, particularly sociology and psychology. This will entail a study of the paradox that although personal construct theory began as a role theory it has not developed in this direction.

Bannister and Fransella identify one of the unsatisfactory features of psychology today as the separation between individual or general psychology and social psychology. They propose a possible solution.

Indeed the integration of social and individual or general psychology (their original separation seems to have been a way of improverishing both) might well centre on re-thinking in construct theory forms, the idea of role.[4]

This sounds a constructive suggestion but it is rather weak. It is not at all apparent why attention to the concept of role would integrate psychology: this must depend significantly on the power of Kelly's concept of role, and perhaps even more importantly on why the discipline of psychology became split in the first place. According to Bannister and Fransella the discipline became split (or presumably developed another split), because 'psychologists have followed custom in establishing social psychology as a mini-psychology, in its own right'. Here, of course, is the most interesting problem in the development of human sciences. Why is it *customary* to separate and specialise to the detriment of both the divorced elements?

Investigation of this question may provide some estimate of the likely success of the programme for integrating psychology set out by Bannister and Fransella. To say that psychologists 'have followed custom' is to give the weakest form of sociological explanation for what happened: weak because the existence of a custom is unclear in what is a relatively new innovating science, and also because even though a custom could be demonstrated it would still be necessary to show why it was followed in this case. It may seem that I am seizing on a sociological point made by psychologists just in passing and criticising it for not meeting sociological criteria. That is true, but for a very clear purpose; that of placing the problem of the split *within* psychology in the context of the problem of the split *between* psychology and sociology. Perhaps disciplines split internally because they are already separated from other relevant disciplines. If this is the case then no amount of rethinking and attempted integration *within* psychology will be as effective as integrating psychology with other relevant disciplines.

Leaving aside for the moment which disciplines are relevant to psychology—it could be philosophy, anthropology, etc.—I propose to examine further Kelly's concept of role as presented by Bannister and Fransella, and particularly for the light it may throw on the separation between psychology and sociology.

Bannister and Fransella introduce Kelly's concept of role in the concept of a criticism of what social psychologists in their separate 'mini-psychology' have done to the concept 'by seeing it too completely in group terms'. They produce the following quotation from Kelly.

Role can be understood in terms of what the person *himself* is doing rather than in terms of his circumstances. There are two traditional notions of role, one the very old notion that role is a course of action which is articulated with the actions of others, so that together you and the other person can produce something. The more recent notion proposed by sociologists and other theorists is that a role is a set of expectations held by others within which a man finds himself encompassed and surrounded. Personal construct theory tries to put role within the context of something a person himself is doing and it springs from a notion that one may attempt to understand others in terms of their outlooks just as a personal construct theory psychologist tries to understand human beings in terms of their outlooks.

So anyone who attempts to understand others in terms of the outlooks they have, rather than their behaviours only, may indeed play a role. This isn't to say that he tries to conform to their outlooks, he may even try to stand them on their heads, but if he tries to understand others by putting on their spectacles and then does something, then that which he does could be considered as a role. So we have three notions of role here. The oldest notion, the notion of a course of activity articulated with the action of others, I suppose that notion could be tied up with the notion of man as the economic entity, 'the economic man'. The more recent notion of man surrounded by a set of expectations, I suppose you can say would be a notion that would undergird the society which had seen itself composed of 'ideological men' conforming to ideas, ideologies. But if we follow the notion of role that comes out of construct theory, I wonder if we might not develop the notion of man as a society composed of 'empathic man' or 'inquiring man'—men who seem to understand and do it by active inquiry, using their own behaviour not as something to act out, but as a means of understanding their world.[5]

The first point about Kelly's discussion is one I have made earlier: he tries to contrast his concept of role with a hopelessly inadequate alternative which makes his own proposal sound quite attractive. When we try to discover what it is he is arguing against it is found to be a stereotype, a caricature or a phantom. He says that there are two 'traditional notions' of role, and the argument is already won, because obviously we want something more recent that 'traditional' and more substantial than a 'notion'. Bannister and Fransella have already reminded us in a subheading that 'A theory is not a notion'.

Kelly goes on with some degree of contradiction to say that the second of the traditional notions was introduced more recently by 'sociologists and other theorists'. This takes role to be 'a set of expectations held by others within which a man finds himself encompassed and surrounded'. It is too obvious how this argument is being loaded against the nameless sociologists and other theorists. He refers only to the expectations of *others*, not to the fact that *one's own* expectations are equally implicit in role theory. And then the weight and redundancy of his words 'encompassed and surrounded' gives away the fact that he is fabricating a set of alternative sociologists and other theorists who produce 'notions' that the person and his aims are completely determined by the society, that is, by the expectations of others. Against this, his own reminder that role must be seen in the context of 'something a person himself is doing' sounds quite an advance.

It is not just Kelly who falls into error when dealing with concepts that are interdisciplinary. Bannister and Fransella introduced the quotation in order to tell us what *social psychologists* had done to the concept of role but the quotation refers to what *sociologists* (and other unspecified theorists) had done to it. They perpetuate the confusion by going on to say that Kelly's concept of role is embedded in the sociality corollary which reads

. . . to the extent that one person construes the construction processes of another he may play a role in a social process involving the other person.

They then comment

This definition relates the 'individual' to the 'social' and makes role more than *simply a socially prescribed dialogue* [my emphasis].[6]

At places like this the worst of Kelly comes through: an ambitious claim is made but not substantiated except by contrast with a misconstrued alternative. The claim is ambitious because at most the definition relates one person to another, not the individual to the social, and this one-to-one interaction model is just a very weak formulation of the social process used by such interesting but limited sociologists as the symbolic interactionists (Blumer, 1962).

If my argument against Bannister and Fransella is to hold, I must at least show why the sociologists' concept of role is something more than 'simply a socially prescribed dialogue'. I can then return to the problem of devising a truly interdisciplinary concept of role and will see what light this throws on splits within, and between, disciplines in the human sciences.

So as to emphasise the ready availability of a reasonably clear account of the sociological concept of role I refer to Coser and Rosenberg's *Sociological Theory: a book of readings*, a deservedly popular standard text published in 1957, revised in 1964 and again in 1969. Role is covered substantially in two sections. Part three, Structural Concepts, begins with a section on Status (a technical term with more than the popular meaning), and here are papers which deal with the most 'structural' aspects of the concept; that is, they seek to bring into prominence the social framework and the ways in which individuals are shaped by, and recruited into, this structure. These papers, if any, will be more likely to present role as a 'socially prescribed dialogue' than papers in the second section—Role-Taking and Reference Groups—which appears in Part two under Self–Other Concepts. How is role treated by the 'structural' theorists?

5.2 STRUCTURAL ROLE THEORY

Park and Burgess (1921) differentiate *status*—a mechanical rule, usually inheritance, which assigns people to places in a society— with *competition*, which is a process of selection in which people compete for the places. Briefly, competition and the division of labour produce 'vocational types', the shop-girl, the policeman, the peddler, etc., which they suggest might be studied.

Linton (1936) uses the term *status* in a different way, to refer to the places available in a society, each defined by rights and duties. A person occupies several statuses. The active aspect of a person's occupation of statuses is called his *role*. Linton then echoes Park and Burgess by distinguishing *ascribed* roles (inherited, or unchosen, roles such as sex and age roles) from *achieved* roles (for which people may compete).

Admittedly, this group of sociologists were close to social determinism. They were inordinately anxious to define their own distinctive subject matter—the social structure—and so the individual is not given much autonomy, or room for manoeuvre amidst the network of Hegelian 'rights and duties' which constitute the society. But Znaniecki (1940) introduces some awareness that there is a variety of groupings within society rather than a single large group. He uses the term 'social circle' to refer to the limited group with which a person's role is most immediately linked and he points out that such groups subscribe to certain values which make their interactions possible. For example the banker and his clients (social circle) accept economic values; the doctor and his patients hygienic values. More importantly, Znaniecki says that a person 'may tend to conform with the demands of his circle or else try to innovate, to become independent of those demands'. Here then is room for the person to make his own contribution to writing the social dialogue.

Hughes (1946) goes further and shows that society frequently produces 'Dilemmas and Contradictions of Status'. Applying Park's concept of the half-breed as 'marginal man' to membership of professional circles, he suggests that in the relatively open society of the United States many technically qualified new entrants to professions find it difficult to gain acceptance in the inner circles of professional groups because they lack the cultural characteristics normally associated with those particular roles. Communication in these circles depends on confidentiality and discretion, for which a high degree of trust is needed, and people with unusual characteristics for that profession—say social class or racial differences—will risk not gaining that trust.

Generalising Hughes' analysis, it seems that people in relatively open and changing societies will find certain roles untenable unless they can change their cultural characteristics—unless they can 'pass'. The crucial point is not whether they are able to pass or not, it is that they will be *forced to choose* what they will try to be. In other words, the socially prescribed dialogue breaks down in societies subject to change (and this must be most modern societies) so that the person is forced into more or less conscious choice and possibly innovation.[7]

The last paper in this section is by Merton (1957) on The Role-Set. Whereas Hughes stressed possible difficulties of a would-be role-taker, Merton notes that a role usually involves relationships with a 'set' of others, rarely with just one other. For example, a teacher relates to his students, his colleagues, his principal, his students' parents, etc., in broadly prescribed ways. The expectations of these various others will frequently conflict (perhaps normally so says Merton) and so there will be social mechanisms for coping with the conflict which might otherwise make the role-set inefficient or un-workable. A person's job is recognised as more important to him than membership of a voluntary association so a man will not be penalised for putting his job first: this is one social mechanism. A second is that differences of power among members of the role-set will set priorities—the teacher's lunch appointment with a colleague can be broken when his principal calls. Thirdly, a person may not be seen in action by members of his role-set (parents are not usually in the classroom). Fourthly, any member of a role-set may not know that his demand conflicts with that of another member. Fifthly, occupants of similar statuses may support each other against threats from members of a role-set, as when teachers support each other against parents of their students. Sixthly, a person may abridge his role-set so as to make the remaining set more workable. The last Merton regards as a limiting case because it is not so much a social mechanism as an individual action which to some extent alters the social structure. Not only is Merton, the sociologist, professionally interested in social structure, he gives it priority over the individual by saying that 'the composition of a role-set is ordinarily not a matter of personal choice', and also 'typically, the individual goes, and the social structure remains'.

Surely Merton is right in his estimate of the chances of an individual changing the social structure: '*typically*' he doesn't, but sometimes he may. Yet this implies no judgement about what is desirable. The few people who alter society may be the essential few who enable it to adapt to changing circumstances. We may recognise in the arts and literature the heroic figure of whatever social standing who comes through the great barrier of social pressure to make his own choice of action which is for this reason *significant* for the rest of us. In contrast we see as tragic the person who fights against all the power of society and yet is bound to lose.

I conclude that even in the group of sociologists *most structurally inclined* and therefore most likely to produce an 'overprescribed' concept of role there has been awareness of the individual's normal and potential contribution to the shaping of social roles—at least since about 1940. Kelly, Bannister and Fransella are therefore in danger of perpetuating a serious misunderstanding of the sociological concept of role. The essential point for my broader argument about the condition of the human sciences is that there is a terrible gap in communication between psychologists and sociologists; a split in the human sciences which is inconceivable in the natural sciences.

If psychologists misinterpret sociologists is the converse true, that sociologists misconceive psychology? I hope to show that this is the case and in doing so will try to test the assertion, made above, that splits within disciplines result from splits between disciplines. This reversal of the direction of criticism will redress the balance which has so far weighed against a group of psychologists who personally are some of the most socially aware and open to interdisciplinary co-operation among their profession.

The reversal of criticism may begin with Merton, the last of the structural role theorists, cited as evidence of a non-deterministic role theory in sociology. Although Merton is technically unimpeachable in his treatment of the concept there are unsatisfactory features in it, and some features of Merton's treatment make the psychologist's attitude to sociology understandable. Firstly, Merton is quick to pick up individual strategies for resolving conflict within a role-set, and label these 'social mechanisms'. When a teacher works in the classroom unobserved by parents, because there is a rule which generally forbids them to be present, this is a social mechanism; but under the same heading, 'insulation of role activities from observability by members of the role-set', are many personal strategies for avoiding contact with members of the role-set who might inhibit one's actions. Merton is technically faultless because as a structural sociologist he consciously picks out structural facts and is not concerned with human action of a more personal kind. That is why he treats the social mechanism described as 'abridgement of the role-set' as a limiting case. It is indeed a limiting case because it is not socially prescribed, it deviates from the typical role-set, and to the extent that it is successful it threatens to change a part of the social structure. Preoccupied with existing social structure Merton has stopped at the boundary line between sociology and psychology, a boundary defined by the limiting case, where personal choice might be exercised and the social structure changed. It is not that personal choice and social change are missed by this theory, it is rather that when he comes across them he chooses to put them beyond a disciplinary boundary and presumably hopes the psychologist, the historian or some other specialist will work out that particular range of problems.

There are other unattractive features of Merton's theory: the analogy of society as a machine is clear from his concept of social *mechanisms*, and elsewhere he speaks of residual conflict in the role-set as like an inefficient machine. He expresses some reservations about the machine analogy and rightly so since it implies that the conflict could be removed and in view of the evaluative connotations of 'inefficiency' that it *should* be removed, even though this area of conflict may be the one in which people become most humanly aware of the need to choose beyond social prescriptions.

So finally I admit a deficiency in the structural sociologists' concept of role, but not the one pointed to by Kelly, Bannister and Fransella. Role is not just a socially prescribed dialogue; however, it is, in the view of Merton, a concept which can be split into two foci of interest, one within sociology and one outside. In short it is *not taken to be an essentially interdisciplinary concept* but two different kinds of concepts which can be worked on independently in two separate disciplines. Such separation is indicated in the *International Encyclopedia of the Social Sciences* where two separate articles, one psychological and one sociological, appear.

Up to this point I have dealt with the *structural* role theorists represented in Coser and Rosenberg's book of readings, giving them priority because they were most likely to accord with the psychologists' misconception of role in sociology. Since they do not fit the stereotype it should be an easy matter to show that the second group of sociologists, the self/other theorists, have a concept of role which is more like Kelly's psychological concept. Indeed I shall try to argue that it is weak precisely because in some respects it is *too much like Kelly's concept*.

5.3 SELF/OTHER ROLE THEORY

After mentioning that William James offered a concept of the social-self more than eighty years ago, Coser and Rosenberg begin their selection with a passage from G. H. Mead. Mead (1934) is famous for his attempt to explain the emergence of the human self. The self is socially created and develops out of man's capacities both to read significant gestures and to play. A person is continually making gestures (using language later on) which attempt to get a response from the other. In trying to call out a response in the other he inevitably calls out that response in himself (particuarly when speaking, because he can hear himself), and so in social interaction he takes the attitude of the other, or takes the role of the other. The parallel with Kelly's concept of role is striking: as Kelly says

> . . . to the extent that one person construes the construction processes of another he may play a role in a social process involving the other person.[8]

Of course it is only a 'parallel' relationship between the approaches and not an identity of interest. However, one aspect of the similarity is worth particular attention. They both use the concept of role as subordinate to a primary concern with cognitive processes, Mead emphasising cognitive socialisation and Kelly (who did not bother much with developmental issues), cognitive interaction. As Duncan (1962) noted

> Mead deals very sparingly with the capacity of human beings to take the role of others. He keeps repeating that mind, self and society arise and develop in the communication of symbols.[9]

I would go so far as to say that neither Kelly nor Mead is a role theorist in any strong sense: role appears in their theories as an inescapable aspect of a communication process, but it is *not worked out as role theory* in its own right.

As to differences between Kelly and Mead, there could hardly be a sharper contrast than that between Kelly's conception of the person as self-inventing and Mead's conception of the self as socially created virtually without residue. And at this early date psychologists could legitimately have charged Mead with setting up an over-prescribed concept of the self. When Mead said that a person takes the role, not of one particular 'other' but of the 'generalised other', thereby internalising the attitudes of his social group or community, he assumed that something consistent enough to be called an attitude could be derived from the often conflicting relationships between various groups of which a person is a member. Actually Mead some-times mentions that a person takes in sectional attitudes, but he does not explore implied conflicts even though (or because?) he could see it all around him in the America of his time. The result is a powerful account of how the social-self is created but only in the context of a peculiarly benign model of society seen as a 'great co-operative community process'.[10]

For the self/other theorists, as for the structural role theorists, the post-war years brought a revision of the earlier sociologists' concern with Hegelian networks of rights and duties. Coser and Rosenberg present a snippet from Sumner (1906) on in-groups and out-groups, followed by selections from Sherif (1953) and Merton and Kitt (1950). These papers confirm that people relate not so much to a 'generalised other' but to 'significant others' (I think this term actually came from C. Wright Mills (1939)). Roles are thus built up in relation to a variety of groups making what may be conflicting demands. In addition, people identify with groups of which they are not actually members; for example the working class voter who identifies with the middle classes and displays 'anticipatory socialisa-tion' by behaving in a middle-class way—sometimes in a more middle-class way than the middle classes! Thus the concept of 'reference groups' eases the determinism of the earlier role theory which depended too heavily on a unitary concept of society.

Having discarded the unitary concept of society, sociologists are warned in the next paper by Levinson (1959) against maintaining a unitary concept of role. He distinguishes three aspects of the concept: there are the structurally given demands, the person's own conception of his role and the concrete actions of the role incumbent. For example, a doctor must be qualified in order to practice (struc-turally given demand) but he may see doctors as having a responsi-bility to work for revolution and the truly communal availability of

Self and Social Context

medical skill (his conception of the role). However, he takes a job in a hierarchical private institution and feels so guilty that he is neither a good doctor nor a good revolutionary (his actions).

If there was any weakness or ambiguity in the earlier sociological concepts which laid them open to criticism or misinterpretation by psychologists, this cannot be said of Levinson's formulation.

> Just as social structure presents massive forces which influence the individual from without toward certain forms of adaptation, so does personality present massive forces from within which lead him to select, create, and synthesize certain forms of adaptation rather than others. Role definition may be seen from one perspective as an aspect of personality. It represents the individual's attempt to structure his social reality, to define his place within it, and to guide his search for meaning and gratification.[11]

With respect to its recognition of a person's own contribution to the definition of role this is beyond criticism, and Levinson's work on patients, psychiatric residents and aides in mental hospitals is there to back up his theory. The limitations are that he uses the concept of 'structure' ambiguously. At one point he refers to *organisational* structure, at another, to *social* structure, and when discussing the fate of 'incongruent' members in an organisation suddenly widens his scope to mention 'structurally incongruent forms of political ideology, occupational role definition, and personality', which continue to exist in the Soviet Union. He asserts that individuals have brought about major structural changes in certain schools, mental hospitals and prisons, and

> Similar ideological and structural transitions are evident in other types of organization, such as corporate business.[12]

The result of these repeated and unexplained shifts of focus is that Levinson uses a *unitary* (because not clearly differentiated) concept of social and organisational structure, in order to attack a *unitary* concept of role.

An important issue missed by Levinson's failure to clarify his concept of structure is the relation of organisationally determined role demands to socially determined role demands: if the organisation is at odds with the society it might find it expedient to change its form of organisation in order to maintain its basic activity (corporate business) and avoid the kind of *social* structural change which would interfere with it (socialise it, for example).

The last three papers deal with the dramatistic model of role-playing and with 'role distance'. Erving Goffman (1959) asserts that in playing their roles people may be cynical about their own performances or quite sincere. They may also move in either direction between the roles of cynicism and sincerity as a result of playing the role. One of his most famous examples is the role of 'mental patient' where one of the effects of playing the role with its, for example, infantilising demands may be a reinforcement of the inadequacy, or labelling process, which forced the person into the role.

In his early work (1959) he describes the person as a performer, trying to present a convincing self by maintaining a consistent definition of a situation and playing his part in it. To the extent that a person can successfully define situations and choose parts in them his role can be seen as something he is trying to do (meeting the Kelly criticism). Goffman does not, and neither must we, overestimate the extent to which we can choose our roles (the earlier distinctions between achieved roles and ascribed roles are relevant and so are the points from Znaniecki on 'social circles', and Hughes on dilemmas and contradictions of status), so there is a strong sense of tension between socially given role demands and self-defined role demands. Goffman appears to resolve this tension in favour of group or social demands when he says

> In analyzing the self then we are drawn from its possessor, from the person who will profit or lose most by it, for he and his body merely provide the peg on which something of collaborative manufacture will be hung for a time.[13]

In *Encounters* (1961), Goffman eased off the social determination by developing the concept of 'role-distance'. A person frequently wishes to express that he is not, or not *only*, the person implied in a particular role-performance. The adult merry-go-round rider who shows that he is not enjoying the ride but is embarked in order to look after a child, collect tickets, etc., is expressing role-distance.

But again Goffman arrives at some apparently contradictory conclusions.

It is right here in manifestations of role distance, that the individual's personal style is to be found. . . . role distance is almost as much subject to role analysis as are the core tasks of roles themselves.[14]

In other words, personal style is to be opened up to sociological analysis, but *analysis in terms of role*.

Rose Coser (1966) detects the contradiction in Goffman's concept and in the last paper of this section seeks to give a sociological account of the disturbing factor of personal style which breaks through when actors show social creativity. Briefly, she holds that social distance is normatively prescribed. It is written into role-prescriptions that people should not play them so committedly that they become 'over-serious', 'stuffed shirts' or 'fanatics'. Life is a continuous process of 'transition between statuses', making it essential that we be ready to move on either developmentally in growing up, or into other statuses as circumstances change.

She explains Goffman's famous examples of role-distance as entailed by the need of actors to resolve sociological ambivalence. That is to say, people commonly find themselves torn by conflicting demands, because their role of the moment cannot completely wipe out their 'other affiliations' (as Goffman had already noted). What Goffman sees as moving away from the role, Coser sees as moving further into what we might call the finer detail of role-specification. The role-prescription would expand to read not just 'Be a qualified and competent surgeon', say, but 'Be a qualified and competent surgeon using resources available to you from other roles (friendly joking to reassure team, etc.), acknowledging the pull of other affiliations (family, golf club, etc.) but not letting them disable you for the role of surgeon on duty, and so on.

Coser criticises Goffman for misusing the concept of role by not confining it to social relationships. In her view

Role requirements . . . refer to a set of expected behaviours that are geared towards maintaining or strengthening one or more patterned relationships.[15]

Goffman may have broadened the concept of role to include certain self-defining behaviours and the contradictory concept of role-distance but Coser swings too far in the opposite direction. Following a definition provided by Talcott Parsons[15A] she takes role-structure as 'the primary focus of the articulation and hence interpenetration between personalities and social systems', whereas role is the 'aspect of what the actor does in his relations with others seen in the context of its functional significance for the social system'. And with this she introduces a unitary functionalist concept of structure which emphasises the maintenance or strengthening of patterned relationships. Conflicting demands due to 'sociological ambivalance' will give a person 'ever more patterns of responses which he can put at the service of conflict resolution'. Other maintenance criteria creep in

> . . . the mature individual, in contrast to the person who does his job, has learned to live up to the demands of his status position with a repertoire of attitudes and inner dispositions which he can call upon freely to solve unexpected and ambiguous situations and in this way to maintain otherwise threatened role relationships.[16]

It is amazing that Coser, whose theory is in part sensitive and clear, and whose expectations of the 'mature individual' are so noble, can assimilate everything to this consensual image of society. Conflict is mentioned as a difficulty to be resolved. By definition, role demands strengthen and maintain relationships. This functionalist model is insensitive to fundamental conflicts of a Marxian kind, or to sectionally defined roles which may demand the destruction of certain patterned relationships in society as a whole.

In Coser's model there is no sense that certain roles are literally forced upon the 'actors'. Criminals, political prisoners, the poverty-stricken and the oppressed are subject to demands which may in the short run maintain and strengthen certain power relationships but in such a way that conflict resolutions may only be possible by the destruction of one or other party to the conflict. I am not saying that all social life is conflict and terror but I am certainly denying that it is all as harmonious and constructively creative as Coser's model.

In a final paragraph Coser likens her sociological process of creative role-playing to Freud's psychological process of sublimation. The person with a strong ego can integrate experience of his past role-relationships and put it *to the use of role-performance*. If such a person is a 'truly creative individual' we must be thankful for the not truly creative individuals who in some circumstances act beyond role demands to exercise personal responsibility and in some cases to break patterned role-relationships.

At the completion of this circle of sociological theories we find a sociologist misunderstanding a psychologist, for Freud's process of sublimation was never so benign. The costs of sublimation to the individual and society may be very high, and so this reference to Freud is superficial, serving only to end the paper with a flourish.

5.4　SOCIOLOGICAL ROLE THEORIES

I have assumed that Coser and Rosenberg's selection of material on role is a fair sample of sociological role theory. It could be argued that accidents of the availability of publication rights will have biased the samples; so too will the American origin of the book, making it unrepresentative of British and European theory. This may be conceded without damaging the first main point of this section, which is to show that sociologists have not, in general, treated role too much in group terms or as a socially prescribed dialogue. For thirty years now there has been some awareness that role prescriptions may not provide for new situations and that role prescriptions may conflict, leaving the person to choose a course of action. If the sample of role theories is broadened to include British theory then this is even more apparent in the work of the social philosophers such as Emmet (1958) who have addressed themselves to the ethical problems of choice of action within *and beyond* roles. In Europe there has also been the long debate on Dahrendorf's 'homo sociologicus' (1968).

If the split between sociologists and psychologists is clearly evidenced (although it still needs to be explained), what of the question of splits within disciplines? It will be useful to examine the Coser and Rosenberg sample of theories presented above to see what patterns of development are discernible within sociology. This, together with the critical points already made in relation to certain of the theories, may also indicate what is left of the concept, and what needs to be added in order to produce an adequate role theory.

The salient feature of sociological role theories is that they elaborate two main themes. The first is concerned with structure and in particular with specifying positions within social structure which persist beyond the incumbency of any single person. The second is focused on face-to-face interaction and the many ways, both obvious and subtle, in which it is defined and managed by the persons involved.

Structural role theorists have at times been too socially deterministic but after the first elementary stages of theory building they were faced with the phenomenon of personal choice between and beyond roles, with its implication of a degree of individual autonomy. Merton's response was to set aside the more individual problems and get on with what he saw as the primary sociological task—a functional analysis of social structure. If he is allowed this definition of the discipline he cannot be criticised for treating the concept of role too structurally. The criticism must be that he failed to grasp the essentially interdisciplinary nature of the concept splitting it along the boundary of his profession. What then were the pressures on the discipline which might account for Merton's definition of it?

At this time sociologists were intellectually insecure (Inkeles, 1959), anxious about the boundaries of their disciplines, the definition of its distinctive subject matter, and their status as scientists. Although one sociologist (Parsons, 1951, 1954) had recognised the interdisciplinary nature of social theory and went on to produce a large-scale systems theory marred by its overconcentration on integrative functions within social systems, Merton deprecated this approach. He saw Parsons' grand theory as a premature attempt to overcome 'the ambiguous status of sociology in contemporary West-European and American societies', an attempt to reduce the

> . . . uncertainty of having accumulated knowledge adequate to the large demands now being laid upon sociology—by policymakers, reformers and reactionaries, by business men and government men, by college presidents and college sophomores . . .[17]

Thus two strong factors bear upon the sociological production process: the professional identity crisis of sociologists and social pressure to deliver the goods. Interestingly it is the social role of sociologists which is used here to explain why they developed certain role-concepts, a 'reflexive' form of explanation that meets phenomenological criteria, and, incidentally, the requirements of personal construct theorists.

There is some support for this interpretation of the development of the sociologist's role from Ben-David.

> Starting perhaps with the studies on the American soldier, and on the authoritarian personality [reference here to T. W. Adorno, 1950], social scientists tended to try and combine practical advice

with theoretically significant contributions to one or another of the social science disciplines. Eventually, they began to consider that the contribution to the discipline was more important than the practical conclusions [reference here to Morris Janowitz, Professionalization of sociology, *Am. J. Sociol.*, July, 1972, and to Edward Shils, The calling of sociology, in Talcott Parsons *et al.*, *Theories of Society*, 1965]. This led to a unidisciplinary approach. Instead of asking where the knowledge to solve a practical problem could be found, researchers broke down the problem into its various aspects—sociological, economic, etc.—and were content to handle only those aspects which concerned their speciality. Because of their conception that social sciences had to resemble the basic natural sciences, they saw this development as an improvement in the status and quality of the social sciences.[18]

Self/other role theorists usually adopt an approach which is in direct contrast to that of the structural theorists. They begin with the minimum unit of social interaction—one person in face-to-face contact with another—and seek to build up larger social units out of this irreducible element. G. H. Mead has had a lasting and important influence on this group of theorists. If anything, there has been a resurgence of his influence on some of the newer schools of phenomenological sociology (Berger and Luckman).

Mead's work contains fascinating contradictions. He writes as a behaviourist tracing the development of human social beings out of antecedents in animal behaviour, and yet he works towards a model of the person as user of language engaged in symbolic interaction— a self who comes into being through the social process of communication.

I have already mentioned his concept of the 'generalised other' with its implication of an organismic society through which the self finds its realisation, and also the modification of generalised other to 'significant others' in C. Wright Mills (1939). What I think needs attention here is Mead's concept of the self, because it reveals something of importance for a critique of this whole line of self/other theorists.

Mead's primary concern was to describe the process of creation of a thinking, social, moral being.

What goes to make up the organized self is the organization of the attitudes which are common to the group. A person is a personality because he belongs to a community, because he takes over the institutions of that community into his own conduct. He takes its language as a medium by which he gets his personality, and then through a process of taking the different roles that all the others furnish he comes to get the attitude of the members of the community. Such, in a certain sense, is the structure of a man's personality.[19]

Nor is it only attitudes that are taken in; the very capacity to think is formed in social interaction.

. . . mind presupposes, and is a product of, the social process.[20]

Mead divides the self into two inseparable but distinguishable aspects, the 'I' and the 'Me'. The 'me' comes in from the society outside; it is the generalised attitudes of the community, the group, the society, the social process, awakened in interaction when the person takes the roles of others. This internalisation of the social structure provides the perfect means of accounting for the capacity of men to behave as they should—as their community would have them behave. Men get the institutions of their community into their own conduct. But notice the easy interchange of all these conceptions of the social—the community, the group, the others, the social process, institutions, the generalised other—and it becomes evident that Mead is failing to discriminate and distinguish the various aspects of structure. If he did make distinctions his primary purpose of accounting for the unitary moral self would not be possible because on his person-to-person model of social interaction there would be too many conflicting and contradictory selves to bring together. And although Mead recognises the possibility of pathological dissociation of the personality into component selves he insists on the original unity of the person.

The phenomenon of dissociation of personality is caused by breaking up of the complete, unitary self into the component selves of which it is composed, and which respectively correspond to different aspects of the social process in which the person is involved, and within which his complete or unitary self has arisen; these aspects being the different social groups to which he belongs within that process.[21]

Now it follows from Mead's failure to distinguish the various aspects of the social which are internalised that the 'me' part of the self will be too conventional and socially determined to possess the moral qualities of choice and action that Mead set out to explain, or to allow for social changes. And so he must develop an autonomous aspect of self to account for the more self-expressive or impulsive actions: this, of course, is the 'I'.

Situations in which self-expression may occur are 'particularly precious' giving rise to 'some of the most exciting and gratifying experiences'. However, the resulting actions may be high or low in value: a mob situation may release vengeful, violent action rather than the self-expressive, independent actions which are possible when a person thinks his own thoughts and takes responsibility for an action carried out, in his own way. 'Impulsive conduct is uncontrolled conduct', and may be violent, but the 'I' is normally limited by the 'me'. The 'I' may contribute its own response to a situation defined by the given 'me'.

> The response is, in the experience of the individual, an expression with which the self is identified. It is such a response which raises him above the institutionalized individual.[22]

There is still a problem in relation to the 'I' because Mead says that it appears in experience only after completion of the act. He believes that we are continually trying to realise this 'I' even though, due to the necessarily unforeseen details of a future action, we shall not know what it is until we have acted.

The distinctive qualities of the 'I', therefore, seem to be impulsiveness, self-expression and indeterminacy. Impulsive behaviour is 'uncontrolled' as against self-expression which takes place when the 'I' uses the 'me' as a means of carrying out what is 'the undertaking that all are interested in'. This is strange because 'the undertaking that all are interested in' (if there is such a thing) would surely come in as the 'me' aspect of self. So there is some confusion here, leaving 'indeterminacy' as the only unmistakable quality of the 'I'. And indeterminacy is not a strong criterion since the person may carry through an action *against* the 'common undertaking' in which the foreseen self (say revolutionary) is so accurate in important respects as to make unforeseen details of the resulting situation and self, trivial.

So I conclude that Mead's concept of self, although valuable in some ways, is spoilt by a certain dichotomy of person and society in which the social comes in as a unitary influence ('Me') which then has to be counteracted by the indeterminacy of the 'I'. The social is unitary because Mead misses conflicts between classes and between societies, and so the individual ('I') has to be found in what may be the trivially indeterminate aspects of action. The fundamental weakness of most role theories may thus be that where the social is made too unitary the individual has to be made unduly autonomous, or indeterminate, in order to allow for the real qualities of human action. This *tendency to polarise self and society* where the social is not sufficiently differentiated is the major weakness of the group of self/other role theorists. It has been shown in Mead; in Levinson, who, similarly, used an undifferentiated concept of 'structure'; in Goffman, who flies between the socially creative user of 'role-distance' and the role determination of this creativity; and finally in Rose Coser, who reinforced the idea that 'role-distance' is normative or socially prescribed.

The general result of these lines of development in role theory is that the self/society relation has been neglected because of a distortion of one or other of the two elements in the relationship. The interdisciplinary nature of the concept of role has never been successfully faced.

The split between the two main relevant disciplines, sociology and psychology, has been reproduced within sociology as two groups of theorists, one structural and one self-orientated, who both swing between structural determinism (the oversocialised man) and individualism (the undersocialised man).

I would hypothesise that the splits within psychology, mentioned by Bannister and Fransella as customary, rest on a similar pattern of developments within that discipline. Basically the contributory factors are professional anxiety, leading to overspecialisation, and a consequent neglect of essentially interdisciplinary concepts or phenomena. It must be emphasised that this is not an argument for simply putting together sociology and psychology, or any other disciplines, in the wishful belief that they will somehow be good for each other. My own experience of such attempts to mix disciplines has been that they often fail badly and drive the participants further apart. There are large areas of sociology and psychology which can be worked on perfectly well without reference to the other discipline —the physiological aspects of psychology and the demographic aspects of sociology, for example. The argument relates only to inter-

disciplinary phenomena like 'role' which are inescapably concerned
with the relation between the social and the personal and so with
the relation between sociology and psychology. I shall return to the
problem of relations between disciplines below when the development of psychology will be explored more fully in the context of its
philosophical origin.

5.5 PERSONAL CONSTRUCT ROLE THEORY

It may now be possible to evaluate personal construct role theory
against the background of a critique of a range of role theories,
whilst keeping a look out for insights into the relations between
disciplines and the development of the human sciences.

The importance of role to Kelly's theory cannot be overestimated.
In its early stages it was known by his students as 'role theory' and as
Kelly said 'it might have been called "role-theory" '. What a curious
contradiction it is that Mair can say

    . . . this central construct in Kelly's theory which indicates how a
    man can enter into meaningful social interaction and under-
    standing with others is only fractionally developed within the
    formal methods suggested by him.[23]

It is patterns such as this—failure to develop the *central construct*
of a theory—that are of great significance in the formation of the
human sciences. Why did it happen? One interpretation would be
that Kelly's theory is essentially interdisciplinary in that it turns upon
the concept of role, but Kelly, partly from modesty, partly from
ignorance, defines role in such a way as to exclude its truly social
aspects so that he can get on with a specialised area of work in
clinical psychology. If this is true then once again the division of
labour strikes at a concept in the human sciences.

When defining role Kelly was quite explicit in his desire to establish a restricted definition.

    We have insisted that the term *role* be reserved for a course of
    activity which is played out in the light of one's construction of
    one or more other persons' construct systems. When one plays a
    role, he behaves according to what he believes another person
    thinks, not merely according to what the other person appears to
    approve or disapprove. One plays a role when he views another

person as a construer. This, of course, is a restricted definition. It is the definition specifically used in the psychology of personal constructs.[24]

And yet this restricted definition is found by Kelly to have profound implications reaching far into social psychology and sociology. He reaches these conclusions in a step-by-step argument which first recognises that the 'ultimate validating criteria' of our constructs must be the 'operation of the construct systems which appear to govern our neighbour's behaviours'. He then recognises that 'group expectancy—governing constructs' act as 'validators of one's own *role-constructs*'. It then follows that psychologists play roles when they necessarily and professionally attempt to construe others' construct systems, and they too must check these constructs against those which the other people actually operate. He next suggests that this method of approach provides a better basis for social psychology than the once prevailing assumption that individual suggestibility could be used to account for group phenomena. His next bid takes in sociology.

Within the present psychological system the phenomenal areas of traditionalism, social controls, law, cultural identification, and ethnic unity can properly be brought into the realm of psychology.[25]

Presumably Kelly's line of thought here is that all these group, societal and cultural phenomena must somehow be embodied in various people's construct systems. A study of their constructs will tell us something about the phenomena. It will be a better explanation than the crude assumption, made by social psychologists, that individual suggestibility can explain group phenomena, and the equally crude assumption, made by sociologists, that people conform to what others want them to do. If I interpret him correctly this means that Kelly is up to an old trick which, by perverse reading of his philosophy of 'constructive alternativism', might be described as the tendency to construct alternative approaches to his own which are at opposite poles to the good qualities of his theory. He then labels these contrast poles 'social psychology', etc., and thus shows the superiority of his position.

The crucial question is whether Kelly's concept of role will take him as far as he believes it will, and the answer must be negative.

Granted that interpersonal, group, societal and cultural phenomena involve construing the construction processes of others, that is role relationships, we only move to the point of acknowledging that human phenomena involve human persons. If we wish to explore the origins, history and present structure of complexes of constructs and the role relationships they make available we shall be severely limited by Kelly's definition of role. His definition is perfectly adapted to therapy. People coming to him because of a virtual inability to construe the construction processes of others or with some persistent distortion in their attempts at such understanding, can be encouraged by means of fixed-role therapy to experiment in relating to others. Trying to play roles and learning to play roles is, when properly done, entirely beneficial in terms of Kelly's theory because many of the social aspects of role-playing—enforced conformity, inducement, manipulation, deceit, and so on—have been carefully defined out of the therapeutic situation. This is excellent for Kelly's purposes but a huge hindrance to social psychologists and sociologists who must attend to the reality of their objects of study and not define them in advance into a more humane and constructive form.

There are other points in Kelly's work where the strain between his narrow definition of role and the more usual broader one shows up. Occasionally he uses 'role' in a much wider sense than he has defined in personal construct theory. When discussing 'guilt', which for Kelly has a particular meaning involving dislodgement from one's core role-structure, he describes core role-structure as

... that part of a person's role structure by which he maintains himself as an integral being.[26]

He then gives as an example the child who gains his core role in relation to mother and father and may experience guilt if he finds he 'has not been acting as his parent's child'. Here it is apparent that core role is culturally and socially prescribed, flowing into the child, through the parents, as a general and partly unconscious influence. At another place Kelly refers to guilt as 'awareness of the loss of one's social role', a much more sociological use of the concept of role than he has specified.

A child construes himself as belonging to his family. He interprets his mother's behaviour. He interprets his father's behaviour. He enacts his presumed part in relation to this interpretation. He comes to identify himself in the practical terms of the enactment. [27]

Although Kelly emphasises that preverbal constructs may be used by the child, this account of socialisation makes a large demand on the child's interpretive resources. It also gives the impression that the child is deciding what part it will play. This may confirm Kelly's general model of man the scientist, experimenting, anticipating and choosing, but it neglects the very great weight of social pressure which has gone into defining the roles of mother, father and child, a formative influence so great that the child's contribution to shaping his constructs is very small at this stage. Indeed it is in this relatively long period of dependence and helplessness that the capacities of the child are given to it, but given to it in the form prescribed by the culture and society. In other words, the ability to construe the constructs of other people is certainly involved in the role relationships of socialisation (as G. H. Mead understood some time ago), but what we need to know is how society is internalised by the child and what the consequences may be (for construing capacities and for other social action potentials) of socialisation into various kinds of social structure.

It is not simply that Kelly's concept of role provides a weak starting point which will not develop very far, it is that he defines out in advance just those kinds of social action which social psychology and sociology must attempt to explain. For when relating to *more than one other*, and this is a vast range of human behaviour, a person must utilise labels and categories, for various groupings of people and various constellations of ideas. Clearly language gives him precisely this facility. And yet for Kelly this kind of behaviour—what he calls '*positional construing of human figures*' in terms of status variables, class concepts and subculture norms—is what the therapist must work against, because it is said to be a failure to construe people *as persons*. Again it is easy to see how necessary Kelly's definition is for the therapeutic situation where positional construing may actually have caused the client's distress (for people are usually more than any positional category will define them as being); but what a complete disablement for the social scientist if 'categories' are ruled out in advance by the definition given to role. Not that the social scientist wishes to use given categories uncritically (Kelly's stereotype) but as one phase in a two-phase operation which consists of grasping the categories normally made available and then questioning and experimenting with these categories in a phenomenological and critical attempt to discover why social phenomena are as they are, and how they might otherwise be.

Personal construct role theory will provide a fine and sensitive method for eliciting verbal constructs which structure certain role relationships. Where these are preverbal or non-verbal it will be usable, but of less certain effectiveness since we do not yet know how to readily elicit and represent these non-verbal constructs. The greatest inadequacy will appear when an attempt is made to elicit constructs (often non-verbal) which are attempts by individuals to construe the constructs of *groups* of others. Although Kelly defines role as 'a course of activity which is played out in the light of one's understanding of the behaviour of *one or more* other people' [my emphasis], he does not explore the social psychological and sociological phenomena which begin to appear as soon as a person attempts to relate to *more than one other*. Of course he is clear at some times about his limited and specialised 'focus of convenience', and I have already shown how well adapted to his chosen field is his concept of role; but at other times his claims about the significance and usefulness of his theory go far into group and social contexts.

It would not seem to be of such great importance that a psychologist makes a slighter greater claim than his theory will actually support, except that this is one of the most familiar patterns in the relations between disciplines in and around the human sciences. These claims together with the usual charges and countercharges of reductionism—of human to animal behaviour, of human experience to social conformity, of the rational disorder of schizophrenia to a disease entity, and so on—are themselves evidence of the division of labour in human sciences being carried to the point of severe misunderstanding.

Nor would it seem particularly dangerous that an extra, if faulty, concept is being offered to human scientists, except that the concept is of a fundamentally individualist kind which, when it has been used before in sociology (by G. H. Mead), has been matched by its very opposite—the concept of a 'generalised other'—as though concepts which are at extremes of individualism or social determinism give rise to their extreme opposites.

Kelly uses a telling image of change within the confines of an existing construct system. Where a person moves to the opposite extreme on one of his construct dimensions he calls it 'slot-rattling', and it is not usually an effective kind of change because it does not explore new dimensions. One way of describing the development of role theory up to the present time would be to describe it as slot-rattling between individual and social approaches because a new dimension has not been found. In this context Karl Mannheim's essay on 'Competition as a Cultural Phenomenon' may provide insight into the present condition of polarised disciplines and areas of disciplines within the human sciences.

> . . . from the point of view of the social sciences, every historical, ideological, sociological piece of knowledge (even should it prove to be Absolute Truth itself) is clearly rooted in and carried by the desire for power and recognition of particular social groups who want to make their interpretation of the world the universal one. [28]

Or as he put it in *Ideology and Utopia*

> Behind every definite question and answer is implicitly or ex-plicitly to be found a model of how fruitful thinking can be carried on. If one were to trace in detail, in each individual case, the origin and the radius of diffusion of a certain thought model one would discover the peculiar affinity it has to the social position of given groups and their manner of interpreting the world. By these groups we mean not merely classes, as a dogmatic type of Marxism would have it, but also generations, status groups, sects, occupational groups, schools, etc. [29]

It is clear that although Mannheim owes and acknowledges a debt to Marx he is seeking to distance himself from 'dogmatic' Marxism by setting up a speciality within sociology, to be called the 'sociology of knowledge'. This speciality will acquire autonomy and a scientifically appropriate degree of objectivity in two ways. One is that although sociologists are intellectuals and therefore predisposed to bourgeois ways of thinking by the well-rewarded positions they are likely to hold, they are at the same time prompted by normal societal developments to see and think in various perspectives. Where different modes of interpretation come into conflict, and this must be the normality of class society, they may 'render one another transparent and establish perspective with reference to each other'. [30] It is here that we may understand criticisms by members of the Frankfurt school, found paradoxical by Martin Jay. [31] Marcuse's criticism that the sociology of knowledge is 'occupied with the untruths, not the truths of previous philosophies' is a response to Mannheim's refusal to discriminate between Marxian claims to knowledge and other claims. There may be untruths in Marx but substantively he makes other competing claims to knowledge 'transparent', not in a reciprocal way but by explaining their form—something they could not do for Marx. By recognising only the untruths in Marx, Mannheim is able to suggest that the sociology of knowledge reigns equally over Marxian and other systems of knowledge: this pluralistic reciprocal, working-through-untruths-towards-truth is Mannheim's 'relationism', criticised by Horkheimer because in its covert assumptions it is a 'metaphysical quest for pure knowledge'.[32] It becomes metaphysical by asserting a generality which refuses to notice that Marx, whatever else he did, took a distinctive step in showing the relation of ideologies to class interests.

Now it becomes clear why Mannheim finds it necessary to reject such a distinctive part of Marx's work, as the second part of his bid for autonomy on the part of the sociology of knowledge.

The study of ideologies has made it its task to unmask the more or less conscious deceptions and disguises of human interest groups, particularly those of political parties. The sociology of knowledge is concerned not so much with distortions due to a deliberate effort to deceive as with the varying ways in which objects present themselves to the subject according to the differences in social settings.[33]

In order to serve sociology, providing it with a subject matter which does not turn round upon the discipline to reveal its ideological functions, Mannheim finds it necessary to break with Marx and to depoliticise the object of study. By drawing the disciplinary boundary at this point he makes the subject matter manageable, at the cost of impoverishing it.

There is another threat to the autonomy of the sociology of knowledge from another direction, that of psychology, which might deal with perceptual questions contained in the idea of perspectives, and also, if Freud is not to be disregarded with the dynamics underlying some kinds of misperception. Mannheim puts out boundary markers in this direction too, by excluding the *'particular'* conception of ideology, concerned with

. . . all those utterances the 'falsity' of which is due to an intentional or unintentional, conscious, semi-conscious, or unconscious, deluding of one's self or others, taking place on a psychological level and structurally resembling lies.[34]

But it has become evident that both psychological and ideological processes are at work even in those areas of investigation which, as theories of personality, seek the status of sciences; so although the sociology of knowledge provides a simply conceived starting point for a sociologist setting out to examine personality theories, the results of this examination break through the boundaries of the discipline of sociology and demand a comprehensive theory encompassing sociological, psychological and ideological problems. In other words, it is only by reversing the normal tendencies toward specialisation and the division of labour in intellectual work that concepts adequate to the phenomena they seek to elucidate can be made available.

Dagenais' assertion that it is not possible to add up the results of separate disciplines and arrive at an adequate explanation of psycho-social phenomena is supported by this finding that disciplines are not (contra Mannheim's assumptions) partial, accurate perspectives but deformed viewpoints. What is needed is a *trans*disciplinary kind of investigation and theory. Whether there is anything of this nature available must be determined by a further more wide-ranging search.

5.6 THE DISCIPLINES MEET — A SYMPOSIUM

Up to this point the discussion of role theory has been deliberately selective in an attempt to *represent* the relation between sociology and psychology as human sciences, whilst using failures in the relationship to explain repeated patterns of inadequacy in formulation and use of the concept of role. Now, as a move towards more effective interdisciplinary theory it will be necessary to examine some recent developments in this field of work and to acknowledge other contributions to role theory from such related disciplines as philosophy and literature. A useful way of broadening the picture may be to look at what is very nearly an interdisciplinary symposium on the concept of role. It is not quite a symposium because the participants did not all meet and so have the opportunity of responding to each other's contributions, but the editor of this particular set of papers[35] did strive to bring about some interaction between the disciplines. There is a transcript of a discussion between a philosopher, a sociologist and a teacher of literature with an interest in the theatre; there is also a paper in reply from one sociologist to another. The editor provides a short overview and it is soon clear that he has very little by way of a significant integration to report. He notes widespread dissatisfaction with the concept of role and mentions what can now be seen as a process of polarisation of knowledge.

> 'Role theory' has tended to be concerned more with one side or other of the abstraction; it has emphasized personality in relation to social psychology or functional normative constraints in relation to deviance and conformity.[36]

He also confirms the sterility of this kind of splitting, commenting that 'Two concepts have not fared better than one'. The six papers which have led the editor to these views then follow.

In order to bring this wide-ranging material within the bounds of a brief discussion and for the sake of relevance to an interdisciplinary purpose it will be necessary to extract the 'central themes' of the papers. If, as Merleau-Ponty suggests, central themes inform the finest detail of substantial written works then the loss of detail will not distort but only crystallise the arguments. I shall also risk taking the papers out of their published order, paying more attention to those which attempt to build interdisciplinary bridges than to those which simply take a position and work out the consequences by normal methods within the usual disciplinary boundaries. The clearest example of the latter category of paper is a perfectly straightforward attempt by Chad Gordon to deploy the concept of role in the context of the human life cycle. For this purpose he adopts an existing definition provided by Turner. It has already been noted that two separate papers, one sociological and one psychological, appear in the *International Encyclopedia of the Social Sciences*, and it was suggested that this held significance for the relation between disciplines. Turner provided the sociological paper of this pair and it is the one now used by Gordon, a social psychologist. He simply sets out a typical ten-stage role succession for 'contemporary urban, middle-class America'. It is a thorough job, resting on the orthodox framework of Parsons, Erikson and Lidz, but it does nothing to develop the concept. In fact it could be argued that uncritical use of the concept only serves to reinforce the ambiguities and weaknesses of Turner's loose sociological definition. Certainly he falls into an oversocialised conception with occasional references to the 'socio-culturally provided structure of reciprocal roles'. Reciprocity is such a doubtful concept here because of the implied consensus model of society when in truth the 'reciprocity' of role-players in unequal power relationships may be nothing but unwilling acceptance on the part of the weaker that for the moment power lies with the stronger. His only fresh contribution is a discussion of the forced relinquish-ment of roles typical of retirement, where the personal consequences can be disastrous. This insight into forced relinquishment of roles is not carried through logically to awareness of the forced imposition of many roles. Still, it could not be expected that Gordon's very general interpretation of Turner's already broad sociological definition would lead far.

> ... a pattern of behaviour and sentiment, organized, in relation
> to presumed motivations, and frequently but not always connected
> to a specific organizational position. [37]

It is difficult to see what behaviour this excludes. Its looseness allows Gordon to include as role-behaviour the efforts of an older man to help a younger man in his organisation—the role of 'sponsor'.

What comes to mind as a description of this paper is Kuhn's term 'normal science': the phase of research in which available concepts are worked through in order to fill in the detail within an established paradigm. [38] It does not advance the conceptual resources presently available but it uses them well enough. Since it does not transcend disciplinary boundaries it offers little of significance for an inter-disciplinary project.

The contribution of Heinrich Popitz, though securely grounded as a sociological paper, is perceptive and rigorous enough to en-counter some boundary questions. Apart from its existence as a fine and careful delineation of the concept of role it is most valuable for the light it throws on the '*homo sociologicus*' debate. This debate, initiated by Dahrendorf in 1958 with a paper described as 'probably the most influential publication in theoretical sociology that has appeared in Germany since the war', is ostensibly about the relation of human nature to man's expected conformity to his social roles. The poignancy of such a theme, in a country where Hitler's followers had pleaded the pressure of orders from above in mitigation of their crimes, can hardly be missed, and it is not surprising that a 'many-sided public dispute took place'.

In relation to sociological theory Dahrendorf seemed to be pro-proposing the abandonment of traditional structural emphases in favour of concentration on description and analysis of the many categories of expectations flowing in to social roles. For example, legal norms which *must* be obeyed, conventional norms which *should* be obeyed, and optional norms which allow the role-taker to do certain things if he wishes. Conceivably such a microanalysis if carried through might reveal the larger social structures (an echo here of Kelly's belief that through personal constructs we might deal with 'social controls, law, cultural identification and ethnic unity'). But the contradition in Dahrendorf's position is that such an approach could only be successful on the assumption of a consensus model of society; and yet he had gained some reputation as a critic of American consensus sociology (Dahrendorf, 1958). The contradiction can be traced back to an earlier stage in Dahrendorf's development.

His attack on American Utopian sociology called for recognition of the ubiquity of conflict in modern societies. As an alternative to both American and Marxian sociology he offered his own theory of conflict which attempted to transcend the old Marxian basis of class antagonism and see conflict as resulting from competition for the relatively scarce roles carrying higher authority in a society. But in order to carry higher authority the scarce roles muct be accepted as legitimate, which is what Marxian sociology specifically denies, except perhaps as a shaky transitional stage. So in avoiding the Marxian position of fundamental conflict (a difficult one to embrace in Cold War Germany) he set up a model where conflict is ubiquitous but institutionalised within a consensus as to the legitimacy of social hierarchy. Within such a model his role theory takes its place.

And now Dahrendorf's position in the debate can be seen more clearly. Firstly, he accepts that sociologists must build a sociological theory which assumes men's conformity to their social roles. Secondly, this '*homo sociologicus*' is an abstraction which we must carefully acknowledge does not capture human nature. The influence of his consensual (authority) model would lead him to the first conclusion. The second is an attempt to rescue the person (human nature) from the implicit overdetermination of his model of society. Does not this repeat, with differences of time, place and theoretical development, G. H. Mead's efforts to rescue his oversocialised person by attributing to him the special private quality of an 'I'?

If so, then the familiar polarisation of concepts of person and society is at work here too.

As Popitz points out, it is neither necessary nor helpful to assume that people behave in conformity with their roles.

Strange to say, in the German discussion Dahrendorf's imputation seems to have been expressly or tacitly accepted. Correspondingly this conformity hypothesis was mixed up with the general discussion of possible conformity effects of sociological theory.[39]

And finally, the most important reflection on the relation between sociology and psychology is found in 'Dahrendorf's suggestion that questions of conformity be delegated *en bloc* to psychology'. Another move (recalling Merton's) to split the concept by means of a disciplinary boundary drawn primarily to suit professional interests, and not with regard to the special qualities of role-phenomena.

If Popitz has taken the discussion forward by disposing of *'homo sociologicus'*, his own proposals for role theory, being rather strictly sociological, do not hold out much promise for *interdisciplinary* advance. He sees the role-concept as touching upon something fundamental to social structures, having a degree of universality which can be set out in a refutable but unrefuted form, and he proposes comparative work across societies with different systems of role-allocation, role-assimilation and role-structures. He suggests that

Lasting societation requires, for example, the setting up of regularities in social behaviour on the basis of agreements about abstractions, the drawing up of sanctionable norms, the relation of normative subsystems to one another, and social generalization of individuals into role-bearers.[40]

The weakness of this view of societation is that it assumes a contract (if not consensus) model of society, and the availability of information and criteria for assessment to an extent as yet undreamt of in industrial society. On the question of agreement about moral standards MacIntyre (1967) said

English society today is at best morally pluralistic in a way that makes the notion of authoritative moral utterance inapplicable; at worst it is a society in which the lack of a shared moral vocabulary makes the use of explicit moral assertion positively pernicious.

What is pernicious is the illusion that is created of a society united not as in fact it is by harsh utilitarian necessities, but by common standards and ideas.[41]

Furthermore, an examination of mass media output would show a process in which standards and criteria are continuously played upon and evoked by special interests, sometimes in a most contradictory way, as when in a tirade against violence they distort the evidence as to its occurrence, or in their regular provision of sexual titillation they feel bound to cover it by moral condemnation or a joking style. Such is the confusion, irrationality and disconnectedness of this kind of social discourse that Popitz's assertions about the minimal requirements of lasting societation—that it entails, for example, 'the setting up of regularities in social behaviour on the basis of agreements about abstractions'—are made to seem unrealistic. Rather than being set up by agreement (the contract model), role relationships emerge, are fallen into, are imposed, are obscured, are kept implicit, etc., by such a variety of processes of which the origins are lost in history, that agreement, even agreement to differ, seems a misdescription. Presumably this is why Popitz relegates to a footnote the observation that

. . . role norms can impose themselves which are aimed at making people blind to their own interests.[42]

Nevertheless it is a tribute to Popitz that, in pursuing the analysis to the point at which self-contradictory interests are noticed, a problem which psychologists and philosophers have grappled with, he has pushed hard against the boundaries of his discipline, possibly a kind of invitation to others who might push through. Later on this invitation will be accepted.

Margaret Coulson contributes a paper which argues against the grain of all role theory: for her the concept introduces such a degree of confusion and mystification that it should be declared redundant. Unlike Popitz, who recognises its limitations and therefore expects it to be unhelpful towards analysis of certain issues—class conflict, for example—Coulson can find no place for the concept at all. The clarity of this position is refreshing and leads to a very crisp evaluation of those who use or fall into conformity or consensus assumptions. But having taken up a position against these role theorists, she displays the familiar tendency to recast knowledge in a form which exaggerates the inadequacies of her opponents. The result is yet another polarisation of person and society.

> At its most general level, role theory implies a sociological view which relates individuals to societies in terms of a process of one-way adjustment and adaptation.[43]

Whilst it can be agreed that this distortion has been the ever present danger of role theory, and that some theorists have erred in this direction, it must be emphasised that a less social-determinist view has been available in the main stream of the discipline at least since the 1940s.

Noticing the widespread use of role theory, which conflicts with the very low valuation she puts upon it, Coulson tries to explain its attractiveness for sociologists. She attributes it to the occupational pressures which bear on the academic teacher: the need to give convincing performances in the stage-like lecturing situation, to gain a good reputation as a basis for professional and scientific rewards and to behave in accordance with an authoritatively defined part in an organised social process. I agree that these are some of the conditions for success as a sociologist; I agree also that such social and occupational pressures are very likely to influence the forms of knowledge produced by these particular intellectual workers. But I find her response to this situation unsatisfactory for a number of reasons. The discovery that distortion has crept into knowledge production does not necessarily indicate total rejection of the product. Whether the product is worth anything will depend on the extent of the distortion and this is a case which needs arguing. Rejection of the concept of role on grounds of its being a peculiarly apt characterisation of the sociologist's own position depends on a demonstration that sociologists' work conditions are *quite unlike* those of other people. Given the many professions and jobs in which performance criteria apply with equal force I cannot accept the conclusions of this argument.

To put it the other way round: if sociologists are involved in social processes through their occupation in a similar way to other people then their concept of role (being determined to some extent by their occupation) will also tend to reflect the structure of other people's occupational situations; it will therefore be relatively accurate and relatively useful. Grounds for rejection of the concept would be the extremely dubious assertion that sociologists are not involved in social processes and therefore are unlikely to capture any social reality in their ideas.

All these arguments stem from assumptions introduced by Coulson, and remaining still within this framework it is possible to turn her argument against her, asking what it is in her own occupational situation which might contribute to her total rejection of the concept? From the description of her post at the time of publication she appears to work in a college of education where presumably her function would be seen as teaching would-be teachers to understand and manage their role resources in their anticipated task of allocating, and imposing, role-potentialities and role-prescriptions. Having shown us that role-analysis takes a particularly functionalist and social determinist form in the area of educational sociology, she rejects the concept partly because of her misconception of it as necessarily determinist and partly because she occupies the particularly distasteful role of *teacher of teachers* of this oppressive form of knowledge. To the extent that we properly understand her position we do not need to stand in it: role therefore remains on the agenda.

Some confirmation of the utility of retaining role theory may be found by assessing Coulson's alternative to it. It is a recommendation to regard school life as a 'structured network of expectations' which, if explored historically and dialectically, would avoid the troublesome concept and, among other things, would adequately recognise social class and power relationships, for 'teachers are themselves not in a position to choose the organisation and processes within the school'. But surely some of the 'structured network of expectations' takes its form from the categories of actors involved, that is, roles, and if the teacher is to some degree powerless this is precisely what can be explored by examining the psychological and sociological dimensions of the role without of course importing the unnecessary and limiting assumptions about consensus or conformity. Such a study will be, as she suggests, necessarily both dialectical and historical. In the case of the powerless teacher it will be no more than a recognition of the forcible imposition of roles, the teacher's function, at times, as agent of this imposition, and consequent alienation which, when experienced outside of the classical industrial context, is that much more difficult to see.

Incidentally, Coulson mentions a further case of the adoption of role as a central concept and then conspicuous failure to develop it: the book by Hans Gerth and C. Wright Mills (1954), *Character and Social Structure*. This may well be the sociological counterpart of Kelly's psychological approach, a repetition of pattern possibly carrying implications for the explanation of developments in human sciences.

A pair of papers by John Urry and Walter Runciman bring into focus the area of social theory most closely related to that of role, namely 'reference group' research. The close relation rests on the fact that as soon as role is viewed as a set[44] of relationships between a person and the various others and groups of others which make up that person's social environment it is possible to investigate the sources and patterns of expectations flowing in from various directions. However, the relevant others in a person's environment depend to some extent on that person's recognition of them; and it has become a commonplace of sociopolitical research that some people see themselves as members of social categories to which they would not be assigned by 'objective' criteria—the well-known case of the manual workers who call themselves middle class instead of working class. Thus it is always to some degree problematical and a matter for investigation which groups are recognised by a person as his relevant others, but, once identified, these expectations flowing in from (perceived) relevant others may provide an explanation for certain actions.

It would be beside the point to evaluate at this stage the points of criticism directed by Urry at Runciman's *Relative Deprivation and Social Justice*, or Runciman's points in reply, although the exchange, arising partly from misunderstandings, may serve as a reminder about this related area of work. There are, however, one or two points in it which bear upon the relations between disciplines.

Before moving into criticism of Runciman, Urry sets up some definitions and appraises the field of reference group theory.

A comparative reference group may be defined as any social object with which an actor compares himself and which consequently acts as a basis of self-evaluation. This notion is based upon the anthropological necessity that where there is a need for self-evaluation and where there are no direct physical standards by which an actor can judge himself he will rely on certain social bases of judgement. It is somewhat surprising that although this has been a clear theme in moral philosophy, contemporary sociology has relatively neglected such considerations.[45]

Again the curious fact emerges that although sociological theory has helped to identify a particular problem it has then been neglected in that discipline although pursued as a clear theme in another: further confirmation that what is needed is an approach which is not inhibited by the boundaries of the disciplines.

Whilst accepting the historical and sociological interest of Runciman's work Urry criticises it as not providing a 'systematic sociological explanation', presumably because it does not proceed from a theoretically generated hypothesis, out to a field study testing the deductive consequences and back to theory with a confirmation, disconfirmation or modification of the hypothesis. This rather strongly professional line of criticism strikes Runciman, apparently, as unfair or irrelevant and provokes the reply

> I do not understand what Urry means when he says that my account is not 'sociological'. But I do not see that it matters. The term when used in this sort of context by people who describe themselves as sociologists usually means no more than that they approve of the sorts of research which they do themselves and disapprove of the sorts which they don't.[46]

And yet Runciman, too, in reply to a later point is capable of specifying the proper context of certain kinds of disputation.

> Urry's concluding remarks about the final section of the book are too fleeting for there to be much purpose in my offering a reply to them. Besides, the proper place for such a controversy would be a journal of philosophy rather than social science.[47]

All this provides another example of the use of professional or disciplinary boundary considerations as elements in what might more productively be rational debates about particular subject matter.

The most direct interaction of the whole symposium produces the most violent clash between disciplines. In the transcript of a discussion between representatives of literature, sociology and philosophy the philosopher's opening remark immediately places the sociologist in a defensive posture.

> I have heard it said that a man is the sum of the roles which he plays. Could you please explain this implausible doctrine to us?[48]

This attack on the sociologist is not exactly unrehearsed, as can be seen by a footnote indicating that an earlier discussion took place before an interdisciplinary faculty group. It may be assumed that having become aware of the limited position held by the sociologist the philosopher wishes to get quickly to the main issues. The sociologist's position certainly is vulnerable: he defines role in terms of normative expectations, sees sociology as a generalising science necessarily concerned with prediction and would like role theory to be a set of confirmed and co-ordinated laws. Pressed by the writer-critic about the distinction between social self and private self he sets up a disciplinary boundary.

The sociologist may also be inspired by humanistic individualism but, in his professional role, he tries to describe and explain regularities in human behaviour.[49]

The writer-critic expresses a more inclusive interest

. . . drama and literature have quite elaborate notions of role as an aspect of fictional creation. But normally these involve an understanding of the complexity of the relationship between patterned expectations, social constraints, and the psychological needs and creative powers of individuals.[50]

The philosopher criticises the sociologist for his positivistic approach, and for his ambiguity on the matter of disciplinary boundaries and the scope of role explanations. The sociologist says at one point

. . . when we come to allocating *human* action between psychology, sociology and social psychology (an uncertain hybrid, usually examining the influence of small groups or small aggregates upon the individual or vice-versa), we must recognise that although they have focussed for historical reasons upon different aspects of human action, the boundaries between them are artificial and increasingly seen as such.[51]

The philosopher is not satisfied with this because

If boundaries are open, each science is free to preserve its pet hypotheses against all refutation. Thus the sociologist can blame exceptions on psychological quirks of the 'individual personality'; the psychologist can appeal to interfering social facts.[52]

The philosopher's criticism is understandable in views of the contradictory stand taken by the sociologist who on the one hand uses disciplinary boundaries to limit his own claims and on the other sees the boundaries as artificial. Furthermore, what a strange view of social psychology it is that sees it, in spite of the 'artificiality' of the boundaries between its parent disciplines, as 'an uncertain hybrid' with such a limited range of interest.

The philosopher's warning must be taken seriously since it distinguishes between use and misuse of fluid boundaries between disciplines. Misuse consists of slipping across disciplinary boundaries in order to consign the difficulties or anomalies of one discipline to a place out of the way in another. *Use* of other disciplines consists of movement into another discipline in search of insights and or substantive results which will be allowed to modify the initial unidisciplinary conceptions regardless of any threats to disciplinary autonomy or to the security of professional identities.

The general picture which emerges from thematic analysis of the 'symposium' is this. That although some sociologists (Coulson) would be rid of the concept together with its many difficulties which so easily turn into mystifications, it is capable of being used to organise mainly descriptive material on the life cycle (Gordon). Furthermore, in the hands of a theorist of some quality (Popitz) it takes the form of a fairly rigorous and sensitive instrument for the investigation of social relationships and social formations. The addition of reference group research to role theory opens up the concept and makes room for less unitary conceptions of both roles and social contexts (Urry and Runciman). The complex relation between human creative powers and social constraints is an integral part of the problem of role (Bradbury). At almost every point the interdisciplinary challenges of role theory have been evaded, distorted or simply refused, mainly because of the professional roles and identities taken up by the various specialists who encounter some aspect of role in the course of their work.

At the very end of the symposium the philosopher puts forward his own view of role theory, saying that he sees it as 'a highly theoretical account of the structure of social duties' akin to the economists' mathematical models of rational behaviour. Whether a mathematical model can yet be produced remains to be seen; however, the mention of social duties may serve to introduce the stream of work in social philosophy which has considered rights and duties in relation to various, usually implicit, models of society. It is a distinctively British contribution to social theory not usually drawn upon in American sociology. What then does the philosopher have to offer towards a more comprehensive and integrated role theory?

5.7 SOME PHILOSOPHICAL APPROACHES AND THEIR IMPLICATIONS

For several reasons philosophers have developed a body of role theory partly independently of the social and behavioural sciences and partly as a direct contribution to this field. The English Idealist philosophers approached role through attempts to clarify ethical problems involving rights and duties, many of which are linked to roles in a social structure. T. H. Green, B. Bosanquet and F. H. Bradley were English liberal philosophers who during the last quarter of the nineteenth and the first quarter of this century used a Platonic and Hegelian foundation for a philosophy which was intended to surpass the Utilitarianism of their immediate predecessors and provide a rational basis for liberal democracy. They were rooted in the individualism of the Utilitarians but sought to show how the individual might find his freedom, self-realisation and truest self through morally significant social relationships. The essay by F. H. Bradley, 'My Station and its Duties',[53] is the most representative document of a school which paid so much attention to the elevating effects of doing one's duty as enjoined by the moral opinions, laws and institutions of their day, that they underplayed the essential conflicts and cross-pressures of class and sectional interests.

The oversocialised morality of their position is understandable as a reaction to the overindividualised morality of the Utilitarians, and the polarity they define has persisted to this day as the issue of personal morality versus social morality, with role morality as an attempt to bridge the gap.

Dorothy Emmet, a contemporary philosopher, has worked on these issues, persistently relating them to sociology. Against the 'alleged autonomy of ethics' she argues the importance of situation and social context as factors in moral decisions. At the same time she criticises neglect of the moral qualities of social acts by sociologists and concludes that

... just as the investigation of the alleged autonomy of sociology suggested that sociologists might do with help from moral philosophers in thinking about the character of moral judgements, so too the investigation of the alleged autonomy of ethics suggests that moralists might do with help from sociologists in enlarging their understanding of the 'situations' in which moral judgements are made.[54]

She also mentions that to her surprise 'ethical systems *per se* are hardly noticed' by anthropologists. The separate disciplines have, it seems, managed a high degree of specialisation. Sociologists deal with the ordinary social act, moral philosophers with the moral social act, psychologists with the development of moral awareness in the child, and anthropologists with the normal act of foreign cultures.

Apart from the interest of her personal contribution to bridging the interdisciplinary void between sociology and philosophy she provides a careful account of role morality, using professions and their ethical codes as examples. It is shown that the functionalist concept of the person as the incumbent of roles is a useful abstraction but one which never provides an exhaustive account of what a man may do. Superficial criticisms asserting the inherent conservatism of functional models are rejected simply by insisting on careful distinctions between the abstraction 'role' and actual human behaviour in situations. She does not excuse the *misuse* of functionalist concepts such as the much criticised homeostatic terms 'equilibrium' and 'consensus' which may be evoked in an unscientific way to imply approval and support for existing social structure.

By applying a degree of philosophical rigour to the concept of role she is able to distinguish role-playing in its relatively unreflective form (the doctor applying practical skills) from role-conflicts, which are seldom absent in any social system (the doctor balancing research against welfare of the patient). The fact that the doctor has the help of an ethical code to guide his decisions does not detract from the essentially moral qualities of the decision. Finally, there will be new situations in which neither role-prescriptions nor ethical codes will be sufficient to decide a course of action when the doctor, or whoever it is, will be thrown back on a personal morality.

The philosopher Bernard Mayo[55] does not like the argument that role-conflicts call upon personal resources for their resolution. He believes that role-prescriptions usually provide guidance on priorities to be observed when conflicts occur. There is an interesting resemblance between these views on conflict and its resolution and the discussions of role-distance, suggesting that the core problem of the relation between self and society reappears in various forms. In Goffman's descriptions, taking distance from a role appears to be a useful personal strategy for avoiding engulfment in the role, although Goffman then holds that distance is gained by setting one role against another.[56] Coser adds to this the idea that role-distance has the important social function of preparing role occupants for their frequent and ultimately inevitable transition out of particular sets of roles.[57] Mayo's version of this is to suggest that moral behaviour—apparently the most private and autonomous behaviour in the last resort—is also behaviour *in a role*.

As I see it, the main differences between Emmet and Mayo are matters of definition. This is not to say that such matters are unimportant since one distinctive quality of philosophical work is its capability for moving definitions around with such scrupulous clarity that alternative and sometimes surprising assertions are made available for further scrutiny: this is the spirit of Mayo's contribution which will now be used to explore another aspect of the relation between philosophy and sociology in their treatment of the concept of role.

Mayo discusses 'role morality' in relation to two other traditionally identifiable positions in the philosophy of ethics: the first is exemplified by Kant's *Grundlegung* which is concerned with qualities of *right acts*; the second addresses itself to the problem of 'being the *right sort of person*', as set forth in Aristotle's *Nicomachean Ethics*. The question for Mayo is not whether there is a third position, role-morality, but how it relates to these other two positions, in particular whether it is distinct from them or whether ,as he is inclined to think, it simply provides a useful new approach to the other two.

Directly against Emmet he says

> . . . a person can perfectly well be regarded as an assemblage of roles, without missing any nuances we may want to catch.[58]

But Mayo is only prepared to assert this in the light of an extremely attenuated concept of role—one he admits would probably be useless to a sociologist—which regards virtually any conduct distinguishable from spontaneous behaviour as role behaviour. The only limitation apart from spontaneity is Mayo's acknowledgement that a person may deliberately choose to act in no role at all

> . . . though to choose to act in no role at all is to choose not to act morally.[59]

As I understand it, Mayo is making a distinction between behaviour which takes serious account of the expectations of others, thereby confirming interlocking expectations between self and others (roles in the attenuated sense), and action which notices the expectations of others but is moved by a decision to ignore all these expectations. Refusing a role is then equivalent to refusing all the expectations of others and understandably on these definitions is a non-moral act.

However, Mayo has simply shifted the ground of discussion for the self/society relationship and must logically turn to the social structural aspect of it: how well integrated and legitimate are the expectations which form such a key element in the moral act—is there a consensus? His answer is that sociologists should not confuse the actual existence of a consensus with the entry into an individual's thinking of the idea of a consensus, the latter and not the former being a necessary condition for moral behaviour. It is clear that the moral philosopher requires a distinction between actual consensus and the individual's idea of a consensus because if progress in ethics had to wait upon, and be limited to, consensual situations it would be hard to find subject matter. But again there are costs as well as benefits in the process of detaching manageable subject matter from the field of the human sciences: in this case philosophy goes in search of the inwardness of individual behaviour based on a consensual model of society, which nevertheless may be only a mistaken idea in an individual's thinking. Sociology is left with massive problems such as the relation between individuals' ideas of consensus and actual consensus, not to mention the appeal to consensus as special pleading by the powerful, the manipulation of consensus by control of communications, for which the philosopher's concept of role will be of little use.

When on the way to his conclusions, the philosopher appears to be offering a refined analysis of the balance between 'requirements' and 'expectations' as the norms controlling role behaviour—a point of some interest to sociologists—he is actually trying to show that 'expectations' will fit his conception of moral behaviour better than the connotation of external force that is carried by the term 'requirements'. And yet the sociologist is faced on every side by the fact that roles commonly carry differential power and are not even open to all in fair competition; that one person or group can 'require' another to behave in a certain way is commonplace.

The naive question as to whether the parent discipline of philosophy has continued to work productively on the person/society relationship even though psychology and sociology have split off from it to form separate disciplines can now be answered. Philosophy itself has undergone a division of labour such that person/society questions are taken care of in a particular speciality. And in spite of the widespread view that philosophy deals with more abstract and general questions which transcend disciplinary boundaries, philosophers can be found defining concepts typically used in other contexts (role, in sociology for example) in such a way that they will be useless in the other context. This process is quite antagonistic to any integrative purpose or to the development of interdisciplinary areas, although it could be argued that a necessary preliminary to integration is precise and particular definition within the separate disciplines. The implications for an interdisciplinary project are that solutions will not be found ready-made in philosophy but there will be relevant work which may, with critical assessment, provide useful insights for a broader design.

Assuming that full respect is given to Mayo's right to fashion a concept which suits his own intellectual purposes we are still left with a problem of assessment, because having moved deliberately away from sociological usefulness he attempts to use this new conception to attack Emmet, a philosopher who seeks to provide a sociologically sound concept of role whilst bearing in mind the ethical implications of the self/society relationship. He rejects Emmet's concept of personal morality in the following way.

> One thing that might be called a personal morality is the morality of the saint, hero, missionary or prophet; someone who conceives himself to have a mission which is for him alone. But this cannot possibly be the sense of 'personal' which is contrasted with 'role-determined', for his actions certainly are decided by (what he conceives to be) his role, even if he is the only one who occupies it, and even if few or none recognize that he does. [60]

A further distinction may clarify this apparent disappearance of the *sociological* concept of role. On Mayo's definition for a person to act in a role it is sufficient that the person projects a possible relationship with others based on their expectations, although he may be alone in seeing it as a desirable relationship. But for Emmet, as I understand her, it is not just a question of whether there is a conceivable relationship available in the role presently or previously occupied. As a result of social change or cultural transposition a person might face situations of the following kind:

(1) conflicting requirements for which there are no precedents which might help to determine priorities;
(2) conflicting expectations for which there are no precedents which might help to determine priorities;
(3) novel situations to which existing and previous role requirements or expectations do not apply.

Perhaps Mayo would reply that the social experience of occupying roles will always provide *general* guidance on what to do. On Mayo's wide definition of role behaviour this is only to say that social experience is relevant to decisions on social action—not a very surprising conclusion; and the sociologist would still need to ask the question whether the occupation of socially (not personally) defined roles always provides guidance on what to do in the above-mentioned situations. Using sociological definitions the answer would obviously be in the negative and this would provide an explanation of the risks involved in projecting a new possible role which, if it does not come to be recognised by some others, puts the person outside society with the possibility of serious sanctions.

Emmet's assertion than in intimate personal relationships there is not always guidance available from existing or previous role-prescriptions to ensure 'right action' would again capture the sense of risk involved in social behaviour, a risk which necessarily calls on personal resources, 'personal morality', there being no social resources in the form of precedents available to assure the outcome.

To the extent that Dorothy Emmet's work has been used by sociologists, and I believe this tends to be the case in Britian but less so in America, their role-concepts have been free of the kind of determinism or oversocialisation which has drawn criticism. However, it is not very complimentary to the theoretical strengths of British sociology to discover that it has hardly touched role theory, and that most of the theoretical work drawn upon by British sociologists has been developed in anthropology. This is a further comment on the strangely separate condition of these human science disciplines that in order to discover a reasonably sophisticated basis for a British contribution to role theory it is necessary to look to a philosopher who has drawn most of her material from anthropology. In fact by 1970, we find this philosopher jointly editing with Alasdair MacIntyre, *another philosopher*, one of the rare *theoretical* works of British sociology. They provide both a comment on the relations between disciplines and an argument for abolishing certain boundaries.

> We do not believe that it is possible any longer to treat social anthropology and sociology as separate disciplines. Accidents of academic history for too long kept apart the study of relatively primitive societies from the study of industrial societies and both from the study of all those societies betwixt and between whose life comprises a great part of human history . . .
>
> The boundaries between such disciplines are not in fact based on what has been already discovered, as they are in the natural sciences, but there is a certain arbitrariness about them, a certain ambiguity. It is partly for this reason that philosophical questions arise for the social scientist himself and not merely for the philosophical observer of the social sciences.[61]

Of course it is not possible to move on from this to suggest that sociology and psychology should be treated as one discipline: it depends on the nature of the boundary problem, and clearly the disciplines of sociology and social anthropology have so far dealt with the *same subject matter* in arbitrarily, accidentally separate contexts. The boundary between sociology and psychology is clearer in that the structures and processes of *societies* are distinguishable from the behaviour and experience of *the person*. But there is some subject matter in common—role-playing, for example—and it is apparent from the earlier discussion of the relations between psychological and sociological theories that role is touched upon by both disciplines without there emerging a specifically interdisciplinary field of work.

Emmet and MacIntyre suggest that in the natural sciences disciplinary boundaries are based on what has been discovered and the implication is that they are by reason of this not arbitrary or ambiguous. Is the boundary between sociology and psychology based on what has been discovered?

It is a difficult question to answer because it is partly historical and partly theoretical. As far as the modern *sciences* of psychology and sociology go they both emerged in the nineteenth century in a period of enthusiasm for the success of positivist natural sciences. Initially their great battles for a distinctive subject matter were with philosophy although the first major work which attempted to establish the term and discipline of sociology, that of August Comte (1830–42), was curious mixture of metaphysical philosophy (the law of three stages) and psychological speculation about the structure of the human mind. Sociology has never lacked theorists who base their explanations of social structural phenomena on assumptions about the biological, physiological or psychological attributes of the person. From Comte's phrenology to Spencer's evolutionary biology to Levi-Strauss' assertions about the binary structure of the human brain, there has been a succession of models of the person built into sociological theories. However, these models of the person, as the examples given might suggest, have not been particularly satisfactory. In a sense the concept of a person, for sociologists, is not as important as the concept of social structure, with the result that the person often seems to have been 'fitted in' after priority has been given to conceptualising social structure. It is this tendency which forms the subject of Dennis Wrong's paper on the 'oversocialised' model of the person.[62] It seems as though an 'image of man' is to be found lurking around the margins of sociological theory—sometimes a credible being, but frequently not so, and providing therefore a point of criticism against the social theory.

For different reasons the person has been pushed to the margins of psychology—a surprising fact since psychology would seem to have the person as its focal point. However, the concept of the person has tended to be neglected in psychology until the relatively recent appearance of person theories—and this work has been characterised as that of a 'dissident' group.[63] Flugel's description of the formative years for the science of psychology provides part of an explanation.

Kant's equation of science with measurement, and his appeal to experience as the only foundation for the formulation of psychological laws, prepared the way both for the separation of philosophy and psychology, and the quantitative developments of the latter that have become so prominent a feature of the last hundred years.

. . . His refusal to consider the will in the light of the category of cause, and his ethical doctrine of the Categorical Imperative, were not calculated to encourage a psychological approach to the phenomena of desire, will, conscience or moral obligation.[64]

In this respect Flugel sees Kant's influence as 'negative'. But there is another possible interpretation.

In order to establish a positivistic and quantitative science of psychology it was essential to find wherever possible—in philosophy, medicine, optics, education—foundations for the new discipline. At the same time it was essential to reject conceptions which might undermine this new approach. Psychology therefore picked up what it needed—experimental methods from the natural sciences, associationism from the *empiricist* philosophers, etc.—and dropped precisely those areas and approaches which dealt with the desiring, willing, morally active person. Not only might the latter undermine scientific psychology, they would also link it so firmly with philosophy that it would not be possible to claim the status of a separate discipline. And so 'person' concepts were submerged for a hundred years and on their reappearance are still treated as 'dissident' and often criticised precisely because they are 'metaphysical' (philosophical).

If this intepretation is correct then it should be possible to find evidence for the division of labour in intellectual work which gradually produces psychology as a discipline; and evidence for the identity crises forced upon the people involved as they reject one possibility and accept another, perhaps torn between almost equally attractive prospects of a mutually exclusive kind. Already it has been shown that the emergence of new personality theories is accompanied by ambivalence towards predecessors as the new theorists filter out what they need from the past and construct around it a new position. In the case of personality theorists it was apparent that a new theory must at least be congruent with the theorist's concept of himself. For theories about phenomena with less direct self-reference, and therefore self-interest, the processes are probably less psychodynamic. But they are still socially dynamic in that the creation of a new distinct intellectual position will probably bring social rewards—something from among that complex of prestige, money and power which have been shown to motivate scientific work.[65] For a new discipline to emerge it is necessary for strong expectation to be created that particular methods pursued in a certain theoretical direction will lead to new knowledge, and it requires considerable incentive to encourage scientists to let go of one such pattern of working assumptions and invest interest in another. What is the evidence for this kind of shift of interest from one set of working assumptions—the basic and partly tacit norms of a scientific group—to another?

Assumptions about what will be discovered are integral to the theoretical activity of disciplines and may provide just that concentration of effort needed to produce useful results: these 'paradigms' or 'disciplinary matrices'[66] as Kuhn calls them are not confined to a theoretical level and may involve well-established practical techniques for handling familiar subject matter. Thus there may be limitations on discovery imposed by the particular repertoire of techniques available to the investigator. This distinction is relevant in that the subject matter of psychology was defined at the origin of the discipline by the application of experimental methods to what had previously been the broader field of philosophy. Ben-David and Collins[67] have described the special circumstances in which the discipline of psychology, and with it the *role* of psychologist as a *natural scientist*, were established. Ben-David and Collins note that

> Originally the subject matter of psychology was divided between speculative philosophy and physiology. Towards 1880, specialized psychological publications came to constitute the bulk of the work in the field, and philosophical psychology was widely disparaged by the 'new psychologists'. The acceleration of production was associated with a growing consciousness among these men of the existence of a distinct field of psychology, and of the need for distinguishing their work from traditional fields.[68]
>
> ... social factors played an important role, independently of intellectual content.[69]
>
> Wundt is undoubtedly the central figure. He had the largest following and he articulated the ideology of the 'philosophical revolution'.[70]

It might be argued that the word ideology here carries no deep meaning but simply refers to the explicit aims and objects of a group. It is true that the word has tended to shift towards this more superficial use recently; however, when a 'revolution' is claimed and the interests (prestige and resolution of role-conflict) of a group are at stake, it seems justifiable to retain some of the original meaning and see the avowedly independent criterion of scientific method being used as a cover for the interests of the group. This would explain the sensitivity of psychologists to scientific status, their ritual citation of scientific guarantors and their late, unwilling and still not fully accepted admittance of the person to the margins of their discipline. Reflexivity has turned its full circle with this role-dependent explanation of why psychologists have avoided or mishandled the concept of role.

The crucial factors were that in Germany physiology had just gone through a period of rapid expansion reaching a limit of about one chair per university by 1870, mostly filled by relatively young men. The prospects of advancement were therefore poor for physiologists. In philosophy, prospects were better since there were twice as many chairs, filled by older men. But philosophy had lost prestige in a long battle against the emergent and highly productive natural sciences and consequently a move into these posts entailed role-conflict for natural scientists anxious not to lose prestige. They resolved this conflict by emphasising empirical, experimental methods which, they claimed, superseded traditional approaches to philosophical problems, making much of philosophy redundant. In a sense their scientific methods guaranteed the superiority of their approach and at the same time enabled them to carry over prestige from their previous field.

Here then at the origins of the discipline is an explanation of the great concern shown by the majority of psychologists for the standing of their subject as a natural science. Furthermore, it is a peculiarly independent account since Ben-David and Collins are seeking primarily to demonstrate the creation of professional scientific roles as part of the sociology of science: to them it is an interesting example of 'role-hybridisation'. It is fascinating to see introduced, from this independent standpoint and from a man who rejects any strong thesis on the social determination of knowledge,[71] the concept of ideology.

Working from a different starting point in medicine and through the history of biological sciences, Robert Young has thrown a beautifully clear light on the emergence of psychology as a science. He attempts to show

... the price which psychology paid by failing to transcend Cartesian dualism, the sensationalist and epistemological biases of associationism and the categories of function of philosophical psychology.[72]

He believes that

. . . historical, philosophical and conceptual studies in the inter-pretation of man's place in nature have a more important part to play than has hitherto been assumed.[72]

This is a fascinating conclusion which if I may turn it to my own purpose, confirms that the emergence of new theories (in this case a theory which founds a new discipline) is frequently characterised by ambivalence towards what has gone before because it forms a body of accepted knowledge which, so to speak, holds the field; further-more, as accepted knowledge it has probably entered into the educa-tion of the rising scholar and is therefore difficult to ignore. Again, because a new discipline must make room for itself it will tend to produce polarisations as it studiously avoids or transposes existing ideas and techniques in order to throw off the old identity, at the same time using too exclusively the new ideas and techniques in which a new identity is being invested.

For Young the fundamental polarisation is the Cartesian dualism of mind/body, which persisted throughout the nineteenth century, and may still be with us, causing the kind of unproductive split between specialities that has already been shown to have serious consequences for certain forms of knowledge.

This book has been concerned with two separable issues, and one of the main conclusions implicit in my argument is that the issues should not be separated.

Gall argued that the faculties used by his predecessors were irrelevant to the lives of organisms, but he failed to analyse his own functions into more basic units. Ferrier adopted a set of useful units and provided an experimental basis for their applica-tion to all parts of the brain, but he failed to transcend the cate-gories of function which his intellectual mentors had perpetuated. The obvious need for the future was a combination of analysis with a biologically significant set of functions. This desideratum has yet to appear.[73]

What can be seen here is psychology being tested for its capacity to relate to two bordering disciplines which imply some substantial interdisciplinary problems: physiology as the physical basis of human function, and evolutionary biology as the contextual and historically developmental aspect of the human being. In both cases the challenge has been refused. The method of experiment, on the model of the physical sciences (psychology's fetish object), has so far pushed aside what it cannot readily handle: the philosophical depth and the biological context of the human person. I have also tried to show that for similar reasons psychology has refused a relationship with sociology and lost the benefit of integrated study of the person in social context.

Observing processes like this forces one to consider whether we should ever be content to attribute changes in the relation between disciplines to 'accidents of academic history'—the reason given by Emmet and MacIntyre for the unjustified separation of sociology and anthropology. There are at least some regular patterns here which begin to provide the basis of an explanation for the relationships between disciplines in the human sciences.

All these, surely, are the personal and social phenomena Kuhn made room for in his work on scientific revolutions. He declined to explore them, preferring to concentrate on paradigm formation as a rather more integral feature of scientific investigation. It is worth noting that Kuhn did not entirely succeed in abstracting paradigm formation from the social structure which supports a paradigm: the postcript to his 1962 publication, added to the 1970 edition, adopts an alternative formulation of paradigm; it becomes 'disiplinary matrix' of which the community of scientists form an important part. Whether it is seen as the identity problem of the discipline of psychology or as a fine differentiation in the division of labour in intellectual work, its consequences for the pursuit of knowledge have been considerable.

What an ambiguous relation between sociology and psychology then appears out of this common area of person concepts. Sociologists have used person concepts but as a means to social structural theories. Psychologists have kept the person out of their discipline or, more recently, have allowed him into the dissident margin of it, where the first crude theories of the person are being formulated. In these circumstances it is perfectly understandable why psychologists and sociologists each deal in stereotypes of the other's concept of role.

Unlike the natural sciences where, as Emmet and MacIntyre say, the disciplinary boundaries are based on what has been discovered, the boundary between disciplines in role theory still rests on *what it is assumed will be discovered* from the standpoint of the separate and in their own way 'biased' disciplines.

The interdisciplinary void between sociology and psychology may now be understood as an area in which there are few incentives to encourage work by either group of specialists. For sociologists there is the danger of being called reductionist, of failing to explain a social fact by reference to other social facts; and for psychologists there is the danger of drawing in subject matter which is difficult to handle by experimental methods and which carries with it the mysteries best left to philosophers.

> ... most psychologists sensibly leave to philosophers the job of investigating the metaphysical self and when they themselves deal with matters relating to the 'self' they are generally referring to the attitudes we hold about ourselves and the traits we are supposed to ascribe to ourselves, in short our 'self-image'.[74]

And the further arguments used to consolidate this split between the mysterious real self and the more accessible self image sound rather less than rigorous.

> ... truth to oneself can cover a multitude of sins. And a man who married a woman because she allowed him to 'be himself' may have chosen a woman with low or no standards of conduct. Rather than portioning the bulk of one's energies to the job of getting to 'know thyself', it would be wiser to direct our attention to a consideration of how we intend to lead our lives. Unbounded preoccupation with oneself looks like a most unsatisfactory strategy for living.[75]

This moralistic exhortation depends on polarising 'unbounded preoccupation with oneself' and 'how we intend to lead our lives', yet another exaggerated opposition, and presumably it does duty as a boundary marker which keeps out subject matter of an unmanageable kind, separating sensible psychologists (the normal role) from the rest.

What I have attempted to show so far in this discussion of role theory and the relation between disciplines is that sociologists and psychologists still deal in stereotypes and misunderstandings of each other's concepts and conclusions. This may not be a problem which does serious damage to the general body of knowledge produced by the separate disciplines but it does have great significance in relation to interdisciplinary phenomena such as personal behaviour and experience in social roles. When a psychologist works on role-phenomena it is difficult to excise the psychological from its context in the social; conversely, the sociologist in devising sociological concepts is continuously generating models of the person by implication. Because both disciplines are beset by the anxieties of maintaining both their productivity and the autonomy which gives them control over rewards for work in their field, they use irrational and defensive strategies against competitors. One such strategy consists of exaggerating differences and distinctions in a way which polarises concepts—for example indeterminate self versus unified society—with consequent distortion of knowledge in both disciplines.

It was noticed that both psychology and sociology found it necessary to expel philosophy: may it be that philosophy took away the problems of role, self and personality and dealt with them adequately? A look at some philosophical contributions will provide the answer.

5.8 A PHILOSOPHICAL MYSTIFICATION

While sociology and psychology, the scientifically precocious children of philosophy, set off in search of their tasks and separate identities, philosophers continued to explore concepts of the person and some of the inevitably role-determined concomitants. There was a period in which British philosophy underwent its own revolution and turned away from metaphysical concepts towards logical positivism and linguistic analysis, but even so there have always been 'dissident' voices calling attention to personal experience and phenomena. Nor was it possible to exclude completely personality and role from linguistic analysis since a significant portion of language deals with these phenomena.

Thus it is possible to find highly relevant work in philosophy even among philosophers who, unlike Emmet and MacIntyre, have not sought to relate it specifically to sociology. Such a case is the work of John Macmurray.

Macmurray criticises the direction taken by modern philosophy.

We began by noting that modern philosophy had been driven by its own logic in the direction of atheism. We may end by recognizing that the nearer it draws to this conclusion the nearer it comes to its own extinction. The opposition of science and religion has compelled philosophy to distinguish itself more and more from religion and to model itself on science. Once philosophy was the handmaid of theology; now it knocks at the door of science and asks for employment as a general cleaner-up. But science has really no need of such assistance. It prefers to tidy up itself.[76]

And so Macmurray would rehabilitate philosophy as a non-dogmatic Natural Theology.

It is interesting to see him describing a process of differentiation of disciplines similar to the one already noted in relation to psychology and sociology, with an added dimension in that, as psychology and sociology head off from philosophy towards science, philosophy splits off from theology and moves *in the same direction* in search of a distinctive and non-trivial subject matter. But unwanted as they are by scientists, philosophers must either settle for the trivial (which is what they have been accused of doing by Marcuse and Gellner[77]) or take up the subject matter of one or other science and attempt to make a distinctive contribution within it. Now it follows from the original affinity of philosophy and theology that whilst philosophers will be capable of contributing their general skills in conceptual and linguistic analysis to the methodological areas of the natural sciences, their ability to take up the subject matter of sciences will depend partly on the closeness of this subject matter to the philosophers' original concerns with theology. Thus in spite of psychology and sociology's neglect of 'theological' matters in an attempt to be scientific in the positivist manner, philosophers will find these *social and behavioural* sciences attractive as subject areas. However, the entry of philosophers to these areas will be a tense affair since the philosophers will be likely to pull these sciences back from the safety and respectability of their status as natural sciences. This, I think, is a good picture of the condition of the social and behavioural sciences: a positivistic style, although no longer the crude positivism of the founding fathers, at war with dissidents and intruders who attack the general orthodoxy in the name of greater humanism, personalism, commitment to evaluation and action in human affairs, mysticism, religiosity, etc.

The possibility that philosophers might enter the social and behavioural sciences and attempt to define a distinctively *human science* is not seriously entertained by Macmurray. His religious standpoint leads him to define a boundary which separates 'the personal' from the impersonal. The personal culminates in God, the great personal Other. Religion is the mode of reflection which subsumes art and science as necessarily impersonal explorations of ends and means, respectively.

> The limitation of attention which constitutes science is necessary to the performance of its function in the economy of personal life. It deals only with questions about matter of fact.[78]

This description simply overlooks the human sciences and polarises religion and science unnecessarily. It also creates the familiar problem of ambivalence towards sources for those human scientists who find Macmurray's description of 'the personal' attractive and who wish to use it to differentiate their own personalistic approach from that of their more orthodox (positivistic) colleagues. They need his beautifully clear analysis of what distinguishes the personal from the physical and the organic; his integrated scheme of action, intention, knowledge and personal relationships which refuses to reduce this defining characteristic of human life to less than human forms of explanation. But they may not wish to equate the personal with religion in Macmurray's way.

There is another interesting example of the pull back from positivism which makes over the phenomenon into a religious entity. Pfuetze attempted to go beyond G. H. Mead's behaviouristic account of the social creation of self and was criticised by Duncan in the following terms.

> It is by far the best commentary on Mead. Pfuetze argues that the corrective to Mead's 'social positivism' is religion while I argue here that it is art. This difference does not in any way affect the cogency and usefulness of Professor Pfuetze's criticism.[79]

Macmurray, whose account of the social creation of self is congruent with Mead's, is now seen to share a common theme with Pfuetze and Duncan—the rescuing of human phenomena from positivism.

Whether it is in the name of art or religion that a theorist reasserts the personal self against varieties of positivism is not of vital importance. What matters is the quality of analysis and description prompted by whatever approach is adopted. With this in mind Macmurray's philosophy may now be evaluated for its contribution to role theory and to the human sciences.

It may seem unjust to look for a contribution to role theory when Macmurray deliberately focuses on self rather than role. For him role is a negative aspect of self, and identification with one's role is possible but not a central phenomenon. The centre of Macmurray's work is selves in personal relation; in community and in communion; and this is the positive form of human relationship which, in terms of his bipolar, dialectical scheme, subordinates its negative. He begins his account of the negative by describing one category of impersonal relationships as 'pragmatic' on the Hobbesian model and it is in this category that the participants would be likely to see others as no more than their legally regulated roles.

> . . . so far as the normal mode of apperception in an actual society is pragmatic, so far as its members are negatively motived in their relations and aggressive or 'practical' in their behaviour, the necessary unity of society can only be achieved by law backed by force.[80]

There is a second subdivision of the impersonal type of relationship: the idealistic or contemplative. These two negative types are subordinated by the single positive type of relationship: the personal. Now it follows from Macmurray's use of a bipolar scheme that he must treat the negative pole as substantially as the positive pole in order to be convincing about either. His failure to deal with role relationships and impersonal relationships (the negative) except as some kind of deviation from the personal (the positive) weakens his claim to have gone to the root of human relationships. He registers the fact that in most societies negative relationships prevail; that Hobbesism 'comes far closer to the normal idea of our social practice than we are prepared to admit';[81] and yet he still asserts that

> Any human society is a unity of persons. This means that its unity as a society is not merely matter of fact, but matter of intention.[82]

Furthermore

> Any human society is a moral entity. Its basis is the universal and necessary intention to maintain the personal relation which makes regards even historically developed social form as in fluid move-

the human individual a person and his life a common life. It is an instantiation of the 'I and You' as the unit of the personal. It is constituted and maintained by loyalty and keeping faith.[83]

In the actual Hobbesian world it is difficult to imagine where Macmurray would find societies where there is equality of basic rights, let alone common access to resources. His apparent description is really a *prescription* for the kind of life that would be beautifully integrated in communion and brotherhood but which barely exists except in friendship and family groups.

The more a society approximates to the family pattern, the more it realises itself as a community . . .[84]

What Macmurray has done is to take a certain kind of intimate social relationship and project the personal qualities found here on to a much larger social unit without giving full weight to the distinctive qualities which emerge with a predominance of impersonal, role-shaped, relationships. Although he discusses the State it is only to contrast Hobbesian pragmatism with Rousseau's idealism, both negative forms which are subordinated by the key positive category of 'community'.

Since we must proceed by contrasting these negative type forms with the positive, it may serve us well if we distinguish between society and community reserving the term community for such personal unities of persons as are based on a positive personal motivation. The members of a community are in communion with one another, and their association is a fellowship. And since such an association exhibits the form of the personal in its fully positive personal character, it will necessarily contain within it and be constituted by its own negative, which is society. Every community is then a society; but not every society is a community.[85]

This leap from recognition of the social creation of self to the assertion of 'community' as the human condition to which societies aspire simply leaves aside all those problems of the relation between the structures of personalities and the structures of societies which make up the human sciences. Of course he allows room for psychologists and sociologists to investigate the *matters of fact* in the relationships, but if they see their work as necessarily evaluative and active they are either trespassing on the area of philosophical analysis Macmurray proposes to call Natural Theology or, if their work is acceptable, they are, in his definitions, natural theologians. This bold claim may follow from his attempt to gather human phenomena into a bipolar scheme with one positive and two negative categories. The immense simplification of such oppositional, bipolar schemata is achieved at some cost to the complexity of human life. The development of such simplified forms of analysis needs to be studied in its own right for it is a recurring theme in the history of ideas. I am not saying that such analyses are *a priori* wrong; rather that they can be used to achieve explanations at such a high level of generality that they do not engage with the reality of social life, or explanations which depend on classifying phenomena according to a criterion which is no more than a preference or belief of the theorist. The psychological self-theorists discussed earlier have often used this form of explanation: Allport, propriate striving; Rogers, self-actualisation; Maslow, metamotivation and self-actualisation. They all contrast a particular kind of motivation (we might call it 'positive') with some other negative kinds which are subordinated in the model of man they most favour.

Whilst it could be shown that many of the philosophically naive self theorists were 'retreating into positive generality', this is not a fair description of Macmurray's work: he chooses more deliberately the philosophical path to God and for him it is a clear advance which takes him over and beyond what he sees as the limitations of the human sciences. However, there are other more subtle contradictions and points of interest in his account of the personal.

Macmurray criticises the main stream of British philosophy—logical positivism to linguistic analysis—and undertakes to go beyond existing conceptions of self. He would reinstate the self as agent by refusing the dualism of conceiving it either as a developing organic system of thought or as a developing organic system of action.

This new standpoint is not merely one alternative among others. It is a more inclusive standpoint. It necessarily includes the 'I think', but in a more fundamental form, as the 'I know'. For if I do something then I know that I do something.

. . . I am aware of the Other, and of myself as dependent upon and limited by the Other.

. . . there is no need to prove existence, since existence and the knowledge of it, are given from the start.[86]

If this is not British then it does seem to be European. Superficially at least it seems to recapitulate the strongly European theme which begins with the dialectical philosophy of Hegel, is grounded by Marx in action by socially related selves on the material and ideological world, and is further developed by the existentialists into a recognition that the Cartesian dualism must be surpassed. Is Macmurray aware of this European tradition? Yes, he is. Unlike the American psychologists who invented 'a kind of existentialism' based on ignorance of the European roots he does acknowledge these sources. But he rejects them in various ways.

The dialectical form of explanation is rejected because although it allows for representation of the two aspects of self—subject and agent—as two successive phases in a process of development, it does not allow them to be subject and agent at one and the same time. Macmurray then moves on to Marx.

> When Karl Marx set out to make the Hegelian social philosophy practical, declaring that philosophies hitherto have only explained the world, while the task is to change it, he could claim that he had merely inverted the dialectic. . . . He did this by substituting the Self as 'worker' for the self as 'thinker', without changing the organic unity-pattern. The result is a dialectic of the practical in place of a dialectic of the theoretical life.[87]

This either/or formulation so favoured by Macmurray and applied here to the relation between Hegel and Marx does no justice to the extent to which Marx supersedes Hegel in a more inclusive explanation which, far from excluding the theoretical aspects of life, actually attempts to show their dependence on the material or economic social formations. To say that Marx 'merely' inverted the dialectic is the give-away. In fact Marx himself had a use for positive–negative oppositions which synthesise in communist society and not as with Macmurray in communion with God.

> In its mystified form, dialectic became the fashion in Germany, because it seemed to transfigure and to glorify the existing state of things. In its rational form it is a scandal and abomination to bourgeoisdom and its doctrinaire professors, because it includes in its comprehension and affirmative recognition of the existing state of things, at the same time also, the recognition of the negation of that state, of its inevitable breaking up; because it

ment, and therefore takes into account its transient nature not less than its momentary existence; because it lets nothing impose on it, and, is in its essence critical and revolutionary.[88]

Macmurray's other reference to Marx is to remark that his criticism of religion 'is almost grotesquely unscientific and *a priori*'. If Marx had studied these complex phenomena

> then he would surely have asked himself whether it accounted for the religion of his own Jewish ancestors as it is expressed in the Old Testament literature. This would have been enough to disprove the hypothesis, or at least to require a drastic revision. For that religion at least is not idealistic in Marx's sense, but materialist. It shows no interest in any other world, but is entirely concerned with the right way to maintain a human community in this world. That some expressions of some form of religion are liable to his criticism I see every reason to believe, perhaps even it may hold of official Christianity in Western Europe in modern times. That would provide good ground for demanding religious reform. But to make it the basis of a theory of religion as such, even of a purely objective and scientific theory, is most unscientific. . . . Such atheism, indeed, strongly suggests the projection of a childish fantasy upon the universe.[89]

Macmurray has universalised Marx's analysis of *religion in particular contexts* and then refuted it by showing that it does not apply everywhere and at all times. Where he admits the relevance of Marx's criticism it is in precisely the context from which Marx derived his criticism, that is, Western Europe in modern times.

With the accusation that Marx projected a childish fantasy onto the universe Macmurray appears to have moved from Marx to Freud. This is so in that he gives an account of childhood which accepts some of Freud's basic ideas. However, he will not allow Freud's dismissal of religion as a projection of childish fantasies, saying that projection is a metaphor with complex meanings such that the adult who tries to realise in his life the form of positive personal relationships experienced in childhood is not indulging in fantasy, but 'seeking to realise his own nature as a person'. It seems that Macmurray wants to have it both ways: Marx's projection of childhood fantasies explains his atheism and discredits it; Freud's explanation of religion in these terms is not allowed to discredit religion because of a special meaning given to the word projection.

Macmurray suggests that the most likely reason for Freud's faulty account of religion is that his data came from abnormal human behaviour. With this commonplace attempt to limit the implications of Freud's work by tying it to the context of abnormal behaviour, Macmurray puts away from himself the radical European tradition which has addressed itself to exactly the same problems and come up with an atheistic critical conclusion which does not allow religion to dominate the human sciences.

It is another good example of the conflict involved in the production of knowledge of the human, and of the need for extremely careful examination of whatever claims to be that knowledge. Macmurray's work has been examined in some detail because it seems to me that he is the philosopher most likely to be called upon by 'humanistic' personality theorists to back up their position. Already he has been cited by some of them,[90] and here I think is the outline of another noteworthy process in the production of knowledge: social and behavioural scientists are usually anxious, for reasons which are clearly based on the historical development of their subjects, about their *scientific* status, and so the best defence against this is to *go in search of a philosophy* which can be used as a support for their position. I risk adding to this an impression, which could bear research, that these same scientists make more frequent use of the *ritual citation*, which is intended to be a guarantee of their bona fides, than do their colleagues in the natural and physical sciences. Often it is Popper who is used in this way, emphasising either the conjectural, imaginative side, or the analytic, deductive side of his thesis as suits their case, but seldom with full appreciation of the implications of a philosophy which denies the need for radically distinctive methods and principles in the human sciences.[91]

It has already been shown that certain self-theorists find themselves in the ambivalent situation of wanting something from a philosophy but needing to evade other implications of it, the result being that they pull apart its logical structure in order to extract some attractive feature. Or, as in the case of George Kelly, they take a superficial look around for a philosophy and then proceed to reinvent some aspect of philosophy which they have not clearly appreciated as existing behind the stereotype they have seen in a quick glance.

Macmurray has tied together so many of the elements which appear in the approach of humanistic self theorists that it is ready-made for them. All is encompassed—interpersonal creation and realisation of self, 'positive' motivation, mysticism, religiosity, religion, symbolic communication, communion and community, mutuality in personal relationships, self-revelation as a process of self-discovery—while the possibly burdensome parts of Marx, Freud and the existentialists are either ignored, rejected by contradictory arguments or dissolved in 'positive' interpretations of their significance.

One does not deny Macmurray the right to his interpretations and religious beliefs but it is essential to evaluate critically theories which do more to mystify than to clarify those social phenomena which occur at the interpenetration of self and society, where our theory is still in such a rudimentary state.

5.9 A PHILOSOPHICAL CLARIFICATION

If some philosophers construct complex theories which mystify as well as clarify, there are others who take up the subject matter of the human sciences and make a contribution which is precisely what it sets out to be. As an example I refer to the paper by Gerald Cohen (1966–7) on beliefs and roles. It is a model of the way in which linguistic analysis can be applied to large and significant theories— freedom, no less—whilst remaining clear and rigorous in its treatment of the phenomena. His thesis is that

> A man must take responsibility for the beliefs which he expresses; he cannot shift it onto some aspect of himself, like his role. Here is a freedom he cannot escape, because he cannot but escape from himself and his situation.
>
> In stating my thesis, I must distinguish what I consider logically impossible, what irrational and what insane. (1) To cite one's role (logically) cannot be to give a ground for a belief one holds, nor can it function as a ground in the thinking of a sane man. (2) A man therefore behaves irrationally when he cites his role to support what he thinks. (3) Only if a man is insane can his beliefs attach to his roles . . .[92]

He carries through his analysis beautifully, relating it to the European intellectual tradition of Hegel, Marx, Freud and Sartre, and then criticises Goffman for that aspect of his work which takes the self as nothing more than the sum of the roles it plays. He notes Goffman's wish to 'combat the touching tendency to keep part of the world safe from sociology', and coolly says

The present inquiry promotes that tendency.[93]

Cohen suggests that

An acceptance of the picture of the self which Goffman offers leads to two equal and opposite distortions in our attitudes to man and society. When the gap between the individual and the roles he plays is denied, a person may receive the callous treatment appropriate to a thing: he may be shifted from role to role without regard to the impact change of station has on him. If the other moment in the assimilation is stressed, if sets of roles are conceived as persons, the social *status quo* is immediately sanctified: when roles constitute selfhood, to change society is to mangle human beings.[94]

It will be obvious that here is another example of a philosopher taking up the subject matter of the social and behavioural sciences and attempting to pull the study out of the 'social positivism' into which it has fallen. It is a matter of serious conflict since nothing less than 'freedom' is at stake.

Cohen has also identified yet another oppositional method of treating the self/society interpenetration, this time at work in the implicit level of Goffman's theory: the polarisation of *totally social self* and *thing*. It is echoed in Macmurray's contrast between the personal and the impersonal in human relationships, and also in the Sartrean scheme as being-in-itself and being-for-the-other. The oppositions are not used in quite the same way by the various theorists, but it is sufficient for the moment to notice similarities of form in the competition and conflict between these different bodies of 'knowledge'. Mannheim's reference to competition as a significant process in the creation of knowledge begins to show some of its essential detail, and theories which assert that 'personal constructs' are bipolar (Kelly and his successors) perhaps take comfort from the regular occurrence of this form of explanation. On the other hand, when the oppositional form of explanation shows itself so frequently as the very cause of particular weaknesses in theories, it may be that bipolar schemes are thrown into more serious question. If this is so then let the 'serious question' be put. Does polarisation, or polarisation of certain kinds, indicate pathology rather than productiveness in description, evaluation and explanation of human social life?

5.10 POLARISATION AND SOCIAL ANALYSIS

To begin at the logical heart of the matter, can it be said that polarisation is integrally misleading independently of the contexts in
which polarised analyses are applied? I think the answer must be in
the negative because as soon as any distinction is recognised between
two kinds of experience, behaviour or social situation (the typical
phenomena of the human sciences) it sets up the possibility of an
axis or dimension between the distinguished elements. Any textbook
on measurement will then remind us that there are various ways of
scaling the dimension. There may be only two positions on the scale
corresponding to the primary distinction which brought it into being,
and yet this crude measurement may be quite adequate for some
purposes. It can be graduated into more, or a great number of
positions, the intervals being equal or unequal and there may or may
not be a true zero. Numbers attached to 'intensive' qualities, for
example 'intelligence', may not be additive; that is one hundred does
not translate into 'twice as intelligent as fifty'.[95]

However, there is a particular quality in polarisation not inevitably
found in ordinary dimensions which mark the distance between
distinct elements: the possibility of extending the dimension between
two known objects (say hard and soft) in opposite directions (mapping out hardness as a quality opposed to softness). The difficulty
that arises is that the polarised dimensions now shoot off towards
'absolute hardness' and 'absolute softness', adding the hazards of
meaninglessness to the normal problems of scaling. Absurdity is
usually avoided by saying that such distinctions are relative and may
be used for practical purposes without any need to explore distant
and possibly spurious implications. It must be noted, however, that
when more complex phenomena typical of the human sciences are
substituted in the above discussion for hardness and softness it
becomes a highly relative and complex kind of description; consider
for example conservatism–radicalism or power–powerlessness.
Nevertheless, the creation of possibly misleading and complex
dimensions is not in itself an explanation of how and why distortions
appear; it is only to notice their potentiality for a certain kind of
misuse. And if there is nothing integrally wrong in the use of these
oppositional schemes then it will be necessary to examine some
examples of use and misuse to see whether there are social and
psychological factors, producing patterns of misuse of what is a

relatively neutral technique of discrimination. In order to exclude the mass of trivial examples which are available it will probably be useful to consider theorists who have given polarisation an important place in their theories and methods; and what better example to begin with than Levi-Strauss, the anthropologist whose work could hardly be referred to without immediate recourse to oppositional schemata and whose influence is sometimes likened to that of a Marx, Freud or Einstein.

Suitable as it is, the example brings out a problem of the kind which is integral to this whole book: how can a British observer read its complexity without the selective distortion which has been shown to operate in the American social-self theorists' interpretation of Freud, or in the American personality theorists encounter with the existentialists? First it may be useful to sketch in the British intellectual scene and its point of view in order to get an approximate idea of the problem.

It calls for a very considerable effort of imagination, almost a willingness to temporarily suspend disbelief, for British, American and probably most non-French scholars who wish to understand and evaluate the massive, evocative, subtle and allusive work on myth that Levi-Strauss has given to the world. From a British standpoint, for example, it is almost inconceivable that there could be an intellectual climate where Hegel is regarded as a philosopher of distinction with a strong relevance for modern social theorists; where Marx is treated as an important scholar whose work still calls for exploration, interpretation and critical testing; where Freud is respected and debated vigorously at a high level of generality in relation to cultural questions; and where the phenomenological and existentialist tradition going back to Husserl is alive and present as a serious body of insight and scholarship. It is a caricature to say of the British scene that it is distinguished by the absence of all the above characteristics, and of course important and very recent changes are in progress; but speaking from my own experience of induction into the intellectual sphere, I know that I was given a view in which Hegel was seen as not currently relevant, although a few quite unusual people did know about him in depth. Marx came over as a person with extreme views on class and state, whose predictions had not come true. Freud was attended to within the psychology of child development and was there subjected to much ridicule, particularly in relation to dream symbolism. Husserl and phenomenology were never mentioned and the only references to existentialism came in through extramural events involving the drama and philosophy of Sartre.

The British (though often of foreign origin) gatekeepers responsible for raising barriers to the Continental tradition were such figures as Bertrand Russell, whose assertion that the whole Hegelian system rested on a logical mistake seemed quite devastating; so too did his remark on Hegel's concept of freedom

> This is a very superfine brand of freedom. It does not mean you will be able to keep out of a concentration camp.[96]

Karl Popper was taken to have dealt with Marx in a very similar fashion: his logical error was to have mistaken a trend, defined in terms of directionally consistent changes over time, for a law of history. As for 'dialectics' this was little more than a trick of verbal self-confirmation.[97] In psychology Hans Eysenck was separating sense from nonsense, using a Popperian philosophy of science to cut Freud down to size with an attractive kind of parody and ridicule. A central complaint, still heard, was that Freud's interpretation of strong denial as a confirmation by its very strength of what is being denied made it impossible to refute him.

Another philosopher of great influence was A. J. Ayer, and I remember reading his *Language, Truth and Logic* with a profound sense of liberation from the weight, danger, threat and anxiety of all the big questions which arise n the Continental tradition, most of them being rendered literally meaningless by the new form of analysis. But of course this retreat into 'objectivity' was nothing but evasion and delay—a superbly efficient defence mechanism betrayed as such by the amount of witty ridicule that went into the arguments, although welcome enough as relief to a so-called 'mature' student cast adrift on these seas of ignorance and mystery.

So now the caricature of the British scene may be said to carry the exaggerated truth of a caricature: it is not that theory was absent, rather was it present with a price-tag of personal credibility.

If the situation had changed substantially over recent years this sketch of the British intellectual scene would not be very helpful towards tacking the problem of understanding the Continental tradition. Changes there certainly have been if only in the greater availability of translated literature and commentaries. But an intellectual style dies no more quickly than a bodily style, of which the intellectual posture is one form of expression. Thus it is possible to see the same patterns of response, which at one time virtually excluded the Continental tradition, active here and now, filtering and interpreting it.[98] Analysis of some examples of this in relation to Levi-Strauss will make it possible to break out of the circle of confusion at the same time as moving toward a critical evaluation of polarisation in the work of Levi-Strauss.

I think it is true to say the Edmund Leach is the best-known critic of Levi-Strauss, 'critic' in this context being taken to include exposition and appreciation of the relevant work. Leach's admirable skill in condensing and presenting arguments together with his unassuming common-sense approach are indeed impressive in the British cultural context, celebrating as they do the qualities of modest, controlled, judicious, empirical appraisal. Yet what a very particular point of view Leach brings to the task. The tone of his introduction is one of gentle warning to the British reader that with Levi-Strauss' background in Hegelian Marxism, some slight influence from existentialism, a love for geology and a gift for music we must expect a curious outcome. And then the most insulating remark of all, embodying the British scientific style of evaluation constructed by Russell, Popper, Eysenck, Ayer and their likeminded colleagues.

> So we need to remember that Levi-Strauss' prime training was in philosophy and law; he consistently behaves as an advocate defending a cause rather than as a scientist searching for ultimate truth.[99]

What is remarkable about this passage is that it not only speaks the language of British empiricism, it exaggerates it to the point where scientific training is seen as conferring the ability for neutral, objective assessment which will lead towards ultimate truth. Not even Popper would embrace the notion of ultimate truth as a scientific prerogative and it seems that Leach's concept of scientific method has taken no account of what Kuhn would call the function of dogma in scientific research.[100] The contrast of philosophy and law with science is remarkable because it is the kind of false polarisation which loads an argument in advance, and mysterious as he may be this is certainly not the way Levi-Strauss uses oppositional categories.

Levi-Strauss builds his approach on some basic observations. Firstly, language can be regarded as a system of discriminations which are present at the phonetic level as contrasts between the kinds of sounds that are used. According to Jakobson[101] these can be seen emerging in a child's gradually developing discriminations of variables such as loudness, pitch, diffuseness, compactness, and the system so created can then be considered as to the use that is made of it in relation to objects, people, experiences, phenomena and so on. The relation will vary with different languages—different sounds for the same objects, for example—and with cultures, since different variables are given varying emphases in different cultural contexts. But whatever minor variations in structure and content occur, language still operates by discrimination, which creates categories, which may then be related to each other.[102] Very often the categories are regarded as oppositions, either dimensionally such as degrees of heat and cold, or in a more qualitative and possibly binary way such as 'living' or 'dead'. Of course there is always the possibility of boundary disputes about the point of death,[103] and it is further possible to construct special scales of death if it is not too frivolous to regard, say, actuarial tables as defining degrees of probability of life and death. But these refinements and elaborations do not alter the basic classificatory function embodied in language and its uses, or the apparently infinite possibilities of constructing classificatory schemes which may be interpreted as binary categories, if we are prepared to define cut-off points. As I understand it, Levi-Strauss asserts that the structure of the human brain facilitates these particular kinds of linguistic, intellectual and cognitive operations and not others; that is why the processes are common across all variations of language and culture.

Secondly, societies typically use myths whether religious or secular to account for their origins and to justify their existing systems of social organisation. A study of these will reveal the structure of social organisations (including their belief systems) which has resulted from the tendency for the human being, given a particular brain structure, to deal with experience in particular ways. Since the myths and social organisations embody a principle of construction it is possible to make a model of this principle and apply it to analysis of the structures. The model can be summarised from Levi-Strauss' directions.

    i. define the phenomenon under study as a relation between two or more terms, real or supposed;

   ii. construct a table of possible permutations between these terms;

iii. take this table as the general object of analysis which, at this level only, can yield necessary connections, the empirical phenomenon considered at the beginning being only one possible combination among others, the complete system of which must be constructed beforehand.[104]

The analytical tool so devised will enable us to relate the apparent variety of myths to an underlying code, thus revealing their hidden meanings—a superb economy of elements and relationships which both control, and may be used to elucidate, complex structures of myth.

It would require a very long digression to follow Levi-Strauss over his immense journey through kinship, totemism, and the myths of South America. Here it will suffice to note that Edmund Leach, even though applying the operational criteria of his own scientistic culture, is satisfied that there is a gain in knowledge.

Our valuation of such an improbable credo can only be assessed in operational terms. If by applying Levi-Strauss' techniques of analysis to an actual body of anthropological materials, we are able to arrive at insights which we did not have before, and these insights throw illumination on other related ethnographic facts, which we had not considered in the first instance, then we may feel that the exercise has been worth while. And let me say at once that in many cases, there *is* a pay-off of this kind.[105]

In spite of these moments of appreciation Leach is greatly troubled by Levi-Strauss' tendency to value the logical coherence of deep structures so highly that he would allow logical perfection to take precedence over documentary material. Leach proclaims basic disagreement with this attitude and creates yet another polarisation in order to deal with it.

for me the real subject matter of social anthropology always remains the actual social behaviour of human beings.[106]

Use of the terms 'real' and 'actual' is intended to ground Leach in his familiar scientific milieu and show how Levi-Strauss becomes fascinated by 'unreal' logical structures. And yet, in just the way he did earlier, Leach has simply *asserted* his own ability to gain direct access to the 'real' and the 'actual' without the intervention of his own logical and conceptual predispositions. Very few philosophers of science would support this position; it is now almost a common-place that theoretical positions or paradigms ('disciplinary matrices' in Kuhn's later formulation) make relevant certain ranges of obser-vations, and enable the scientist to accumulate anomalies for a con-siderable period without abandoning a particular position. This I take it is a reasonable translation of Levi-Strauss' point that logically perfect structures may throw doubt on documentary materials partly because even on documents there are no self-evident and 'raw' facts.

So I conclude that bipolar or binary schemes of analysis are not *necessarily* disabling or mystifying for social analysis; it depends how they are used, and Levi-Strauss comes out very well on this par-ticular test as Leach so generously points out. The related conclusion is more central to the evaluation of theories of self and social con-text: that where there is a clash of intellectual styles, false polarisa-tions may be used to bring knowledge within the perceptual and stylistic limits of an interpreter—even in the case of such a sophisti-cated and sensitive interpreter as Edmund Leach. In other words, false polarisations tend to occur where there is a clash of professional interests; in this case a very British anthropologist threatened by a methodological style and body of high level assertions greatly at variance with his own.

Another British anthropologist (although I note her affection for her Bog-Irish ancestors) who has brought a similar pattern of criticism to Levi-Strauss is Mary Douglas.

He seems to offer a perspective in which social controls on the human body can be included in a vast psycho-sociological analysis of controlling schemata (*Mythologiques* 1964, 1966, 1968), but he cannot come up with anything interesting about cultural variations (which are local and limited) since his sights are set on what is universal and unlimited to any one place or time. His analysis of symbolism lacks an essential ingredient. It has no hypothesis. Its predictions are impregnably, utterly irrefutable. Given the materials for analysis (any limited cultural field), given the technique of analysis (selection of pairs of contrasted elements) there is no possibility of an analyst going forth to display the structures underlying symbolic behaviour and coming home dis-countenanced. He will succeed, because he takes with him a tool designed for revealing structures and because the general hypo-thesis only requires him to reveal them.

... Levi-Strauss has given us a technique. It is for us to refine it for our own problems. To be useful the structural analysis of symbols has somehow to be related to a hypothesis about role structure.[107]

Perhaps it is the ambitious quality of Levi-Strauss' project which attracts this kind of tough criticism. Levi-Strauss has a general hypothesis which is also no hypothesis! And yet he has given us a technique which is worth refining. What more is it reasonable to ask of a human scientist? What have the greatest contributors, Marx, Freud, Durkheim, Weber, given but a technique (other critics have said 'method') worth developing because it clearly has some potential. Possibly the hidden contrast here is between 'techniques' and 'results'. If so it would be cavalier to dismiss the volumes of *Mythologiques*. Is it not that there is a considerable difference in the level of generality at which the two theorists have chosen to work, Levi-Strauss at the typically high level of Continental theory and Douglas in what might be called the middle range, more encouraged in the British intellectual circles, there being no evaluative connotation in the terms high and middle here?

After registering once again the great difficulties of communication across different cultural expressions of the same discipline it is now possible to see that Mary Douglas is struggling to create a means of linking the various levels of analysis in the human sciences, and her way of doing this involves exploration of *the interdisciplinary area of role structure*. Her contribution will later be seen as of cardinal importance for the creation of a truly interdisciplinary concept of role.

Before leaving this discussion of polarisation in social analysis it will be necessary to look at a psychological theory to see how the technique or method has been used in this discipline; whether it is integrally harmful as an approach and whether there are patterns of use and misuse akin to those at the sociological level. A fine example is available in George Kelly, the theorist whose work has already been discussed from various aspects. As far as I can trace, personal construct theory was developed quite independently of structural anthropology and yet it relies significantly on binary discriminations or polarities.

Kelly's use of polarisation occurs in relation to his assumptions about the structure of human construing processes, and again in the method or technique he proposes for appraising these construing processes. His model of a person, it will be recalled, is that of a scientist, continuously trying to anticipate events by operating and revising discriminations of difference and similarity among experienced phenomena. The discriminations are like polarised dimensions devised by a person to give order and structure to his perceptions, so providing him with a basis for acting in a relatively planned and purposeful way. Examples of such discriminations would be hard/soft, hostile/friendly, like-me/unlike-me, and so on, limited only by the capacity of the person to handle the range of dimensions so devised.

Although the potential number of dimensions (henceforward 'personal constructs') is very great, there is a hierarchical structure which brings the multitude of detailed and specific constructs under the control of a smaller number of superordinate constructs. Thus for a given context of a person's life it is possible to elicit a relatively few constructs (numbered, say, in tens), hierarchically arranged, which the person uses to make sense of his experience. The basic method for eliciting constructs is to obtain from a person a list of the people and objects (elements) of some significance in their life. These elements are then taken in threes and the person is asked to split the threes into units of two and one, the two being alike in some respect which differentiates them from the other one. For example, John and Mary are both friendly as against Joe who is aloof. Assuming these elements do really carry significance for the person concerned it is possible to study the content of a person's construing, its dimensionality and the structures of the dimensionalised life space.

As to structure, superordination/subordination has already been mentioned, to which may be added as many other relationships as the investigator can recognise: for example, exclusiveness, inclusiveness, grouping into factors, the limits here being set only by the capacity of the psychologist to produce constructs about the relation between constructs. Taken over all, the structure will depend on the kinds of constructs used—for example, comprehensive, specific, propositional or preemptive—as well as on the relations between the constructs.

Evidence has begun to accumulate on various aspects of Kelly's theory: Bannister has derived an explanation of schizophrenia from it and tested this in relation to diagnosis and therapy; Fransella has investigated and designed a therapy for stuttering based on personal construct theory; many other psychologists have tested particular assertions woven into the theory although as far as I can judge nobody has yet found a way of testing the most basic assumptions about the universality of human binary construing processes. My view is that this is untestable because of Kelly's willingness to see any change in construing as an 'elaboration' of a construct system— even suicide, when being alive can no longer be tolerated in relation to prevailing constructs. But I also think that testability is not a final criterion which must be used for every element of a theory: it is permissible for metaphysical assumptions to be used and, although not testable by particular experiments or observations, the assumptions will be subject to judgement after a sometimes considerable period of exploration has gone into the theories generated by them. Levi-Strauss, similarly, was criticised by Douglas for his irrefutable theory but I suggest that such criticism is premature in relation to both theorists.

In summary it can be said that Kelly's assumptions about the centrality of construing in human activity, together with his assertions about the structure of personal constructs, provide a programme and method for mapping this aspect of human life, a programme which is attracting a certain amount of rather confirmatory evidence.

Now before moving to a conclusion about the consequences of building personal constructs into a dichotomised or bipolar form, I should like to note some very striking patterns of relationship between the work of Levi-Strauss and Kelly, bearing in mind that they came independently within different disciplines to their formulations. Might the relationships show something about the tendency for human minds to create independently, similar or transformable patterns structured in the dichotomous fashion that is integral to both theories?

The source of Levi-Strauss' assertion about the binary form of human mental productions is his belief that the brain works only in this way. Kelly's assertion about dichotomy is that it is integral to the process of discrimination in that likeness implies unlikeness with the result that all construing has this oppositional form. Levi-Strauss suggests that the consequences of human dichotomous thought come back in mysterious and greatly transformed structures of myth which enable societies to persist since the myths give meaning to the extremely varied lives which are led in various societies. The myths have a mysterious form because they deal with virtually unanswerable questions about the origins of societies, the creation of sex differences (and so on in the manner of the Genesis stories). The similarities of underlying form are universal, resulting from the universal brain structure of the human being; and the deep structure is so inescapable as a form of expression that in a sense the myth 'speaks the person'. The qualified cultural determinism of this theory arises from the fact that the focal point of Levi-Strauss' work is the highly abstract structure of myths which he believes can be elucidated using the powerful analytical tool of binary transformations.

Kelly focuses on a quite different point: he is interested in the human capacity to dichotomously construe personal experience and so *devise* a personal (con) structure which gives meaning to life and enables it to be managed more or less successfully. The dimension *they* polarise is the familiar one of society (culture)/individual: Levi-Strauss seems to regard initiatives and determining influences coming down to the person, whilst Kelly sees the person as making choices which result in certain cultural and societal superstructures.

So, the anthropologist focuses on culture and rearranges personal phenomena to fit in with his master scheme; the psychologist focuses on the person and rearranges collective phenomena to fit in with his model of the person. Both are technically correct at the level of investigation required by their separate disciplines. Both lose credibility when they move beyond their disciplinary boundaries: Levi-Strauss when he chooses a primarily physiological model for the brain,[108] Kelly when he takes culture to be like an accumulation of scientific results arrived at by the human 'scientist', a serious over-estimation of the human capacity to behave scientifically in everyday life. Their separation into bounded disciplinary groups with a specialised way of viewing the world can be understood as consequent upon the division of labour and the need to protect group property and interests; what is not so clear is why the separate specialists seem inevitably to make reference to phenomena 'belonging' to another speciality. Here I think it is necessary to conclude that where phenomena arise on the foundation of a process of mediation between two co-determinants—culture (society)/the person—it is not possible simply to refrain from considering the action of any particular one, each being present by implication in consideration of the other. It will be remembered that the present study began from the observation, among others, that models of man generate models of society and vice versa, making political and ethical neutrality unavailable to human scientists. It is encouraging to see that Robert Young has detected other examples of the deleterious effects of splitting certain subject matters, some mentioned above,[109] and another in his discussion of Marxist and Kuhnian approaches to his own discipline, the history of science.[110]

Another starting point for the present study was the thesis that scientific or any other knowledge is not generated by a cool, impersonal, objective human activity; instead new knowledge enters competitively as its exponent tries to displace predecessors, often getting into extremely ambivalent relationships when something of what has gone before is wanted as a component of the new knowledge. The problem is to detach the wanted components from their undesired context and this is where a splitting process with full psychoanalytic connotations is often employed. A further example of this acquisition strategy is employed by Kelly in relation to Freud. I concentrate on Kelly's reaction to Freud's concept of the unconscious since this will lead well into a final assessment of the consequences of polarisation in social and psychological analysis.

After setting out the primarily verbal and therefore more readily symbolised constructs, Kelly goes on to deal with many aspects of what he calls 'covert construction'. Covert construction often involves preverbal constructs.

A preverbal construct is one which continues to be used even though it has no consistent word symbol.[111]

When words are not available other symbols may be used although these are likely to be less definite and somewhat difficult to communicate.

The therapist will have to infer, from the occasions on which the client claims he has the indescribable feelings and from such fragments of description as he is able to offer, what the elements are and how they are construed.[112]

Preverbal constructs usually originate in childhood.

Generally, if the client construes the therapist, through transference, by means of an essentially preverbal construct, the therapist should be alert to the possibility that the client is envisioning some kind of child-like dependency relationship to the therapist.[113]

A person may cover preverbal constructs with a profuse overlay of verbalisation often ending in confusion. Preverbal constructs may also appear in dreams.

As to the unconscious, preverbal construction will substitute for this 'too ready cover for ambiguity', along with other terms such as submergence, suspension, subordination, impermeability and loosening. It will be sufficient for my purpose to concentrate on submergence and suspension since these relate most directly to the unconscious.

Submergence occurs when one pole of a construct is 'less available for application to events'. For example, a person may repeatedly emphasise that all people are good to him/her, as a way of denying the polar opposite that at least some people are bad to him/her. In this case the likeness end is readily available but the contrast end submerged. It can be the other way round with the contrast end available and the likeness end submerged.

> For example, the client offers a series of descriptions of incidents and people which, judging from the contextual grouping, are conspicuously nonsexual in content. Elements which could be subjected to sexual construction are consistently omitted. There are no slips of the tongue, nothing that could possibly be given a sexual interpretation. . . . One has to infer the submerged end of his sexual construct from the scrupulous contextual grouping of the contrast elements.[114]

Submergence is apparent in many dreams; it may also be a way of protecting the self from reappraisal in relation to the submerged pole.

It can hardly have escaped attention that Freud, though not formally acknowledged, is entering this system in a very far-reaching way. Again I would turn Kelly's theory against him and ask rhetorically, 'What pole is here submerged for you?' When he moves on to suspension it is even more apparent what is happening.

> The phenomena which are popularly identified as 'forgetting', 'dissociation', and 'repression' can all be handled within the theoretical framework of the psychology of personal constructs in much the same way.[115]

The intensely personal reaction both to Freud and to any other kind of determinant of individual human construing is well indicated by the passage

The decision not to use the notion of an 'unconscious' follows from our systematic position. This is a psychology of *personal* constructs. We assume that personal constructs exist. If a client does not construe things in the way we do, we assume that he construes them in some other way, not that he really must construe them the way we do but is unaware of it. If later he comes to construe them the way we do, that is a new construction for him, not a revelation of a subconscious construction which we have helped him to bring to the fore. Our constructs are our own. There is no need to reify them in the client's 'unconscious'.[116]

It is also possible to see how use of a model of human construing cognate with the binary model applied by Levi-Strauss to myth leads Kelly to exactly the opposite conclusion, a sharp reminder to those who suggest unification of the human sciences on the basis of a common method (I admit to being excited at one time by these superficial similarities). But it does suggest the relative neutrality of a method which can produce such different conclusions.

There is by now no need to dwell on the familiar process in the production of knowledge which consists of reaction to an explicit or implicit competing standpoint or predecessor. Instead it will now be easy to move to a judgement on the significance of polarisation in Kelly's work. It is clear that he sets up *by definition* a system of construing and construct analysis which is polarised only in the very weak sense that it consists of binary discriminations; for example me/not-me, sexual/not-sexual. These binary categories can of course accommodate contrasts (say red/green in a colour spectrum), incompatibles (Freudian therapy/personal construct therapy/, and conflicts (capitalism/communism). However, the successful use of a grid of personal constructs does not carry any strong implication that *all* construing is dichotomous; indeed Kelly's many references to submerged poles imply that construing often does not take dichotomous form. I assume he would not take shelter behind the doubtful argument that 'normal' construing is dichotomous but the balance is upset in clinically relevant conditions. So again the conclusion remains that polarisation is not necessarily or integrally misleading: there is a certain loss of information when many different qualities of discrimination are cast into binary form, a perfectly acceptable procedure for many purposes. It is the claim that it is the *only* form of construing, and correct analysis thereof, that is a mistake—confusion by Kelly of *the efficacy of binary analysis for some purposes* with what happens in human experience and action.

Perhaps Kelly's habit of throwing competing theories out to the far ends of contrast dimensions in order to open up space in a field where he would obviously like to begin again as though nothing had gone before, led him to elevate his own intellectual strategies into universal human qualities.

His reaction to the unnamed Freud was highly ambivalent and perhaps needs further explanation. This is available if Kelly's conflictual social situation or role is taken into account: an American therapist wanting to offer without payment relatively short-term counselling in an area where even the bland American version of Freudianism would be an esoteric and subversive theory to be identified with. The consequence is that when he refers to Freud it is usually in a jokingly defensive tone, ridiculing the theory he had once been foolish enough to adopt.[117]

In an attempt to start clinical psychology all over again he devised a pragmatic, common-sense, individualistic model of man and a sharply defined tool of scientific, quantifiable analysis; a transformation into his own cultural context of the psychoanalytic psychology originating in Europe. It certainly incorporates and celebrates the myths of his own locality, like a Levi-Straussian transformation—different words but the same structure with a few inverted elements to enable it to be fitted into a different cultural setting. It is ironic that the man he would least agree with on the social formation of the person provides such a good explanatory framework for Kelly's weaknesses; and that the psychology apparently most capable of being integrated with Levi-Strauss' structuralism is in fact the most distant in its conclusions.

Both Levi-Strauss and Kelly see themselves as applying a 'dialectical' method of analysis to social and personal phenomena, the source for Levi-Strauss being the Hegel/Marx tradition, for Kelly more simply his view that the person proceeds continuously from experiment, to an answer or resolution, which provides the grounding for further exploration and movement, and so on. Thus dialectical analysis does not need to be identified with Marx. Like the oppositional categories on which it rests, dialectical analysis is neither privileged nor condemned in advance; everything depends on how it is used. It is therefore suggested that by rigorously critical evaluation it is possible to move over the boundaries mapped out by particular disciplines, both dialectical and otherwise, in search of the fundamental problems which encourage the integration of work on certain substantial interdisciplinary phenomena.

The question which initiated this excursion into philosophical approaches to role and self rested on the recognition that sociology and psychology were at one time contained within philosophy. The division of labour in intellectual work allowed for the separation and specialisation of the two disciplines but at the cost of disvaluing transdisciplinary problems of which the role/self relation is a leading example. Could it be said that the parent discipline has retained the role/self problem and solved it in a more unitary way than has been possible in the newly differentiated specialities?

The indications are that British philosophy has not retained a generalist approach; it has not kept hold of the problems of role and self to solve their mysteries and provide great insights. Instead philosophy has undergone such a far-reaching differentiation that these problems arise in the distinct areas of social philosophy and moral philosophy, although conceptual and linguistic analysis sometimes draw them in as examples. Within social philosophy and moral philosophy the polarisations which hinder interdisciplinary work—collectivism and individualism—reappear, and in spite of the professed aim of philosophers that they should make their criteria explicit[118] they are still capable of falling into mystification, distortion and bias. Of course there are particular and valuable contributions to be found but in each case these have then to be disentangled and worked into a different context. The basic problem remains but resources for attacking it continue to accumulate.

5.11 THE RELATIONS BETWEEN DISCIPLINES

If any general conclusion receives support from exploration of polarisation in social analysis it is the one suggested by Mannheim, who took it from Marx: that bodies of knowledge and even philosophical criteria do not float in a social vacuum; they are very frequently attached to, and express the interests of, social groups. In the continuous process of competition between intellectual formations attached to various groups, polarisation tends to occur where there is a conflict of interests. One consequence of such conflicts is that groups must strive for real or apparent differentiation from each other so that when they attack the other there is no chance of themselves being likened to, or identified with, what they attack.

A further interesting consequence of non-extreme conflict situations—that is to say, where violence is ruled out and the war is one of words—is that groups sharing the same sphere of potential influence, but with not very radically different knowledge to offer in return for a monopoly of occupational control, will tend to provide very similar services, but will be at great pains to claim distinctiveness for themselves. These attempts to set up non-rational distinctions will take competing groups into the irrationalities of parody, ridicule and exaggeration typical of ideological battles between political groups. Some examples may allow this comparison between political processes and interprofessional processes to be substantiated: the first will be to outline party political conflicts in Britain and then compare these with interprofessional conflicts in the United States.

British Labour and Conservative parties have carried through virtually identical measures to control and restructure the economy and yet they endeavour to call their interventions by different names. When election time comes round the programmes offered to the electorate are clearly differentiated so as to appear to embody the interests of capital and labour. But since a sectional appeal limits its own range of attraction both parties find it necessary to address themselves to the interests of the nation as a whole, what they sometimes refer to as competing for the middle ground. What they can be seen to be doing is *using* the two major interest groups as a means of gaining or holding on to power, and they turn round on their adopted interest groups whenever it seems that their own power can thereby be maximised.

There are many interesting consequences of these party political manoeuvres. Whenever party actions converge (as in controlling the economy) there are calls for a coalition. However rational this may seem as a way of conserving the energy lost in party conflict, enabling the best team to be chosen free of party consideration, it is near suicidal, except in the abnormal circumstances of wartime, for a party to admit that it does not really stem from one of the major interest groups. It is also a serious threat to the two-party system which purports to hold an alternative government in readiness (and does so in a trivial sense) if both parties appear to confirm that a one-party (totalitarian!) constitution is best. The contradictions and ambivalences of this delicately balanced system give rise to complex ideological structures containing claims to information, explanation and predictive power. It is the plausibility of the claims which then influences which of the parties shall take political power.[119]

The relation of interest groups to power and ideological processes is readily seen at the societal level, although I admit that not everybody would agree with this particular, greatly abbreviated, analysis. Assuming for purposes of argument that it is correct, how does the professional group compare with the political party? Can the same elements of interests, power and ideological processes be discovered in the competition or conflict between professions?

A recent book by Terence Johnson[120] attempts to show that just these elements are relevant to any proper understanding of professions. He asserts that although the original impetus to study professions came from a sense that they were important parts of the occupational and power structure, these considerations have given way in recent decades to functionalist accounts or trait models. Functionalist accounts mislead by assuming consensus as to the value of professions in upholding and furthering the most important aims of societies. Talcott Parsons' particular error lies in attributing cognitive rationality not only to the use of knowledge in providing a service but also to the nature of relationships between professionals and their colleagues and clients. It is plausible, for example, that a chemist might be superbly rational in his manipulation of knowledge and techniques but at the same time jealous of his colleagues and in a highly ambivalent relationship to the large corporation which employs him.

Trait models of professions attempt to list the characteristics of professional activity—skill based on a body of abstract knowledge, a code of ethics, etc.—as though some essential quality will be revealed by describing and comparing the many examples. Wittgenstein's reminder that there can be families of comparable examples without a particular 'essence', that the rope which attaches ship to shore contains no single fibre that covers the whole distance, serves to show the limitations of this approach.

Johnson argues that attention must now be paid to the varieties of professional occupations, to their historically specific nature and to the fact that

... each type ... has varying consequences for occupational

practice and is the product of different institutionalised forms of control.[121]

The comparison with political parties now becomes feasible. A profession, like a political party, depends on an interest group in the sense that its practitioners offer a service based on complex knowledge and techniques which will be used to further the interests of the relevant people (clients). Similarly a profession must be convincing enough in its 'programme' to gain the confidence of clients who pay dearly for its services, individually or through the State, and may have to wait some time before the benefits are apparent. In this sense a profession uses the needs of a sectional interest group to justify its monopoly control of an occupation. In addition, a profession needs to convince the State and general public that its service furthers not only a sectional interest but those of the nation as a whole (the more so where a service, like medical care, depends on State mediation). The position of the normally well paid middle-class practitioners themselves is a delicate one, particularly where, with the spread of State-mediated services to poorer groups, professionals are no longer simply exchanging services with equally prosperous middle-class peers. The interests of practitioners must be made to appear consonant with those of the client group and the State, even though there is likely to be a discrepancy and there may be serious conflict. It is precisely at this point that professions are forced into the arena of ideological interchange in order to reconcile their contradictory and ambivalent power relationship.

William Goode provides an example of professional groups fighting for control of the areas of sociology, psychology and medicine.[122] Although Goode does not use the language of ideological analysis, I suggest that the events he describes will bear this kind of interpretation.

It is a common sociological observation that when vivid claims issue in conflict, each side is likely to develop stereotypes and misconceptions about the other, especially in formal contexts, while by contrast some individual members from each side may develop congenial, respectful working relationships across the lines.[123]

My point in placing Goode's example into the context of ideological conflict is that in his account the stereotypes and misconceptions could simply be random mistakes in perception. As I see it the 'mistakes' have a consistent direction and serve to discredit the other group or limit its sphere of competence.

Goode describes how clinical psychologists have pushed the discipline of psychology towards professionalisation. It seems that there is a line of pressure flowing down from the psychiatric area of medicine towards clinical psychology stemming from the fact that they both practise psychotherapy. In order to compete with their more firmly established medical colleagues clinical psychologists desire a similar kind of professional identity, and being a very large section of the discipline of psychology, perhaps a half, they have affected the position of the whole subject group.

On the other side of psychology stands sociology, sharing with psychology the field of social psychology, since there are sociologically trained and psychologically trained social psychologists. Psychologists have put pressure on sociology to either regulate the training of their social psychologists or forbid them to use the term psychologist. This has the obvious purpose of avoiding 'multiportal' entry which might dilute the professionalism of psychologists or pose further threats to a group already under attack from the medical side. Sociologists and psychologists have agreed that sociologically trained social psychologists will not call themselves psychologists, but the seriousness of the pressures involved can be judged by Goode's statement that

> ... the state and national psychological associations paid little heed to our legitimate claims in the field of social psychology until our protests were organized sufficiently well to defeat legislation here and there.[124]

What offends Goode is the deplorable implication that

> ... our organization is thereby forced to act as a guild rather than a scientific society.[125]

He recommends sociologists not to follow the path of psychology and seek monoply control of the kind exemplified in their 'guild' activities. To him monopoly control of a scientific field is impossible or undesirable: a better model would be the academic in, for example, economics, who offers consultation on his scientific skills under control of the ethic of science rather than restrictive guild regulations.

If the seriousness of these power struggles between more or less professionalised disciplinary groups has been demonstrated, the irrationality inherent in the processes can be shown in relation to psychotherapy where on the one hand clinical psychologists and psychiatrists have been unable to establish the distinctiveness of their approaches and on the other they both refuse to submit to a test of their relative competence. Goode explains the latter point by saying that submission to any competent higher authority is an admission that the professionals are not sole arbiters of standards. Furthermore, Goode sees the relative scarcity of studies which test the effectiveness of various therapies as a defensive strategy against the probably embarrassing truth that there really are very few differences and that the efficacy of all methods is still in doubt.

> . . . this pattern might be cited as the hallmark of the emerging profession, which typically survives by faith, not by proof of works.[126]

I have set out these examples of conflict between disciplines at some length, although still too superficially in relation to the importance of the theme, in order to account for some of the peculiar irrationalities which characterise the relations between disciplines, irrationalities which stand in sharp contrast to the professed rationality of the search for knowledge, and its productive applications, within each discipline. Stereotypes and misconceptions can be seen to rest not not only on mistakes or limitations of perception but on power struggles in which it serves a very clear purpose, though not always a conscious purpose, to misrepresent competitors. This *ideological* interchange sometimes goes back, as in the case of sociology and psychology, to the conditions of origin of the disciplines. It is the group counterpart of that more individual phenomenon displayed by the self-theorists when they try to make space for themselves amidst the competing and often similar theories which hold a particular field. That is to say, there is a filtering effect on incoming knowledge and a shaping effect on outgoing knowledge-claims, brought about by the self-concept of the theorist, serving to protect his personal identity: the group counterpart consists of the conflictual effort to establish and maintain professional identity. By itself this process would account for the existence of an 'interdisciplinary void' in the place where a rich and productive role theory might be.

Accounting for the lack of work at a certain interdisciplinary interface is only one part of the story: what of the equally interesting consequences for knowledge production? It might be argued that in spite of external conflicts and conditions, disciplines are still capable of developing an internal organisation which sustains the objectivity of their findings. In my view there is no convincing evidence that any philosophical principles, scientific ethics, norms of science or scientific methods can confer immunity from the external interactions between disciplines and their social contexts. Furthermore I agree with Young's comments on Kuhn, the philosopher of science whose work is most sensitive to the problems of the internal autonomy and social context of disciplines, that

> . . . his analysis of the relationship between 'internal' and 'external' factors has reinforced the very distinction which he appeared at one time to be bringing into question. Having produced a lucid analysis of the dilemma, he has gone on to stress the internal factors at the expense of the external ones, thereby failing even to address himself to the issue of their mutual interpenetration and the deeper claim that they are constitutive of each other.[127]

I contend that the various examples already adduced—the self-theorists and relations between disciplines in the human sciences—show that there are many consequences of this interpenetration of the internal and external factors, although probably no single generalisable pattern. Johnson does suggest, however, that there may be a pattern which is common to the professions.

> Theoretical knowledge is, then, less important than knowledge which is applicable to the current practical needs of the patron. Practitioners are more likely to stress monist explanations which can be simply and immediately applied in policy or therapy. A stress on knowledge of this kind protects the practitioner in his need to *know* and *do*. Thus, medicine in the period of oligarchic patronage in England stressed monistic explanations of all disease, and blood letting was a simply derived therapy.[128]

Or, more generally

> Variations in the organisational and structural locations of practitioners will not only lead to differences in attitudes regarding the occupational community, but also to differences in the types of knowledge and ideologies espoused.[129]

The condition of the discipline and profession of psychology in Britain is of some interest here. Not only does it provide insights into the relations between more and less well-established professions in the medical, psychiatric and psychotherapeutic fields comparable to the American example already discussed, it also stands at a critical point in its professionalisation—the point at which it must choose from available resources a body of knowledge on which to base an effective form of therapy. Tizard, in his presidential address to the British Psychological Society, puts it this way

At least one thing is clear about the contemporary situation: the reason behaviour modification has become so popular so quickly is that it promised to fill what can now be acknowledged as a therapeutic vacuum.[130]

And in regard to the relations between professions

When we compare the position of psychology in society with that of the sister profession of *medicine*, the contrast is as great as that between the underdeveloped countries of the third world and the major industrial powers. Medicine is a well-developed discipline compared with psychology. Doctors are members of a respectable, highly paid and much respected profession of long standing. They have at their disposal powerful therapeutic techniques which enable them at other times to get away with anything— even the useless and expensive remedies that still constitute the bulk of medical practice.[131]

Already this is some indication of a conflict situation similar to the American situation of twenty years ago: are there comparable processes at work and if so what are the consequences for knowledge production?

Hearnshaw suggests that British psychology of the period 1892–1939 is marked by four features: a widespread faith in psychometrics; a marked antipathy to theory; a tendency to regard it as a biological rather than a social science; and a concern for 'applications'. He attributes this predominantly biological approach to the influence of Darwin and Galton, and yet this biological emphasis 'never really fulfilled its early promise'.[132] Only in the last decade has there been any significant development in *social* psychology with the establishment of chairs at the London School of Economics, Sussex and Bristol. These developments have not changed substantially the generally atheoretical, psychometric, biological and, to some extent, applied character of the discipline.

The first sign of monopolisation of resources and practice—that crude precondition of effective professionalisation—appears in 1934 when a Professional Standards Committee was set up to study the problem of psychological testing. There was concern that these products of the psychometric interests of psychologists were being used and even devised by the untrained and this seems to have been the spur to consider more general aspects of the psychologists's professional role because

. . . further discussions led to the formulation of a new constitution, which would allow the Society to seek incorporation. This constitution provided for different classes of membership, and hence created the possibility of a kind of 'register' of psychologists which could provide a basis for protecting the public from inefficiency and charlatanism. In October 1941 the Society took the first step in formally accepting its professional responsibilities by becoming incorporated.[133]

Here is a most striking parallel to the American experience, even to the use of 'charlatanism' to describe competitors. It is noticeable that professionalisation is justified as protection of the public and that no mention is made of monopolisation. Later when a British Psychological Society committee comes to consider the question of registration, the duality of interest is more apparent because without it

. . . there is no protection either for the public against unqualified practitioners or for the reputation of psychologists.[134]

But this is a point I shall return to after following some lines of advancement for professional psychologists.

It is not very surprising that their monopoly of testing secured a professional role for psychologists, firstly in relation to education and secondly in relation to psychiatry. It was the only distinctive resource made available by the discipline: their biologism was overshadowed by biology itself and their atheoretical approach was typical of most British disciplines rather than any singular quality of psychology. Leaving aside educational psychology which is less relevant here, it can be seen that psychologists were able to gain a modest foothold in the psychiatric and medical fields.

At the beginning, psychologists functioned as psychological testers, concerned with the measurement of intelligence and other psychological functions.[135]

By 1973 the growth of clinical psychology within the context of a National Health Service has been so substantial that the Department of Health and Social Security is calling for evidence on the Role of Psychologists in the Health Services. The British Psychological Society's report refers to the wide range of activities undertaken in assessment, therapy, research, ward management, institutional and communication problems, and in teaching. Behaviour therapy is a significant factor in therapy.

> *Behaviour therapy* in its various forms represents a striking example of practically useful methods developing from the basic research and theory of many experimental psychologists. The expansion of this form of therapy has been so rapid that already practitioners often have to specialize within this approach (e.g. focusing attention primarily on deconditioning procedures or operant procedures). There are now a number of journals solely devoted to behaviour therapy.[136]

It is also noted that clinical psychologists are involved in rehabilitation and training, psychotherapy and counselling, and experiential group methods. The work of Rogers (client-centred therapy), Ellis (rational–emotive therapy), Perls (Gestalt therapy) and Kelly (personal construct therapy) is made use of.

In relation to the possible extension of all these activities the BPS evidence is a very clear bid for autonomy and for a better status as against psychiatry. It argues that

> *the principles and techniques of assessment, modification and research have general applicability* . . .
> Psychiatric settings have provided the major context in which the skills of clinical psychologists have been usefully developed and demonstrated. It is appreciated that the association between psychology and psychiatry has been to the benefit of both professions and will continue to be so in the future. Nevertheless, the skills of clinical psychologists have useful applications beyond psychiatry and mental illness.[137]

Basically these further applications within the National Health Service would mobilise all available psychophysical knowledge of human sensory functions to assess and monitor patients over the whole range of medical treatments and services. Behaviour modification would be used to help chronic patients and the handicapped, to relieve the anxiety which usually attends hospitalisation, and against the ailments which can best be tackled through attitude change, notably smoking, drug abuse, alcoholism and venereal disease. Research, too, would widen its scope and might be interdisciplinary in relation to other specialists.

The crucial point of autonomy in relation to psychiatry is again addressed in the context of organisation of services.

> Psychological services will be provided to Departments of Psychiatry but such services will not be organized and administered as parts of departments of psychiatry. Such an arrangement will, it is hoped, adhere to the principle of the NHS reorganization document (Cmnd 5055, p. 57, 4.2): 'To allow for the exercise of professional discretion in their work, professional people are most suitably managed by members of their own professions'.[138]

It is further considered desirable that patients should be referred directly to psychologists in some cases and that general practitioners or other medical specialists should temporarily transfer over-all responsibility for a patient to a psychologist where a substantial psychological contribution to care makes this advisable. Thus psychologists would play a similar role to the specialist or consultant in medical services.

The typical professional concern with multiportal entry is in evidence when it is recommended that the one form of training not leading to a higher degree or diploma, but consisting of three years' supervision under a senior psychologist, be done away with. It is further emphasised that a clinical psychologist combines the roles of scientist and clinician.

The underlying strategy of these various proposals is obviously to seek comparable status and power to that of the medical practitioner and at the same time to define a distinctive sphere of competence which will ensure autonomy even when working alongside (and certainly no longer under) psychiatrists or other professionals. Although autonomy depends on rejection of the 'medical model', for some areas of behavioural dysfunction there is paradoxically no better professional model for the psychologist to emulate. This is carried through even to the extent of proposing legal registration for psychologists. There seems to be a fairly strong connection between developments in clinical psychology and the proposal to seek registration which came before a Special General Meeting in 1974. Earlier that year the Secretary General said

> . . . it seems likely that the issue of the professional registration of psychologists will loom large; partly because the Foster Report highlighted the oddities of some of those who practise psychotherapy for gain; partly because the Trethowan Committee is attempting to outline the role of the clinical psychologist in the Health Service and will shortly publish a Consultative Document; and partly because of the rapid development of interest in psychotherapy as an art, craft or science, both by would-be practitioners and by would-be clients seeking fulfilment by any method that holds out hope for a richer, fuller life.[139]

After circulation of a discussion document the question of legal registration was explored at a Special General Meeting in October 1974. The Chairman of the Society's Committee on the Legal Registration of Psychologists in the United Kingdom set out arguments for and against, emphasised that once a Bill had been introduced to Parliament the Society would be unable to determine its final form, and that although likely to be well represented on any controlling body psychologists would not be in sole charge. Various points of view were expressed.

1. That any Bill should seek to set up a Register for psychologists as a whole, and not be restricted to psychologists in certain applied fields only (e.g. clinical, educational, occupational, etc.).
2. That great care would need to be taken in defining the criteria for eligibility for registration in order not to crystallize psychological roles in a way which might prevent their further development.
3. That University Departments often greatly benefited, both in teaching and research, from the work of such other specialists as physiologists, ethologists, anthropologists, sociologists and philosophers, and care would have to be taken to ensure that such people were not disadvantaged from the registration of psychologists.

The Committee was asked to continue its work with the possibility of advising that an appropriate resolution be brought to the next

Annual General Meeting. The voting figures were 27 for, 9 against with 3 abstentions.

At the AGM in April 1975, which took place in the midst of a conference attended by over a thousand members, a special session on legal registration produced a straw vote which revealed an even balance of viewpoint; proportions of two for, two against and one abstaining. The attendance of about two hunded members probably now represented more accurately the views of the Society's five thousand members of whom about six hundred belong to the Division of Clinical Psychology. Thus the British situation is as yet quite unlike the balance of power within American psychology because, as Goode pointed out, nearly half of American psychologists are in the clinical field. If the growth rate of clinical psychology continues—the Division more than doubled its size between 1968 and 1974—it may be anticipated that another few years will bring a different outcome.

There is evidence of considerable strain within the discipline as clinical psychologists work out their relationships to their colleagues in other specialties. A Working Party Report on Training in Psychotherapy suggested that

> Neither psychoanalysis nor any development in psychotherapy has ever tended to become an important stream in British academic psychology. Academic psychology has tended to become sterile and fragmented, frequently obsessed with animal analogues and very rarely using the concept of the whole person developing over a lifetime as its focus. Currently, this concretistic model of psychology as a 'science' is proving so disappointing to students that it is under vehement political attack and suffering from desertions to humanistic psychology or other forms of radical alternative.[141]

The Report notes that many clinical psychologists are still used inappropriately as 'testers' and that they find difficulty in working therapeutically in a context 'which is dominated by the medical model'. Deploring the virtual absence of substantial training facilities within universities, they say

> It can be argued that an area such as the navigational problems of the rat has been over-used and that the kind of human interaction involved in psychotherapy might well provide a focus of study for the psychology student.[142]

This suggestion that psychotherapy might become a focus of study instead of a fringe area (often called 'unscientific' by mainstream psychologists) is reinforced by Davis, who argues quite explicitly that the true paradigm for psychology not only should be, but already has been, clinical work.

> . . . experimental psychology, unlike its scientific predecessors, became academically established without the customary preliminary for the establishment of a science, namely the reception by the majority of its specialists of a paradigm (Kuhn, 1970, p.19). It is against this singular scientific background that it may be possible to evaluate the academic profession's reaction to the impact of the very live paradigm candidate which has for many years dominated the psychological scene because of its manifest ability to confront the phenomena of human life.[143]

Tizard in his presidential address notes the conflict within the discipline, institutionalised by the existence of a Scientific Affairs Board and a Professional Affairs Board, and seeks to learn from the history of its development.

> . . . a belief in the interdependence of scientific and professional psychology was expressed by many of our most illustrious predecessors. Examining what they thought, and perhaps where they went wrong, may help us with some of our own problems.[144]

He reviews the contributions of Myers and Burt and concludes that

> We can look back then at a whole era in which those who were using psychology in industry, education and the clinical field drew from the prevailing psychological theory of the time the lesson that to apply psychology was to assign individuals to points in a multidimensional matrix. This, it was thought, would enable them to be sorted into appropriate categories, for which there were appropriate educational or occupational niches, or appropriate forms of remedial treatment.[145]

He then recalls that the Second World War gave a new impetus to operational research and made apparent the social relevance of psychology. Academic psychology slipped back after the war although applied psychology units were established at Cambridge and the Institute of Psychiatry and in these places theory and practice were brought together around general problems of social relevance. This and later work by, for example, Tizard's own Thomas Coram Research Unit[146] will provide the basis of a more environmental, 'functional' type of investigation which gives due importance to the institutional and sociocultural contexts that influence human behaviour, and will show the gross limitations of previous diagnostic and remedial efforts. Such a psychology will not only be richer in content but will be directly relevant to *social policy*, particularly in the areas of child care and education.

I realise that Tizard's view, although presidential, is not necessarily representative of the discipline of psychology as a whole. Nevertheless, it seems a matter of some significance that his proposals point the way towards interdisciplinary or transdisciplinary work between psychology and sociology. It may well indicate that, faced with its crises and strains over professionalisation, legal registration and the need to find a role which is respected and useful, psychology is being forced towards consideration of the whole person in social context, even though the original foundation of the discipline depended on setting aside these problems in order to carve out a disciplinary identity. What prospects are there for the emergence of significant interdisciplinary developments?

A recent study of interdisciplinarity[147] provides an excellent account of recent attempts to work across disciplinary boundaries, making it possible to ask whether the problem of relations between disciplines has been mitigated by new academic developments. The study is concerned with a wide range of disciplines covering the natural and social sciences; its mood is very constructive, reflecting the wish of the authors to appreciate the reasons for increasing interest in this kind of course and to recognise achievements in the field. At the same time they work thoroughly over a number of case studies and give due prominence to various failures and difficulties which emerge. The picture would be more complete if it could be extended to include the negative cases where interdisciplinarity has been resisted to the point of preventing it from happening, or where it has never occurred to specialists that links might be desirable.

A distinction is recognised between joint honours courses in which the links might be merely fortuitous and interdisciplinary courses in which 'we expect some of the links to be planned'.[148] Four broad approaches are noted.

First those which make links or build bridges between two

disciplines (not always clearly distinguishable from joint honours); secondly, those organised on a broad faculty basis (natural sciences, social science, etc.); those based on the study of an area or period; and a rather variegated group focused on a 'theme' or 'problem'.[149]

The departmental structure of universities and polytechnics is said to work in favour of single or combined honours and somewhat against interdisciplinary ventures. Even where schools of studies or unit courses have been devised these may create their own kinds of difficulties. Courses which depend on departmental co-operation and finance are particularly conducive to role-strain in that

> All the professional academic pressures that work upon academics —publications, career prospects, the opinion of colleagues—will tend to divert commitment away from the hybrid course.[150]

This is a sobering thought when read against the importance attached to role-hybridisation[151] and dual-role-occupation[152] by Ben-David and by Mulkay in their studies of scientific creativity.

Although in rare cases new departments have been created—the Department of International Relations at Birmingham—the expense and forward implications of such a radical step preclude it as a general solution. And although schools of studies are designed to facilitate the gradual, exploratory development of interdisciplinary work, this tends to be at the cost of administrative complexity and, if option courses proliferate, serious malintegration.

The problem is not confined to institutional pressures.

> We have to take account of a professional structure as well as an institutional structure, and of both of these in relation to the structure of knowledge.[153]

It is suggested that in some subject areas, history being one example, the 'craft model' of a profession predominates: this is a closed and esoteric form of professional grouping with a tendency to develop its own tacit criteria of fitness to join, based on an apprenticeship and personal acceptability rather than formal qualifications. Such a group may develop its own language and implicit norms. But it is not just language difficulties which keep some specialists apart; it has to be recognised that teachers can be so fundamentally opposed that they simply cannot work together to plan and monitor a course. One could refer to genetic and environmentalist accounts of individual and racial differences to show that fundamental differences of view might be involved. The problem extends even to the subject matter and texts.

It is hard to grasp how deeply the literature on almost all subjects has been influenced by the conceptions proper only to that subject. The teachers launch themselves into an interdisciplinary effort to integrate the basic concepts of several subjects, and almost every book the student reads undoes their work.[154]

The authors consider most of the examples dealt with so far to fall within the 'relativist' interpretation of the growth of knowledge and would contrast this with the objectivist approach. The objectivist approach holds that 'objective knowledge of the real world' can be obtained by the application of a principle such as Popper's criterion of falsifiability, and to the extent that this has been done disciplines and bodies of knowledge reflect the structure of the real world. Basically they see the two approaches as incompatible although they find some room for reconciliation where knowledge can be seen as structured in levels and where knowledge in a particular domain is incomplete. My own view is that the contrast between relativist and objectivist approaches is drawn too sharply: relativist views are not independent of the real world and objectivists such as Popper never claim completeness or the absence of 'levels' of knowledge. Possibly this polarisation accounts for the view that in well-developed disciplines borderline shifts are more likely than any disturbance of the core of a discipline. Given that the anomalies which accumulate in any research programme or disciplinary matrix *do not fit in* and cannot therefore be explained, it must be left open whether they will have only marginal significance or be subversive of disciplinary cores. Both Popper (objectivist) and Kuhn (relativist) allow the possibility of revolutions.

It may be true of the general body of scientific disciplines that *trans*disciplinary developments ('establishing a common system of axioms for a set of disciplines') are 'the most rarefied possibility'.[155] However, in the social sciences, where division of the subject matter followed by specialisation and professionalisation has created such arbitrary and irrational subdivisions, it may be that pursuit of this rare possibility is both practical and necessary. It need not be a common system of axioms which brings together whole disciplines but a common system which spans the most conspicuous voids, such as the area of role.

One of the most interesting findings of the study of interdisciplinarity is that, of the fifteen readily identifiable interdisciplinary developments in Britain, only one takes in psychology proper; two developments take in *social* psychology and only one of these (cultural studies at Birmingham) relates it to sociology. Taylor has confirmed the split into sociological and psychological versions of social psychology and from experience of both types of departments warns against the false hope that it provides integration.[156] The one case which takes in psychology proper only confirms its tendency to be regarded as a natural science since its partners are philosophy, linguistics and computing, with an emphasis on artificial intelligence: this development, called 'cognitive studies' at the University of Sussex, is proving unattractive as an option to anthropology students but is a very popular third-year option for students majoring in logic with physics, or logic with mathematics. In other words, the only interdisciplinary development involving psychology proper enlists it as a discipline dealing with human cognition and moves it away from, rather than towards, the social.

A further cause for regret in relation to cognitive studies is that it is the one programme which approaches a transdisciplinary and critical emphasis of the kind being attempted in the present study.

> ... the rationale is not that we have a group of independently viable subjects which can usefully collaborate in tackling certain borderline problems. Rather, my argument is that if any one of these disciplines is practised in ignorance of the concepts, methods, theories, and problems of others, then there is a serious risk that inadequate sets of descriptive concepts will be used, problems will be poorly formulated, shallow empirical investigations will be made, woolly and obscure metaphors and slogans will pass for explanatory theories, conceptual confusions will go undetected, and the rich store of knowledge embedded in common sense will not be properly utilised.[157]

What an excellent description of the problem, and of knowledge in the human sciences. But without proper awareness of how these disciplines were driven apart and thereby in some respects impoverished, there is rather small chance of fitting them together into new, productive integrations. In other words, it is no 'accident of history' that the disciplines of sociology and psychology are separate, each producing their own version of social psychology: it is rather that historical, social and personal processes of an understandable kind have forced them apart and any integration, for however limited a purpose, will fail unless these processes are taken into account. It is an open question whether integration can actually take place without a change in the balance of forces which led to separation; without a change in the cultural setting which sets a particular value on knowledge of various kinds, a change in the institutions and professions which set their own kinds of boundaries, a change in the role pressures which both facilitate and hinder certain kinds of investigation and a change in the consciousness of the producers of knowledge. In this context it seems possible to say that the search for knowledge across all these boundaries is a revolutionary activity.

I will now draw together the main points arising out of this investigation of the development of certain disciplines, the relations between disciplines and some recent attempts at interdisciplinary teaching.

The familiar process of competition between groups identified with particular bodies of knowledge leads to criticism, which frequently spills over into ridicule and parody as positions are polarised by the conflict of interests. Amidst this cut and thrust, groups are striving to achieve credibility for their claims and there is usually the sense that a public of potential clients is watching and may withdraw support. For example, when Eysenck ridiculed the British Psychological Society report on Training in Psychotherapy by saying that its criteria did not exclude such practices as tea-leaf reading, it brought forth a letter suggesting that 'for the good of the profession' such personal feuding should be carried on in private.[158] This misses the point that competition between bodies of knowledge is not reducible to a personal feud and that to exclude these conflicts in the interest of public relations is to misrepresent the discipline.

Conflicts of interest in the field investigated are principally between psychology and medicine, secondarily within psychology between 'academic' and 'applied' groupings, and further between competing specialisms within psychotherapy. In Britain the 'scientism' of Eysenck, allied to behaviour therapy, is at odds with the 'unscientific' clinical variants of Kelly, Rogers, Perls and Ellis. Strangely, Freud and his British successors in object relations theory are not seen as major contenders, and yet careful analysis has shown that Freud is present as a central component of at least Kelly's and Rogers' theories, although in the disguised form which follows from their reaction to his work. To a large extent then the conflicts here are a shadow play, with the real contenders hidden in a secret struggle. This accounts for the ideological nature of the battles—the sudden verbal violence of the clashes which can only be understood in the light of a deeper analysis of what is going on.

Without some reflexive understanding by human science specialists of the dynamics they are locked into, it seems unlikely that the specialisms will become more productive. The exchanges which take place are so distant from real issues, so distorted by polarisation, so 'symptomatic' rather than communicative, that the specialisms seem bound to the endless, compulsive repetition of their mistakes.

As for interdisciplinary collaboration, how could it be expected that disciplines locked into their own systems of oblique communications would communicate successfully over the professional chasms between disciplines. Does not deeper analysis positively predict all the factors which emerged in the study of interdisciplinarity?

Recalling Goode's recommendation that sociologists should not seek 'guild control' but should practise an academic kind of professional activity controlled by the ethic of science, is this still a serious possibility now that it can be seen how deeply penetrated by professional considerations the academy really is? Nor is it so very clear what the ethic of science might be. And again is it not just too late? Already sociology, the most diffuse of disciplines, has its professional body, the British Sociological Association, within which a group of 'applied' sociologists, the Social Administration Association, is attempting to differentiate itself and gain independent access to research funds. This latter move may be due to their unwillingness to be associated with a discipline which has undergone constant vilification and ridicule in governmental, academic and wider circles because of its supposed role in fomenting criticism and disturbance.[159] Just as psychology came under attack and is now fighting its way towards useful respectability with clinical psychology leading the way, so now is sociology the ready scapegoat for social ills. If it is possible to describe the Social Administration Association as concerned with social therapy, or societal therapy, they present an uncannily accurate mirror image of the psychotherapists within psychology as they attempt to lead sociology back to acceptability through its useful applications. Since the exchanges involved are no more rational than in cases already investigated, the costs in knowledge may be very great.

It is as well to remember in relation to all this that the single most important determinant of the rapid growth of behaviour therapy and the other surface therapies is that there is a social need and they come cheaper than analysis. The counterpart at the societal level is a concern for 'welfare' that gains its credibility only against a background of severe social crisis.

REFERENCES

1 P. J. Heine. *Personality and Social Theory*, Penguin, Harmondsworth, Middx (1972), p. xvii

2 P. Worsley. The distribution of power in industrial society. In *The Development of Industrial Society* (ed. P. Halmos), Sociological Review Monograph 8, University of Keele, Keele, Staffs (1964), p. 15

3 B. Morris. Reflections on role analysis, *Br. J. Sociol.*, 22 (1971), 408

4 D. Bannister and F. Fransella. *Inquiring Man*, Penguin, Harmondsworth, Middx (1971), p. 50

5 G. A. Kelly. Transcript of a tape-recorded discussion with Fay Fransella (1966)

6 D. Bannister and F. Fransella. *Inquiring Man*. Penguin, Harmondsworth, Middx (1971), p. 50

7 W. J. Goode. A theory of role strain, *Am. Sociol. Rev.*, 25 (1960), 483–96
   For the logical and quite far-reaching development of Hughes' observation

8 G. A. Kelly. *The Psychology of Personal Constructs*, Norton, New York (1955), p. 95

9 H. D. Duncan. *Communication and Social Order*, Oxford University Press, Oxford (1968), p. 101

10 G. H. Mead. *Mind, Self and Society*, University of Chicago Press, Chicago and London (1934), p. 186

11 D. J. Levinson. Role, personality and social structure. In *Sociological Theory* (eds. L. Coser and B. Rosenberg), Collier-Macmillan, New York and London (1969), p. 305

12 D. J. Levinson. ibid., p. 308
13 E. Goffman. *The Presentation of Self in Everyday Life*, Double-day Anchor, New York (1959), p. 253
14 E. Goffman. *Encounters*, Bobbs-Merrill, Indianapolis, Ind. (1961), p. 152
15 R. L. Coser. Role distance, sociological ambivalence and transitional status systems. In *Sociological Theory* (eds. L. Coser and B. Rosenberg), Collier-Macmillan, New York and London (1969), p. 328
15A T. Parsons. *The Social System*, Free Press, New York (1951), p. 25
16 R. L. Coser. Role distance, sociological ambivalence and transitional status systems. In *Sociological Theory* (eds L. Coser and B. Rosenberg), Collier-Macmillan, New York and London (1969), p. 335
17 R. K. Merton. *Social Theory and Social Structure*, The Free Press, New York (1957), p. 7
18 J. Ben-David. How to organise research in the social sciences, *Daedalus*, **102**, 2 (1973), 42
19 G. H. Mead. *Mind, Self and Society*, University of Chicago Press, Chicago and London, p. 280
20 ibid., p. 243
21 ibid., p. 209
22 ibid., p. 239
23 J. M. Mair. In *Perspectives in Personal Construct Theory* (ed. D. Bannister), Academic Press, New York and London (1970)
24 G. A. Kelly. *The Psychology of Personal Constructs*, Norton, New York (1955), p. 177
25 ibid., p. 179
26 ibid., p. 503
27 ibid., p. 503
28 K. Mannheim. Competition as a cultural phenomenon. In *Essays on the Sociology of Knowledge*, Routledge, London (1952), p. 197
29 K. Mannheim. *Ideology and Utopia*, Routledge, London (1936), p. 247
30 ibid., p. 253
31 M. Jay. *The Dialectical Imagination*, Heinemann (London 1973), p. 64
32 M. Jay. Quoting Horkheimer, ibid., p. 64

33 K. Mannheim. *Ideology and Utopia*, Routledge, London (1936), p. 238
34 ibid., p. 238
35 J. A. Jackson (ed.) *Role*, Cambridge University Press, London (1972)
36 ibid., p. 2
37 C. Gordon. Role and value development across the life cycle. In *Role* (ed. J. A. Jackson), Cambridge University Press, London (1972), p. 74
38 T. S. Kuhn. *The Structure of Scientific Revolutions*, University of Chicago Press, Chicago and London (1970)
39 H. Popitz. Social role as an element of social theory. In *Role* (ed. J. A. Jackson), Cambridge University Press, London (1972), p. 36
40 ibid., p. 38
41 A. MacIntyre. *Secularization and Moral Change*, Oxford University Press, Oxford (1967), p. 57
42 H. Popitz. In *Role* (ed. J. A. Jackson), Cambridge University Press, London (1972), p. 35
43 M. Coulson. Role: a redundant concept in sociology? In *Role* (ed. J. A. Jackson), Cambridge University Press, London (1972), p. 109
44 R. K. Merton. The role-set. In *Sociological Theory* (eds L. Coser and B. Rosenberg), Collier-Macmillan, New York and London (1969), p. 365
45 J. Urry. Role performance and social comparision processes. In *Role* (ed. J. A. Jackson), Cambridge University Press, London (1972), p. 130
46 W. G. Runciman. Reply to Mr Urry. In *Role* (ed. J. A. Jackson), Cambridge University Press, London (1972), p. 145
47 ibid., p. 147
48 M. Hollis. The man and the mask: a discussion of role theory. In *Role* (ed. J. A. Jackson), Cambridge University Press, London (1972), p. 41
49 B. Heading. op. cit., p. 45
50 M. Bradbury. op. cit., p. 47
51 B. Heading. op. cit., p. 55
52 M. Hollis. op. cit., p. 62
53 F. H. Bradley. *Ethical Studies* (1876), Clarendon, Oxford (1927)

54 D. Emmet. *Rules, Roles and Relationships*, Macmillan, London and Basingstoke (1966), p. 54
55 B. Mayo. The moral agent. In *The Human Agent*, Macmillan, London and Basingstoke (1968), p. 47
56 E. Goffman. *Encounters*, Bobbs-Merrill, Indianapolis, Ind. (1961)
57 R. L. Coser. In *Sociological Theory* (eds L. Coser and B. Rosenberg), Collier-Macmillan, New York and London (1969), p. 318
58 B. Mayo. ibid., p. 51
59 ibid., p. 52
60 ibid., p. 62
61 D. Emmet and A. MacIntyre. *Sociological Theory and Philosophical Analysis*, Macmillan, London and Basingstoke (1970), p. xii
62 D. Wrong. In *Sociological Theory* (eds L. Coser and B. Rosenberg), Collier-Macmillan, New York and London (1969), p. 122
63 C. S. Hall and G. Lindzey. *Theories of Personality*, Wiley, New York and Chichester (1957), p. 4
64 J. C. Flugel. *A Hundred Years of Psychology*, Duckworth, London (1951) p. 14
65 M. Mulkay. *The Social Process of Innovation*, Macmillan, London and Basingstoke (1972)
66 T. S. Kuhn. *The Structure of Scientific Revolutions*, University of Chicago Press, Chicago and London (1970)
67 J. Ben-David and R. Collins. Social factors in the origin of a new science: the case of psychology, *Am. Sociol. Rev.*, **31**, 4 (1966), 451–65
68 ibid., p. 452
69 ibid., p. 453
70 ibid., p. 463
71 J. Ben-David. *The Scientist's Role in Society*, Prentice-Hall, Englewood Cliffs, NJ, and Hemel Hempstead, Herts. (1971) p. 7
72 R. M. Young. *Mind, Brain and Adaptation in the 19th Century*, Clarendon, Oxford (1970), p. 252
73 ibid., p. 249
74 J. Laidlaw. Is 'real self' a useful topic for first year psychology courses? *Bull. Br. Psychol. Soc.*, **27** (1974), 129

75 ibid., p. 130
76 J. Macmurray. *The Form of the Personal*, vol. 2, *Persons in Relation*, Faber, London (1961), p. 224
77 Although approaching from Marxian and non-Marxian directions they agree in this judgement of linguistic philosophy. H. Marcuse. *One Dimensional Man*, Beacon Press, Boston, Mass (1964), and E. Gellner. *Words and Things*, Gollancz, London (1959)
78 J. Macmurray. *The Form of the Personal*, vol. 2, *Persons in Relation*, Faber, London (1961), p. 218
79 H. D. Duncan. *Communication and Social Order*, Oxford University Press, Oxford (1968), p. 106, referring to P. Pfuetze, *The Social Self*, Bookman Associates, Copenhagen (1954).
80 J. Macmurray. *The Form of the Personal*, vol. 2, *Persons in Relation*, Faber, London (1961), p. 136
81 ibid., p. 136
82 ibid., p. 127
83 ibid., p. 128
84 ibid., p. 155
85 ibid., p. 146
86 ibid., p. 209
87 *The Form of the Personal*, vol. 1, *The Self as Agent*, Faber, London (1957), p. 97
88 K. Marx. *Capital*, vol. I, Lawrence & Wishart, London (1970)
89 J. Macmurray. *Persons in Relation*, Faber, London (1961), p. 153
90 See, for example, D. Bannister (ed.), *Perspectives in Personal Construct Theory*, Academic Press, New York and London (1970), p. 184 (quoted by J. M. M. Mair)
91 K. Popper. *The Poverty of Historicism*, Routledge, London (1957), p. 135
92 G. Cohen. Beliefs and roles, *Proc. Aristotelian Soc.*, **67** (1966–7), 18
93 ibid., p. 33, footnote
94 ibid., p. 33
95 M. R. Cohen and E. Nagel. *An Introduction to Logic and Scientific Method*, Routledge, London (1934), p. 294
96 B. Russell. *A History of Western Philosophy*, Allen & Unwin, London (1946), p. 764
97 K. Popper. What is dialectic? *Mind*, **49** (1940), 403 ff.
98 A. Wilden. *System and Structure*, Tavistock, London (1972), p. xix

99 E. Leach. *Levi-Strauss*, Fontana, London (1970), p. 20

100 T. S. Kuhn. *The Structure of Scientific Revolutions*, University of Chicago Press, Chicago and London (1962), 1970, p. 14

101 R. Jakobson and M. Halle. *Fundamentals of Language*, Mouton, The Hague (1956)

102 F. de Saussure. *Course in General Linguistics*, Philosophical Library, New York (1959)

103 D. Sudnow. *Passing On: The Social Organization of Dying*, Prentice-Hall, Englewood Cliffs, NJ, and Hemel Hempstead, Herts. (1967)

104 E. Leach. *Levi-Strauss*, Fontana, London (1970), p. 25

105 ibid., p. 56

106 ibid., p. 98

107 M. Douglas. *Natural Symbols*, Penguin, Harmondsworth, Middx (1973), p. 94 (Barrie & Rockliff, London, 1970).

108 A. Wilden. *System and Structure*, Tavistock, London (1972), p. 243

109 R. M. Young. *Mind, Brain and Adaptation in the 19th Century*, Clarendon, London (1970), p. 7

110 R. M. Young. The historiographic and ideological contexts of the 19th century debate on man's place in nature. In *Changing Perspectives in the History of Science* (eds M. Teich and R. M. Young), Heinemann, London (1972)

111 G. A. Kelly. *The Psychology of Personal Constructs*, Norton, New York (1955), p. 459

112 ibid., p. 461

113 ibid., p. 461

114 ibid., p. 469

115 ibid., p. 471

116 ibid., p. 466

117 G. A. Kelly. *Clinical Psychology and Personality* (ed. B. A. Maher), Wiley, New York and Chichester (1969)

118 P. Winch. *The Idea of a Social Science*, Routledge, London (1958), p. 102

119 J. Trenaman and D. McQuail. *Television and the Political Image*, Methuen, London (1959)

120 T. J. Johnson. *Professions and Power*, Macmillan, London and Basingstoke (1972)

121 ibid., p. 85

122 W. J. Goode. Encroachment, charlatanism and the emerging profession: psychology, sociology and medicine, *Am. Sociol. Rev.*, **25**, (1960), 902–14
123 ibid., p. 904
124 ibid., p. 905
125 ibid., p. 905
126 ibid., p. 912
127 R. M. Young. The historiographic and ideological contexts of the 19th century debate on man's place in nature. In *Changing Perspectives in the History of Science* (eds M. Teich and R. M. Young), Heinemann, London (1972), p. 409
128 T. J. Johnson. *Professions and Power*, Macmillan, London and Basingstoke (1972), p. 72
129 ibid., p. 82
130 J. Tizard. Psychology and social policy, *Bull. Br. Psychol. Soc.*, **29** (1976), p. 230
131 ibid., p. 229
132 L. S. Hearnshaw. *Bull. Br. Psychol. Soc.*, Supplement (1969), p. 7
133 R. J. Audley. *Bull. Br. Psychol. Soc.*, Supplement (1969), p. 17
134 British Psychological Society Committee on Legal Registration of Psychologists in the UK. Discussion Document, *Bull. Br. Psychol. Soc.*, **27** (1974), 461
135 British Psychological Society. Report to the DHSS on the Role of Psychologists in the Health Services, *Bull. Br. Psychol. Soc.*, **26** (1973), 310
136 ibid., p. 312
137 ibid., p. 313
138 ibid., p. 319
139 British Psychological Society. Secretary-General's newsletter, *Bull. Br. Psychol. Soc.*, **27** (1974), 106
140 British Psychological Society. Committee on Legal Registration of Psychologists in the UK. Discussion Document, *Bull. Br. Psychol. Soc.*, **27** (1974), 561
141 British Psychological Society. Report of Working Party on Training in Psychotherapy, *Bull. Br. Psychol. Soc.*, **28** (1975), 10
142 ibid., p. 18
143 H. Davis. Clinical practice and the paradigm for psychology, *Bull. Br. Psychol. Soc.*, **29** (1976), 326

144 J. Tizard. Psychology and social policy, *Bull. Br. Psychol. Soc.*, **29** (1976), p. 225
145 ibid., p. 228
146 J. Tizard, P. Moss and J. Perry. *All Our Children*, Temple Smith/New Society, London (1976)
147 Group for Research and Innovation in Higher Education. *Interdisciplinarity*, Nuffield Foundation, London (1975). (Acknowledgements to Dr A. Mansell for this reference)
148 ibid., p. 7
149 ibid., p. 10
150 ibid., p. 13
151 J. Ben-David and R. Collins. Social factors in the origin of a new science: the case of psychology, *Am. Sociol. Rev.*, **31**, 4 (1966), 451–65
152 M. Mulkay. *The Social Process of Innovation*, Macmillan, London and Basingstoke (1972)
153 Group for Research and Innovation in Higher Education. *Interdisciplinarity*, Nuffield Foundation, London (1975), p. 23
154 ibid., p. 35
155 ibid., p. 47
156 L. Taylor. Psychology and sociology: interdisciplinary teaching, *Bull, Br. Psychol. Soc.*, **20** (1967), 11
157 Group for Research and Innovation in Higher Education. *Interdisciplinarity*, Nuffield Foundation, London (1975), p. 44
158 K. A. Nichols. *Bull. Br. Psychol. Soc.*, **28** (1975), 214
159 D. Martin (ed.) *Anarchy and Culture*, Routledge, London (1969)

6
British Existentialism

I have suggested that in the field of personality theories there are many implicit as well as explicit lines of communication between individual theories and schools of thought, along which move attitudes, actions and reactions to form, in a dynamic way, new claims to knowledge in the human sciences. This form of analysis serves both to locate knowledge in its sociohistorical context and to make visible personal processes of selection, distortion, attenuation and interpretation at work right at the heart of the human activity of knowledge production. In general it seems the task has been to keep out threatening knowledge or viewpoints which might in a particular situation embarrass or misidentify certain theorists. It is also clear that some generalisation is possible to the extent that one can trace typical patterns of transformation between, say, European and American existentialism, or typical patterns of reaction to Freud.

Almost in the form of a socially given experiment there is a group of British existentialists, Ronald Laing, David Cooper and Aaron Esterson who have embraced European, and particularly Sartre's, existentialism so fully and directly that it hardly seems possible to speak of selection or distortion. And yet Britain, generally, has been no more receptive to radical European ideas than the United States.[1] How then may this be accounted for? How have Sartre's ideas been used? What forms of knowledge have emerged and how do these relate to the general body of personality theories current in Britain?

Undoubtedly the strongest theme shared by the British existentialists is a reaction: to exclusively organic or genetic explanations of schizophrenia; to diagnostic use of the ambiguous term schizophrenia in relation to a wide range of unusual behaviours and experiences; to medical and psychiatric forms of treatment or confinement which take little notice of the experience and social contextual position of the person; and to the viewpoint which sees only undesirable, diseased qualities in the schizophrenic person's manner of living. The reaction begins at a point of collison between the

established medicopsychiatric professions and the developing
insights and wishes of a group of workers in the state psychiatric
institutions who were thwarted at every turn by existing conditions
and forms of organisation.

It is not easy to appreciate just how bad conditions were at this
formative time for the group. The 1959 Mental Health Act gives
some indication of the public fear and ignorance which allowed the
mental hospitals to fall into low priority within a health service that
was poorly resourced and understaffed. The only practicable methods
of treatment were quick surgical, electrical, or drug therapies which
were 'empirical' rather than theoretically grounded and served more
to bring patients under control than cure them. These were nevertheless hailed as a great advance on the past. All this in institutions
usually built in the massive, nineteenth century custodial style with
minimal amenities and poor food.

Extreme conditions of this kind help to explain the difference
between the reaction of the British existentialists and some of the
typical patterns of reaction found in the American theorists. Whereas
the American theorists filter out more radical elements of existentialist theory, the British existentialists can hardly find a theory
radical enough to make sense of their experience. What a contrast
there is between the experience of Americans such as Allport, Rogers,
Kelly and Maslow with their primarily middle-class, often student,
not extremely disturbed counselling clients, and the experience of
the British group into whose care come largely working-class
patients with the full range of disturbances, into hospitals already
overflowing with the most deteriorated and hopeless patients—a
half-alive record of the failure of these state institutions.

So the British existentialists' reaction takes them from the safe
centre to the very edge: instead of a retreat into positive generality
it is a full scale attack on the boundaries of social knowledge and
social norms. Of course it does not mean that, because they move
into a situation of confrontation between extreme experience and
radical theory, all their responses are thereby guaranteed to produce
useful knowledge or effective action. It only means that their
inclusion strategies for knowledge are relatively free from one
typical distorting process: it still remains to examine the body of
theory they bring in, and further to assess what particular use they
make of it.

They begin from the position of insiders having received a conventional training in psychological medicine, enabling them to hold responsible posts in state mental hospitals. Their situation is then complicated by the fact that their responsibility is not grounded on the power to act effectively: not only do they have insufficient time to devote significant attention to any one patient, they are also growing in the conviction that the skills they have been given are the wrong ones. They see interpersonal and social factors at work in the problems they have to deal with and have no resources for handling them. So the search begins through the psychological and social disciplines for relevant and useful knowledge. Unfortunately, there was virtually nothing available in Britain. It must be remembered that this was before the great expansion of social and behavioural sciences in the new universities of the early nineteen-sixties. It was a time at which psychology was tied to a particularly positivistic model of investigation for reasons I have tried to indicate by reference to the history of the discipline and to its relations with other disciplines in the human sciences. For similar and sometimes reciprocal reasons sociology was in the grip of a barely articulated positivism which neglected psychosocial mediations as the forbidden 'psychologism' that Durkheim had warned against. There was very little theoretical work going on: anthropology remained separated from sociology, and philosophers such as MacIntyre and Winch had not yet entered sociology in a substantial way. The bulk of sociological output was concerned with survey and empirical work on problems of educational achievement, community structure and planning, or problems of the welfare state. For a group concerned essentially with the interpenetration of psychic and social phenomena the British scene was barren in the extreme. Neither the content of the separate disciplines of sociology and psychology nor their lack of integration could serve them.

This divergence between sociology and social psychology can be illustrated from many fields. In the study of conflict and war there have been mutually exclusive social and psychological explanations. In studies of social stratification, the psychological approach seems to have produced a particular account of class and status in subjective terms, which is contrasted with the sociological account in terms of objective factors, rather than systematic investigation of the psychological aspects of a significant element in the social structure. The 'psychology of politics' hardly deserves to be mentioned, so remote does it appear from the most obvious facts of political structure and behaviour. In almost every field of enquiry it could be shown that psychology and sociology constitute for the most part two separate universes of discourse.[2]

In these circumstances where else could the British existentialists turn but to foreign sources?

American social and behavioural sciences had to offer at this time a nascent area of work on patterns of communication. Searles had provided what Laing called a pioneering effort to explain how a person might be 'driven crazy' in some circumstances,[3] and Bateson, Jackson, Haley and Weakland had presented their famous double-bind hypothesis. It is these sources that Laing made use of in his first more tentative explorations of *The Divided Self* (1960) and *The Self and Others* (1961). As they become available, the works of Goffman, *Asylums: Essays on the Social Situation of Mental Patients* (1961), Szasz, *The Myth of Mental Illness* (1962), and Scheff, *Social Conditions for Rationality* (1964), are brought in. However, it is a reflection on the condition of American social and behavioural sciences that for various reasons (some partly explored in respect of personality theories) none of these sources is politically radical; certainly not in a way that would answer to the extreme experience of the British group. They were useful as a start and may have provided just a little support in very lean times but they have not remained central to development of the new body of work; that is to say they have remained in the footnotes rather than being moved to the centre of the text. Even Bateson and his colleagues' double-bind theory, which has sometimes been criticised as though it formed the core of the British group's theory, has been put back in its place by Laing; this in spite of his very great admiration for Bateson's perceptiveness

I use the phrase less frequently now, because in Bateson's sense, it's got a very precise meaning and I think there is something to be said for allowing that precision to remain.[4]

The fact is that American social and behavioural sciences, though infinitely larger and more theoretically developed than their British counterparts, had nothing very substantial to offer.

The perfect answer to the British group's needs was much closer to hand. Jean Paul Sartre's immense attempt to humanise Marxism by fusing it with his own very active interpretation of phenomenology and existentialism spoke both to the feeling-laden complexities of role, self and group interaction and to the broader political issues implicit in the institutionalisation of psychiatric practice. These issues of political control were being pulled rapidly out of their normal obscurity by events covering a large part of the world as the 1960s brought disturbance and disaffection to the United States, China, Britain, Vietnam, India, Czechoslovakia, Ireland, Japan, France, Germany, Africa and elsewhere. The purpose of these conflicts was quite different from the World War II aim of stopping the self-evidently bad Hitler: these were civil disturbances which mobilised and at the same time threw into question the internal control systems of states, although internal forces were sometimes backed by external and imperialist powers. In a deepening series of crises the first-line control systems of police and army were revealed as a clumsy and often brutal power available to governments and authorities of many different kinds. It is then a short step to criticism of the second-line control systems—families, education systems and mass media of communication.

No longer could the trouble be put down to a few dissatisfied agitators, although this reflex action of authority was still frequently triggered; nor could it be attributed to the other common explanation, a lack of communication. On the contrary, communication had risen to such new heights of efficiency and pervasiveness that it had itself been put forward as at least a contributory cause of the conflagrations. More especially the quality and form of mass communication with its primarily commercial, propagandist and manipulative functions had been advanced as a cause of many modern social problems becoming a major subject of concern for the British New Left of the 1960s. Two other factors press hard into this social dynamic: disillusionment with the 'Old Left', exemplified by the ossification of Russia as an experiment in communism, and the quiescence and apparent contentedness of working-class groups in the advanced capitalist societies, thus directing left and right-wing intellectuals, from their different standpoints and in different terms, to problems of false consciousness, alienation and ideology. Clearly many of these phenomena are related but the concept which resonates through all the social and personal levels of the difficulties —after all, Marx himself had given it four distinguishable meanings —is *alienation*.[5] It is in just these terms that Sartre presents it, adding his own nuances, and it is in just these terms that the British existentialists take it up.

Reason and Violence (1964) marks the point at which Sartre's philosophy, already drawn upon by Laing in its earlier less political stages is taken up, translated, condensed and made available by Laing and Cooper to English-speaking readers in a substantial way as the work of a decade, 1950–60. To enter and explore the dense, ambiguous flux of Sartre's writing, absorbing it sensitively and crystallising it into one-tenth of its original size is a feat of such magnitude that only a labour of love could sustain it. Their success can be judged by the author's own commendation in a foreword. Laing and Cooper's reservations about the theory they translated are slight: they express uneasiness at the critical treatment of Kardiner.

> Such criticism, though necessary, does less than justice to Kardiner's work which, however tendentious its solutions, at least clearly outlines the problems posed by work such as Ruth Benedict's, in which relations between institutions in society are discussed analogically in terms of one-person pathology. [6]

It is interesting to see them at this stage resisting the criticism which might limit their own tendency, much exaggerated later on, to apply concepts from one-person or interactional pathology to the institutional structures of societies. It will also be recalled that Maslow was able to borrow Ruth Benedict's concept of 'synergy' to falsely integrate his organismic model of the person with a social context. They further assert that

> Sartre does not deal adequately with later work in group dynamics that is indebted to Lewin, nor with the work of Talcott Parsons, Bales, Shils, and others. [7]

This very generous account of American work, set so firmly in structural functionalism and shot through with organismic analogies which prevent its liberation from a natural science model, is actually a misconceived reservation. More will need to be said about the British existentialists' sociological weaknesses, but on their own ground of psychoanalysis they say with some authority that Sartre deals with only a limited range of psychoanalytic writing, with the result that his analysis of Jean Genet lacks the important dimension of unconscious phantasy. In short, their only well-founded reservation relates to the completeness of Sartre's work, not to its substance. What they would add presumably is something from the British psychoanalytic tradition in which they were trained and which Laing, at least, had already deployed in his earlier studies—the tradition which runs through Freud, Klein, Fairbairn and Winnicott, developing the Freudian ideas through Klein's exploration of very early childhood experience, Fairbairn's formulation of object relations and Winnicott's sensitive paediatric and psychoanalytic studies of growing children. For the moment this interesting line of succession must be set aside but not without registering the fact that the British existentialists have this area of resistance to Sartre's work. This will help to explain some important subsequent and distinct directions taken by various members of the group.

Before differentiating the group it will be useful to examine in outline just what Marxist existentialism could give to their common purpose. The Marxian critique of society gives them a weapon for attack on the institutions that obstruct and offend them; this in the double sense of the psychiatric institutions themselves and again the institutional structure of society. It is the latter which regulates the mental hospitals, giving controlling power to the medical profession, a profession of high status and with such a studied seriousness and propriety in its practice that it might be a model of the bourgeois values Sartre attacks so scathingly.

Sartre's sensitivity to the nuances of human feeling and experience, together with a confident phenomenological stance which enables him to explore these areas not as side issues or epiphenomena of some more objective biomedical reality, but as central subject matter of a human science, gives the British existentialists a sense that they are going to the heart of the matter in human relationships, rather than moving to a lunatic fringe of human experience and to the margins of their discipline.

Sartre's aim of synthesising knowledge over several disciplines taking into account self, role, and group membership promises to clarify the relation between psychic or personality structures and the formative influences of the family, social groups and institutions.

Possibly above all else Sartre, from his roots in European phenomenology, offers them a rigorous science, in Husserl's sense, to set against the institutionalised form of British science which is not only unsuitable for their particular purposes but, to the extent that it segregates and regulates medicopsychiatric knowledge, psychology and other disciplines, is integral to the oppressive practice they want to get rid of. The importance of this clash of philosophies and paradigms *of science* is impossible to over-emphasise, being one of the major themes of this study. It is too large a theme to be resolved in the context of setting out and criticising the work of the British existentialists but it will be possible to locate and sharpen the issues involved in the different formulations.

Earlier, when looking at polarisation as a factor in the production of knowledge, it was necessary to differentiate the intellectual climates of Europe and Britain. The dominant British intellectual concerns within the philosophy of science were linked to the name of Popper. It was unusual, at the time when British existentialists were so much in need of techniques and resources of a human science, to find any work which did not base itself on a Popperian philosophy of science; and this of course denied the conception of a separate logic or method for the social and behavioural sciences.[8] It was Popper who ridiculed dialectical arguments or methods of analysis until the word dialectical became an indicator of all things unscientific and tendentious. Similarly, psychoanalysis was his constantly given example of the untestable assertion which, in virtue of that quality, disqualified itself from serious consideration. For him, sociology's main task would be to study the unintended consequences of human action, which, if harmful, might be put right by the only rational method available—piecemeal social engineering —since no more comprehensive programme for social change could have a scientific basis. This was *established* science in many senses: it was politically unchallenged by the existence of two major political parties both practising piecemeal reform; it was accepted throughout the natural sciences with which medical, psychiatric and psychological sciences identified themselves; it enabled the medical profession to claim an objective basis for its authority over mental illness, to the exclusion, or controlled admission in a subservient role, of psychoanalysis and other psychological therapies. Psychology has by now, however, made the most of its identification with the natural sciences and its stock of rationally programmed behaviour therapies, to gain a strong foothold for clinical psychology in mental hospitals.

Given all this it can be seen that every interesting direction of development that attracted the British existentialists was guarded by definitions which would invalidate them as unscientific. This was *their own alienation* to which Sartre brought relief and new light. They could, with this philosophy, challenge existing definitions of scientific method, subject matter and disciplinary boundaries.

Sartre sees the various theories of sociology and psychoanalysis as more or less partial realisations of some moment or moments in the dialectic. Since they are not grasped by dialectical reason they are blown up into total theories, and inevitably run into contradictions which their authors try to deal with by *ad hoc* hypotheses, or simply ignore.[9]

They note his distinction between dialectical and non-dialectical subject matters.

History and the Social are the only true realms of dialectical reason.[10]

And they rejoice in the dialectical concept of continuous movement in human relationships as social beings act to totalise, detotalise and retotalise human situations. Since totalisation is a key term in Sartre's philosophy, and is adhered to by the British group throughout, it will probably be worth pausing at this stage to consider it more fully.

As I understand it, Sartre addresses himself to the problem of conceptualising social phenomena and produces the term totalisation to deal with four problems. Firstly, there is the problem of finding the best descriptive term for referring to the relationships that exist within a group of people, whatever its size, at a given point in time. Although brutally simple external forces can operate to produce uniformity of action, say going to war, there is an infinite complexity of interpersonal perceptions, feelings and actions which reflect the personal wishes, purposes and intentions of the people involved. The term totalisation emphasises the interconnectedness of any social unit and the sense in which its 'structure' depends on a certain consistency and directedness on the part of all the people involved. The phenomenological term 'intentionality' is a probable source of this kind of emphasis.

Secondly, Sartre wishes to recognise ubiquitous change taking place over time so that any totalisation of a given moment is open to detotalisation as a particular pattern of human relationships shifts, consequent upon changes in the intentionality of the people involved, leading towards retotalisation as a new situation emerges. Thus any present situation is a result of detotalisation and retotalisation of a previous situation. Putting it this way draws attention to the historical depths of any group and the special quality of situations which come about through a succession of earlier situations. At the same time it serves as a reminder that groups and societies show a directedness toward the future which significantly influences present actions.

Thirdly, by resting social structures on the human choices which together constitute that structure, Sartre keeps human agency at the centre of his theory. This places responsibility for what people are in their own hands, a heavy burden for them to carry in the present condition of the world, but it throws out the challenge to use this power of choice to change the world for the better. Such a conception is held to be superior to previous models and theories which, by their reliance on physical or organismic interpretations or analogies, overlook or undervalue this most distinctive quality of human action and experience.

Fourthly, having kept the subject matter fully human, so to speak, Sartre is able to unite the human scientist with the human subject matter. The human scientist is directed towards the subject matter in a way similar to that of other participants: any analysis or inter-pretation of a situation is both 'interested' and 'responsible' for influencing its future condition. The human scientist may therefore 'totalise' a situation in the sense that it is comprehended, and can, in imagination and possibly in fact, detotalise it, break it down and retotalise it or bring about a new situation.

Sartre's general strategy is clear although its formulation is dense. By concentrating on the distinctively human qualities of social formations and the distinctively human action of knowing them, he leaves no room for the 'bad faith' of any claim that one's actions are socially determined (by his role, for example, in the earlier discussion by Cohen),[11] or that observation and theory can be detached and objective. This homology of human scientist and subject matter is not a completely new idea: a technical form of participant observa-tion has long been recognised in sociology, and as Sprott observed

Relatively orderly courses of decision-making and so on take place in the way they do because the participants assume that they will, and act on these assumptions; this consensus provides a framework which prompts, constrains, and limits the sorts of actions which are envisaged.

The fact that we have, and share, these models in our minds and that from time to time we contemplate them, means that we are all, in some sense, sociologists.[12]

But it has never received quite the Sartrean emphasis, which goes against the grain of the more mechanistic Marxist materialism and at the same time rejects the fetishisation of objectivity by the social and behavioural sciences.

Consistently, Sartre criticises Freud's concept of the unconscious because it allows a person to slip away from responsibility by claiming that some actions are determined by unconscious forces. It is slightly unfair to concentrate on unconscious determination in Freud rather that the therapeutic aim which is to recover and choose again the unconscious directions one has fallen into. However, Sartre does acknowledge the possibility of unconscious as well as social influences, for he suggests that in choosing from a field of possibilities to realise one of them, the person contributes to the making of history.

The agent's project then assumes a reality, *which the agent himself may not know*, but which by the conflicts it manifests and which give rise to it, influences the course of events.[13]

I suggest that this philosophy, an immense synthesis of personal and social phenomena, a paradigm of human choice extending toward the future and implying action of a social and political kind, supplies the perfect basis for British existentialism. As a group they have never gone beyond it although there is a tendency for them to develop their separate personal uses and interpretations of the fundamental position. These three variations on a theme provide fascinating cross-perspectives on existentialism as well as a very good account of the present condition of British existentialism. I shall now trace their three separate projects, beginning with Ronald Laing.

6.1 R. D. LAING

It will be remembered that the one substantial reservation Ronald Laing expressed (together with Cooper) toward Sartre's work was that he had covered too limited an area of psychoanalysis. Presumably he was thinking of the vigorous developments of Freud's ideas going on in Britain, a very important body of knowledge to Laing because he had been trained within its context and had already made some use of these new concepts in his earlier books. Although he used a number of sources—Klein, Bion (on group processes), Milner and Winnicott—it seems that his main debt is to Klein. Not only does he add a Kleinian emphasis on very early experience when speaking of his attitude to psychoanalysis,[14] he also says that he wanted to be very close to Klein.

> When I was in analysis with Charles Rycroft at the London British Institute of Psychoanalysis . . . I wanted to be supervised by Melanie Klein. Protocol required that my analyst first check out the 'lie of the land', and he reported back to me that Melanie Klein was unable to supervise me, because she didn't consider *him* as properly analysed.[15]

And this also serves to indicate that the field of psychoanalysis in Britain contains its different viewpoints. At a rough description, it is probably correct to say that Freudians and Kleinians (claiming to have achieved a development of Freud's ideas, but not always accepted as such by Freudians) predominate, with some representation of Adler and Jung.

Of course the best test of lines of influence is to compare the conceptualisation that is used, and the result of this is to confirm that Klein, although not necessarily acknowledged at every step, is greatly present.

> . . . in the patients here considered, the splitting is not simply a temporary reaction to a specific situation of greater danger, which is reversible when the danger is past. It is, on the contrary, a basic orientation to life, and if it is followed back through their lives one usually finds that they seem, in fact, to have emerged from the early months of infancy with this split already under way.[16]

He also puts a similar emphasis on aggression,[17] orality, and the fate of the self in relation to reality.[18] Although at the same time he must sense a sharp difference in that Klein pays little or no attention the social context or political issues: perhaps this accounts for the lack of detailed acknowledgement by Laing.

On the existentialist side Laing does give clearer acknowledgement to the general tradition of Kierkegaard, Jaspers, Heidegger, Sartre, Binswanger and Tillich, noting at the same time important points of divergence. And then shows how important to him is the work of Sartre by describing his contributions as 'brilliant phenomenological accounts',[19] or in other complimentary terms.[20] In short, the centre of gravity of Laing's work is an attempt to synthesise a basically Kleinian psychoanalysis with the existentialism of Sartre whose own treatment of psychoanalysis Laing regarded as too limited.

As Laing moves toward greater involvement with the work of Sartre in translating *Reason and Violence*, and as Sartre's work becomes more Marxian and sociocritical, Laing begins to change the tone of his writing. From the patient explanatory mood of *The Divided Self* (1960), written in 1957, he moves to the kind of expression contained in an introduction to a 1965 edition of the same book where he says that 'normality' and 'adjustment' may be seen as 'the abdication of ecstasy' or 'the betrayal of our true potentialities'. His alienation at the time of writing consisted of a kind of puzzlement that he could not actually find the 'signs and symptoms' supposed to be characteristic of schizophrenics and he carefully sets out the sense and beauty of schizophrenic communication, hoping no doubt that there will be something of revolution in psychiatry. By 1964 very little had changed in psychiatry, and the general social and political scene was getting more and more violent and irrational. With *The Politics of Experience, and the Bird of Paradise* (1967), the most famous and infamous statements ring out. It is a great refusal to enter into complicity with the alienated and alienating processes of the modern world; a protest at the psychological and physical violence which is perpetuated in the name of normality and goodness. It is a cry of rage at the harm that is being done by the conceptually mutilating definitions placed on people within the context of dehumanised and mystifying systems of knowledge which perpetuate our blindness to what we are and to what we might be. It speaks of the tragedy of a missed opportunity to be different, less tormented, more authentic selves.

> We are bemused and crazed creatures, strangers to our true selves, to one another, and to the spiritual and material world—mad, even from an ideal standpoint we can glimpse but not adopt.[21]

Many difficulties enter at this point as Laing ties up an extreme social criticism with the alternative of 'true selves'. To clarify matters I will examine first the true self conception in relation to personality structure before going on to raise some sociological and political points. The concept of a true self appears to have placed Laing in the company of the natural self-theorists and self-actualisers such as Maslow and Rogers. This is not quite so because Laing provides some very sensitive definitions and reservations which just about save his concept. For example, he distinguishes carefully between inner self and true self: the inner self may be phantasticised and therefore not true.[22] Inner states have no special privilege over outer ones and the true self depends for its sustenance on dialectical relationships with other persons. The false self is that which operates to preserve the inner self from unbearable encounters with reality, as when an hysterically happy false self obscures the unhappiness of the inner self. No matter what mutilation the inner self has suffered it cannot be completely disposed of.

> The task in therapy then comes to be to make contact with the original self of the individual which, or who, we must believe is still a *possibility*.[23]

It is the concept of an original self which causes most difficulty. It is unlikely that it means simply the pretherapy self which, until entering therapy, had managed to cope with life, because, even though there may have been periods of apparent 'normality' in a schizophrenic's life, Laing makes it clear that he expects to find the roots of the difficulty in very early infancy (the Kleinian emphasis). In that sense the pretherapy self has been heading for breakdown for some time. This must mean therefore that Laing is looking toward the early infant self as a source of possibility for the true self. At this stage

> . . . the early ego is largely unorganized, though, in keeping with the whole trend of physiological and psychological growth, it has from the beginning a tendency towards integration.[24]

This is a reasonable working hypothesis for a clinician: it is clearly stated, supported by other British analysts such as Winnicott and Fairbairn and open to investigation. It is, however, a very long way from here to political and sociological questions which must be concerned not only with the inescapable fact that incoming experience impinges on the pristine ego, to split it and lay down the broad outline of later patterns, but also with the social qualities of incoming experience in early infancy and throughout life. When he moves to the political level of analysis it is not very informative to counterpose the original self and an alienated social condition in which we are all mad.

It might be argued that true self is not the same as original self and that true self can be given a slightly more social and political interpretation. This is so, for it could be said that true self is simply a relative term which refers to the *possibility* that at any particular moment a person may, particularly with the help of a therapist or other dialectically relating person, transcend one or more contradictions in behaviour or experience. That is to say, the inner self may, for example, take back a projection which sustains part of a false self system acting as a barrier to non-contradictory communication and relationships. In contradistinction the false self can, by definition, never make such a gain, for its aims are all phantasies incapable of satisfaction, its communications always oblique and misleading, its actions always secretly moved by the inner self which, by its need for a false self, shows that it is split. The false self can only multiply its contradictions, the true self has transcended at least one, and using its 'original' resources has a tendency toward integration. There is a danger that the original self will be used in a confusing way, as in the nature mysticism of Maslow and Rogers, but apart from this one can only say that Laing's scheme is a possible way of organising the discourse of therapy. Unfortunately, it offers virtually nothing by way of social and political analysis; not even when he introduces new, more interpersonal concepts in an attempt to go beyond the usual psychoanalytic basis of explanation. In fact these new concepts often seem to add little except new terminology; for example, his extensive use of the word 'mapping' to refer to the process whereby social forms are imposed on the family, and family structures are taken into personality structure as part of political socialisation.[25] In an essay of 1967[26] he sets out a case which is intended to show that internalisation is concerned not so much with other persons in the form of parents or siblings but with the patterns of interaction between others. What is taken in is a patterned sequence of events of fairly long duration, much like the section of a complete film contained on one reel. The case was that of a girl who had been used as an objectified go-between for the parents and grandparents who made her transmit messages when they were not speaking to each other. Laing emphasises that the girl had been affected by patterns of interaction which caused her to retreat into reveries about a game of tennis, including the belief that she was a tennis ball, knocked from one player to another.

> Her personality is not somewhere inside her, 'in' intrapsychic structures or what-not; it is the way she experiences her world and acts in it, in and between herself and others. [27]

The jibe at Freud is obvious enough and echoes quite uncannily the ridiculing criticism brought by Sullivan against Freud.

> This dynamism (the self-system) is an explanatory conception; it is not a thing, a region, or what not, such as superegos, egos, ids, and so on. [28]

The ambivalence of Laing's attitude to Freud is quite dramatically confirmed when in a revision of the same paper[29] Laing drops this formulation. The similarity between Sullivan and Laing may be more than accidental since Laing has referred approvingly to Sullivan's approach, presumably because it is interpersonal in its terminology.

When drawn into political discussion and action of the kind represented by the 1967 Dialectics of Liberation Conference, Laing has very little of a political contribution to make, except to apply his categories derived from personal interactions to various large-scale, destructive, societal activities such as the Vietnam war. He attempts to unite these greatly disparate levels by reference to successively higher meta-levels, or more and more inclusive systems. To his credit, he professes little knowledge of the mediations between these levels and systems. [30] It is sometimes suggested that Laing was pushed into the political limelight by those who wished to make a cult figure of him; when there he did what he could with what he had available. This seems to neglect his willingness to put politics into the titles of two books, *The Politics of Experience* and *The Politics of the Family*. It does not matter that the books were obviously rather hastily assembled earlier papers containing very little political analysis, except perhaps that this throws greater doubt on his ability to recognise political analysis, let alone produce it.

In a book written with Phillipson and Lee, *Interpersonal Perception*, Laing attempted to provide a method for detecting discrepancies in interpersonal perceptions, experiences and attributions by looking not only at what each person thinks of the other but at what person-thinks-other-thinks of the relationship. It is a useful step towards introducing an element of reflexivity into such assessments. Even here, however, after saying that there is no necessary isomorphism between personal and other kinds of relationships, he speculates on East–West cold war absurdities and says

> *The West reasons:* 'We do not want to make the first move, but we are not sure whether East does or not' [my italics].[31]

This is deeply confusing. The West does not reason. Social action on the part of a major political bloc emerges from the interaction of politicians, interest groups, administrators, secret service organisations and other social forces which are completely overlooked by person-to-person analogies and bear no relation at all to concepts of original self or true self. In other words, Laing's over-ambitious use of his limited resources leads him into plausible inaccuracies—dare I call them mystifications?

When Laing actually states his revolutionary position it consists of a polarisation of extreme possibilities between which he adopts an intermediate position.

> In our society at certain times, this interlaced set of systems may lend itself to revolutionary change, not at the extreme micro or macro ends; that is not through the individual pirouette of solitary repentance on the one hand or by a seizure of the machinery of state on the other; but by sudden, structural, radical qualitative changes in the intermediate system levels: changes in a factory, a hospital, a school, a university, a set of schools, or a whole area of industry, medicine, education, etc.[32]

To conceive that changes of whatever nature in one relatively small unit of society would change or lead to the change of a whole society seems quite unrealistic, a gross underestimate of the resilience of all the remaining institutional structures and their capacity to bring any particular unit under control. Of course he did not have at this time the example of Chile to show that even where a kind of revolution had been achieved by means of electoral institutions there is sufficient power in other institutions (and more than sufficient when aided by international capital) to overthrow it by force. In fact it is a peculiarly self-centred view that revolution will be brought about when responsible professionals, like himself, demystify professional practice and reveal its violent, oppressive, more sinister purposes. Laing's views on this persist if we may judge by his prickly response to a member of the Movement on a recent American tour, and by these remarks on that occasion

> Two years ago . . . ninety-five per cent of the professors of psychiatry in America regarded me as schizophrenic. Now these are the people charged with the system of mind control in this country.
>
> This is my contribution to the revolution: to learn how to dismantle that bit of state control from within, because you're not going to dismantle it from without. It means you've got to get *to* the minds of the people in control to see if they can be changed.[33]

Suddenly I am reminded of Jourard's fantasy that a change of mind from the president down might revolutionise society or Rogers' fantasy that shadow teams would accompany political delegations, to meet each other on a personal basis, and so remove misconceptions from the interchanges by adding a truly human element to them. Perhaps then the final image is one that Laing himself staged at Hunter College where he was expected to deliver a lecture as part of a celebrity tour of America. Sitting alone in a single spotlight on a silken rug he says

> I am a student of my own nature. I can only tell you how my own life has gone.[34]

6.2 D. G. COOPER

David Cooper's distinctive contributions to British existentialism are that he documented conditions in psychiatric hospitals and tested the limits of change in these institutions at a formative time for the group. Proceeding from the hypothesis that untenable family roles underlie the hospitalisation of schizophrenics, he designed a form of therapy which included families in the assessment and alleviation of these problems. As a further development of the logic of this position he tried to provide a therapeutic unit, Villa 21, to act as a counter-culture against the family, seen as creator of the estranged and alienated condition of schizophrenia, and against the typical hospital treatment which confirms and freezes the condition, thereafter containing it by sedation and/or confinement.

In addition, he has reached farther politically than other members of the group (although whether his reach exceeds his grasp is a question to be considered), has lived very close to the personal and institutionalised alienation of radical anti-psychiatry, and given most extreme expression to the anguish and struggle of the existentialists' position.

He shared with Laing the task of translating and presenting, in *Reason and Violence*, the philosophy of Sartre, and seems by the unreserved tribute in his later book, *The Death of the Family*, to have remained closer to Laing than to Esterson. He is so close that at times it seem impossible to distinguish them; their division of labour in *Reason and Violence* is not clear in spite of separately attributed chapters. What seems significant for later developments is that Cooper presents with great force and engagement Sartre's case study of Genet, constantly referring back to it as though it is for him the exemplar of existentialism. At the same time he is eager to liberate himself from the analytic rationality associated with his training and with the domination of psychiatry by a disease-entity, natural-science model perpetuated by the medical establishment. For this purpose he contrasts and polarises two types of rationality:[35] the analytic and the dialectical. Dialectical rationality has already been described in relation to its strategic importance for the British existentialists.

In *Psychiatry and Anti-Psychiatry* (1967) Cooper reports his Villa 21 experiment together with his application of dialectical rationality to a new family-interpersonal model of schizophrenia. Theoretically the work does not go beyond the Sartrean position contained in *Reason and Violence*; it is, however, more simply, quite elegantly, written with frequent glances toward Oriental philosophies and many telling references to such people as Aries on childhood, Artaud on his own treatment for madness and Parsons on the family. Against Parsons' functionalist treatment of the family, which binds the person into social institutions under the integrative idea of a value consensus (primarily being-for-others), he argues the virtues of deviation (primarily being-for-oneself).

One is even tempted to ponder on the daring hypothesis that in the 'psychotic' families the identified schizophrenic patient member by his psychotic episode is trying to break free of an alienated system and is, therefore, in some sense less 'ill' or at least less alienated than the 'normal' offspring of the 'normal' families.[36]

This tendency to romanticise schizophrenia is reinforced by his reported experience of moving with some surprise and relief from normal (alienated) committee meetings into therapy groups in Villa 21.

> Few of the people in the Villa had any significant organized talent but there was a sort of diffused fragmentary genius, perhaps something more between people than in them.
>
> . . .
>
> I remember thinking once that schizophrenics were the strangled poets of our age.[37]

Like Laing, he is not entirely satisfied with American attempts to develop the double-bind hypothesis, preferring to define more generally the resources of metacommunication—communications about communications—which may be used to demystify interactions in families and groups. He acknowledges that unconscious phantasy is present in these interactions but decides to give it second priority. After presenting a case study quite as illuminating as those contained in *Sanity, Madness and the Family*, he becomes quite strongly aware that the dimension of unconscious phantasy he criticised as missing from Sartre's study of Genet is being neglected.

> . . . the exchanges in family groups call out for psychoanalytic interpretation . . .
>
> We have, however, excluded this mode of studying the interactions in order that we might bring clearly into view the complex interrelation of acts and intentions—the interrelation of decision systems. Without this latter framework of understanding, 'pure' psychoanalytic work may flounder far from the central issue— Eric's progressive choice of himself in the face of the choices the others make about him.[38]

Concentration on choice is useful in itself and a clear realisation of Sartre's approach. Yet it shows what a difficult task the British existentialists had set themselves by criticising Sartre for neglecting unconscious phantasy. Cooper had by this time made insufficient progress to integrate the two approaches; Laing's attempts to unite them were tending to oscillate between perceptive case studies and superficial, global political assertions; Esterson worked quietly on towards his later publication of *The Leaves of Spring*.

Cooper's Villa 21 experiment sought to create an environment in which young schizophrenics could experience confirming relationships, frequent interaction and 'meeting' in a demystifying atmosphere, freedom from the usual occupational diversions of hospital life, freedom to choose what to do and in so doing 'choose themselves' as responsible human beings. Staff were specially selected for their capacity to bear the predictable anguish of this degree of choice, against which their normal protection of a uniform and an institutionally defined role would no longer be available to them. The resulting dynamics were understandably powerful. Hospital organisation was threatened to the core by Villa 21: the rigid role segregation with its professional jealousies, the rituals of cleanliness, the orderly routines, the belief that hospitals can do things for patients. Rumours surrounded the activities, multiplying and amplifying incidents. The strain on staff was tremendous because they were required to cross the borderline between sanity and madness. By the time *Psychiatry and Anti-psychiatry* was published Cooper was speaking in the past tense about his involvement in the experiment. Realising he had gone beyond the limits of institutional change, he left the hospital in the belief that only in the community could such units exist. Through the newly formed Philadelphia Association, houses would be provided to afford asylum and sanctuary in which people—some of them professionally qualified therapists—could help each other, as and when they were able, on the journey through madness, free from the alienating pressures of any hospital. And then, in a book which had argued the irrelevance of establishment demands for quantification and proof, Cooper provides 'an ironic addendum' which shows with the help of chi-squared and Yates' correction the effectiveness of conjoint family and milieu therapy. This indicates a degree of exaggeration in the polarised contrast of analytic with dialectical rationality.

The 1967 Dialectics of Liberation Conference was a high point of Cooper's political activity. As well as taking a leading part, he edited the proceedings,[39] including his own summary speech. As I know from personal experience, the atmosphere was heady, pushing Cooper towards portentous, although still basically Sartrean, rhetoric.

If we re-interiorize our exteriorized power by uniting in our cultural revolution, we shall soon see what is left of them. We shall see men who have dehumanized themselves and would further dehumanize us. We shall see men who are terrorized by the vision of human autonomy and spontaneity.[40]

To which is added an extremely romantic view of schizophrenia.

'Schizophrenia is simply the project—usually an abortive one thanks to social interference—to rediscover a pristine wholeness that really lies outside one's history but which is pointed to by one's history.[41]

The similarity to Laing's view is apparent.

And finally Cooper closed the conference with proposals for action that brought a deadening anticlimax to the whole affair: we should burn our television sets and newspapers and tear up our newspapers in public; we should tear up our ballot papers and establish transnational centres of revolutionary consciousness such as were being formed by Cooper and his colleagues—an Anti-University, an Institute of Phenomenological Studies and houses for schizophrenics, all more relevant to a revolution in professional consciousness than the overthrow of a state.

By the time of writing *The Death of the Family* (1971) Cooper has moved even further in exploration over the borderline between sanity and madness as conventionally defined; over the borderline between bourgeois alienation and existential freedom. Having lived his Sartrean philosophy in an alien hospital institution to the point of being expelled like the schizophrenic victim of a family's irrationality; having carried the burden of speaking the material powerlessness of the Dialectics of Liberation Conference where the gap between actual power and the imagined possibilities of some of the world's greatest visionaries was almost too much to bear, he throws off the reins of caution to rage against the family as perpetrator of the most personal mutilations in exploitative societies. The only social and political analysis is, like Laing's, occasional use of single person or family interactional concepts of pathology in relation to larger units of social organisation, the half-argued justification for this being the tendency for many forms of organisation to reproduce the structure of the family. There is a desperate search for more desirable human qualities, once again into madness and now into childhood.

... every child, before family indoctrination passes a certain point and primary school indoctrination begins, is, germinally at least, an artist, a visionary and a revolutionary.[42]

A further close parallel to Laing, in his concepts of original self and true self.

Proposals for revolution now become very personal in their focus. What is needed, in addition to centres of revolutionary consciousness, is a 'love and madness revolution' in which alienated self structures are taken apart so that we can rebuild ourselves without personal taboos: this will 'revolutionize the whole society'.[43] I fail to see how this is to be reconciled with his earlier suggestion for Villa 21, now repeated, that 'temple prostitutes' should have been used to sexually initiate the young men, so ending the mystification of sexual segregation in hospitals.

The outstanding quality of Cooper's work is therefore not so much lucidity and consistency as personal courage in setting out his experiences and fantasies in all their anguish and contradiction. He has never carried through the promise of adding to it theoretically, but there is a sense in which he is willing to display his own unconscious phantasy in the uncontrolled writing of a 'strangled poet'. Like Genet, whose existential choice he presented so passionately in *Reason and Violence*, he attempts to *choose* madness and alienation, and indeed lived through the kind of spiritual and bodily crisis he sees as death and rebirth.[44] The final irony is that he was helped through by members of his family,[45] yet another sense in which he has moved from writing about the ironies of the present situation into living them.

6.3 A. ESTERSON

Aaron Esterson was co-author with Laing of the book which forms the pivotal empirical study of British existentialism: *Sanity, Madness and the Family* (1964). By 1970, and earlier if publication time is allowed for, he can be found headed in an independent direction in the form of his book, *The Leaves of Spring*. In this he acknowledges his indebtedness to Laing, Cooper and Paul Senft, but takes care to differentiate his own approach by reporting that the material had been intended as his contribution to a second volume in the *Sanity, Madness and the Family* series.

But as my research proceeded it seemed more appropriate that it should be embodied in a work by myself alone.

The reader is strongly urged to pay close attention to the
definitions of various of the terms I have used. Many of these will
be familiar, being currently employed by others, including Dr R. D.
Laing, but not necessarily in the sense in which I am using them.[46]

In setting out his starting point Esterson begins with the
philosopher John Macmurray, acknowledging at the same time the
dialectical method of investigation coming down through Marx,
Hegel and Sartre. I find this reference to Macmurray puzzling. As
was indicated above, Macmurray's approach is compatible neither
with Marx, Hegel, Sartre nor Freud. It will be recalled that his over-
simplified and idealised integration of the personal, the family,
community and God contained elements of contradiction and
mystification which can perhaps best be indicated briefly by comparison with Laing. Just as Laing projects onto higher levels of
social organisation the mutilating processes which he sees in the
family and in the treatment of schizophrenics, so by inversion
Macmurray projects the good *personal* relationships he sees in
family situations onto the higher levels of society and ultimately the
universe. It is not that Esterson actually draws much from
Macmurray, there being only one further reference to his work, so I
assume that in what is by now a familiar pattern in the human
sciences, theorists feel bound to link themselves to some philosophical position no matter how contradictory the source may be
and no matter how little real significance it has for working out their
theory. Two grounds of explanation for this already discovered are
the original monopoly of the subject matter possessed by philosophy,
and the need for scientific guarantors by theorists and groups
staking claims to knowledge and competing for credibility. For
Esterson it may be important to show that he has some resources
available independently of Laing and Cooper's translation of
Sartre: this struggle for a distinctive identity would be perfectly
understandable on the part of a person who has suffered criticism
which might better have been directed at Laing or Cooper and whose
contribution to the pivotal work of British existentialism has tended
to be overshadowed by the more spectacular activities of Laing and
Cooper.

To the extent that Macmurray's philosophical position is tenable,
it would provide Esterson with a parallel to the Sartrean contrast
between praxis and process—the *personal* (open only to philoso-

phical scrutiny) and the *impersonal* (available to scientific analysis). And Esterson no less than his colleagues needs some defence against the likelihood that his alien position within the British medico-psychological field will be made truly alienated by invalidation of his work and himself as unscientific. It will later be seen that the expected attack does indeed come.

Esterson moves on to affirm the Sartrean distinction between praxis and process, and it is soon clear from references and text that Sartre is a major inspiration. The first two concepts he deploys in relation to his data are straight from this source: 'serial group' and 'altered identity'. Changing Sartre's example of a bus-queue to that of a gang of labourers, Esterson sets out an exemplar of 'serial' relationships for the British existentialists. A serial group consists of people brought together for a purpose which resides outside the group (the contract for labour), having as their 'serial object' the task they are to perform (digging a hole) or the common object (bus, for bus-queue) which unites their similar movements. The 'serial object' may be a shared phantasy as in the case of prejudice against the Jew, Red, Black, etc.

Altered or 'alterated' identity is for a person

. . . Whom he feels himself to be in the eyes of the other. [47]

It is then possible to take up the history of the Danzig family, one of the eleven families reported on briefly in *Sanity, Madness and the Family*, detotalising and retotalising the basic group practice until it becomes intelligible in relation to serial objects and altered identities. Without these new concepts and new method of analysis the Danzig family group presents nothing but a confused, inconsistent jumble of contradictory purposes, views and attributions, beyond understanding and beyond controlled intervention.

For example, it is not apparent, until the nature of the relationship between the parents is understood, why the daughter's behaviour is so threatening to the rest of the family that she has eventually to be expelled as 'sick'. The marriage had been prompted and arranged as a common-sense, contractual link within the strongly defined roles laid down by the Jewish faith. Its serial object is 'public opinion' which demands respectability and also defines very tightly what they are to be for each other; and since they are both locked in this alienated condition of being-for-the-other they cannot communicate other than to reinforce the stereotype or confirm the implacable power of public opinion. A structure of such fragility produces little personal satisfaction so that gratification has to be sought obliquely and vicariously through their children, a self-defeating process because these hidden relationships create irregularities which cannot be handled or tolerated by those who must walk the razor edge of respectability.

Within this family of four (a younger child was not included in the study) there are several permutations of possible relationships. Esterson explicates these at both conscious and unconscious levels using 'current psychoanalytic theory' to interpret unconscious phantasy relations between family members. By 'current psychoanalytic theory' Esterson means something slightly different from his existentialist colleagues, Laing and Cooper. He is closer to Freud, though aware of Klein's importance, and his interpretations of unconscious phantasy in the Danzig family are relatively orthodox, based on the organ-modes and Oedipal processes. His knowledge of the Jewish faith and practice brings together in a most satisfying way some deeper aspects of Freud's theory with the praxis and process of a Jewish family. In every sense it is a completion and fulfilment of the promise contained in the earlier brief report in *Sanity, Madness and the Family*.

It will be recalled that Laing and Cooper, when making available Sartre's philosophy, expressed dissatisfaction at Sartre's limited treatment of psychoanalysis. This seemed promising in that some strengths of the British psychoanalytic tradition might then have been integrated with Sartre's transdisciplinary, explicitly political, theories and methods. What has happened is that Esterson has carried through this promise by remaining close to the rich data of the family studies. Esterson, the least spectacular of the British existentialists, is the only one to have produced a clearly stated theory, thoroughly grounded empirically, which incorporates analysis of unconscious phantasy into an investigation of family patterns in families where one member has been diagnosed as schizophrenic. He has placed on the agenda, discussion of a dialectical human science which deals with personal experience and relates it to a social context. Since it opens up a field for investigation and shows by example what can be done, it will be taken forward into the concluding discussion where these few and precious resources for a human science will be assessed.

Before leaving the British existentialists it will be useful to see what kinds of defensive measures are deployed by the intellectual community most likely to be threatened by the serious presentation of a dialectical human science. It has already been suggested that Popper's great influence on the British intellectual scene is such as to make the very word 'dialectical' a shibboleth indicating allegiance to violent, totalitarian, irrational beliefs. In relation to a recent debate he said

> I did not go out of my way to attack Adorno and the 'dialectical' school of Frankfurt (Adorno, Horkheimer, Habermas, *et al.*) which I never regarded as important, unless perhaps from a political point of view; and in 1960 I was not even aware of the political influence of this school. Although today I should not hesitate to describe this influence by such terms as 'irrationalist' and 'intelligence destroying', I could never take their methodology (whatever that may mean) seriously from either an intellectual or scholarly point of view.[48]

The violence of this language and its dependence on splitting the intellectual and scholarly from the political is clear enough. No doubt it reflects Popper's view that '*critical reason is the only alternative to violence so far discovered*'.[49] In a sense it is better to debate violently than to fight. And yet, is this not a slightly irresponsible and unrealistic attitude to the production of ideas? It may be that intellectuals can engage in 'violent' disputation without harming each other but as soon as the knowledge so produced is taken up and used by other social groups with conflicting interests it may be used to justify violence of the other, more brutally effective kind. Popper's demarcationist attitude maintains satisfyingly pure categories but at the cost of creating an out-group of dangerous people, beyond understanding. He too should have learned this particular lesson of history.

Practical deployment of the anti-dialectical viewpoint comes in a review by Eysenck[50] of *The Leaves of Spring*, under the heading 'The Madness of Dialectics', (a 'witty' inversion of Esterson's subtitle, 'A Study in the Dialectics of Madness'). Eysenck begins by telling a story about his clash with Cooper in public debate. Cooper did not, as threatened, 'shout slogans to the sound of a violin', but introduced an American draft-dodger and conducted a noisy, political debate around his experiences, declining to listen to Eysenck. One does not need to approve of this treatment of Eysenck to see that he is using the story to ridicule Esterson whose views and personal style are clearly distinct from those of Cooper. Having 'set up' Esterson in this way, the rest of the review repeats similar distancing strategies: for example, Esterson's *footnote* references to the Tibetan Buddhist tradition and to the Kabbalist Tree of life, which accompany an otherwise clear discussion of self-consciousness, are referred to as passages beyond his comprehension. The spirit of the review is contained in the judgement that it is a confused mixture of confused Sartrean and Hegelian sources.

> ... it clearly bears little relation to orthodox scientific or medical-psychiatric writings or practice, but delights in word-spinning and freedom from all restrictions of logic and fact.[51]

It seems strange that a work of so little relevance and so little substance needs review, but then we have seen just how important such boundary maintenance activities as parody, stereotyping and refusal to understand are as processes in the production of knowledge. Whatever psychological and sociological understanding of these processes can be gained will be worth having since it may provide just a little alternative to the kind of 'directed ignorance' which limits human enquiry.

REFERENCES

1 A. Wilden. *System and Structure*, Tavistock, London (1972), p. xix
2 T. B. Bottomore. *Sociology*, Allen & Unwin, London (1962), p. 60 (2nd edn, 1971)
3 H. F. Searles. The effort to drive the other person crazy—an element in the aetiology and psychotherapy of schizophrenia, *Br. J. Med. Psychol* **32**, (1959), 1
4 R. I. Evans. *R. D. Laing: The Man and His Ideas*, Dutton, New York (1976), p. 27
5 K. Marx. *Economic and Philosophical Manuscripts of 1844* (transl. M. Milligan), Lawrence & Wishart, London (1961)
6 R. D. Laing and D. Cooper. *Reason and Violence*, Tavistock, London (1964), p. 22
7 ibid., p. 22
8 K. Popper. *The Poverty of Historicism*, Routledge, London (1957), p. 135

9 R. D. Laing and D. Cooper. *Reason and Violence*, Tavistock, London (1964), p. 15
10 ibid., p. 98
11 G. Cohen. Beliefs and roles, *Proc. Aristotelian Soc.*, **67** (1966–7)
12 W. J. H. Sprott. *Sociology at the Seven Dials*, Athlone Press, London (1962), p. 5
13 R. D. Laing and D. Cooper. *Reason and Violence*, Tavistock, London (1964), p. 52
14 R. I. Evans. *R. D. Laing: The Man and His Ideas*, Dutton, New York (1976), p. 5
15 ibid., p. 3
16 R. D. Laing. *The Divided Self*, Penguin, Harmondsworth, Middx (1965), p. 79 (Tavistock, London, 1960)
17 ibid., p. 85
18 ibid., p. 161
19 ibid., p. 95
20 ibid., pp. 84 and 47
21 R. D. Laing. *The Politics of Experience and the Bird of Paradise*, Penguin, Harmondsworth, Middx (1967), p. 12
22 R. D. Laing. *The Divided Self*, Penguin, Harmondsworth, Middx (1965), p. 202 (Tavistock, London, 1960)
23 ibid., p. 158
24 H. Segal. *Introduction to the Work of Melanie Klein*, Hogarth, London (1973), p. 24
25 R. D. Laing. *The Politics of the Family*, Penguin, Harmondsworth, Middx (1976), p. 92 (Tavistock, London, 1971)
26 R. D. Laing. Individual and family structure. In *The Predicament of the Family* (ed. P. Lomas), Hogarth, London (1967)
27 R. D. Laing. ibid., p. 123
28 H. S. Sullivan. *Interpersonal Psychiatry*, Tavistock, London (1955), p. 167
29 R. D. Laing. *The Politics of the Family*, Penguin, Harmondsworth, (1976) (Tavistock, London, 1971)
30 R. D. Laing. The obvious. In *The Dialectics of Liberation*, (ed. D. Cooper), Penguin, Harmondsworth, Middx (1968), p. 16
31 R. D. Laing, H. Phillipson and A. R. Lee. *Interpersonal Perception*, Tavistock, London (1966), p. 138
32 R. D. Laing. The obvious. In *The Dialectics of Liberation* (ed. D. Cooper), Penguin, Harmondsworth, Middx (1968)

33 R. I. Evans. *R. D. Laing: The Man and His Ideas*, Dutton, New York (1976), p. lxvi
34 ibid., p. lxxv
35 D. Cooper. Two types of rationality, *New Left Review*, **29**, Jan.–Feb. (1965), 62–8
36 D. Cooper. *Psychiatry and Anti-psychiatry*, Tavistock (1967), p. 37
37 ibid., p. 109
38 ibid., p. 72
39 D. Cooper (ed.). *The Dialectics of Liberation*, Penguin, Harmondsworth, Middx (1968)
40 ibid., p. 198
41 ibid., p. 201
42 D. Cooper. *The Death of the Family*, Penguin, Harmondsworth, Middx (1971), p. 27
43 ibid., p. 107
44 ibid., p. 157
45 ibid., p. 157
46 A. Esterson. *The Leaves of Spring*, Penguin, Harmondsworth, Middx (1972), p. ix (Tavistock, London, 1970)
47 ibid., p. 39
48 K. Popper. In *The Positivist Dispute in German Sociology* (eds T. W. Adorno, H. Albert, R. Dahrendorf, J. Habermas, H. Pilot and K. R. Popper), Heinemann (1976), p. 289
49 ibid., p. 292
50 H. J. Eysenck. The madness of dialectics, *New Society*, 17 Dec. (1970)
51 ibid.

7
British Psychoanalysis

I cannot pretend to give anything like a comprehensive account of British psychoanalysis in this section: partly it is a matter of limitations on space in a study which must cover a lot of ground in order to make some basic comparisons; partly it is lack of experience and of that deeper sensitivity to subject matter which comes with committed practice in a discipline. Once again I take a risk and seek the central theme which informs the work and thus allows it to be brought into relation with other disciplines in a fresh way.

The central theme of British psychoanalysis is 'object relations theory'. This distinctive development of Freud's ideas moves through Klein's work (based firmly on instincts) to the concepts of object relations (centred on the ego) and consequently to a consideration of self as the human subject affected by and possibly able to transcend the object relations processes and their consequences. Some difficulties which arise are that self is conceived as possessing *pure, original, whole, real* or *true* states which offer criteria of success in therapy. These special potentialities of the self are sometimes idealised, used as mystifications and pseudo-explanations, or as the psychoanalytic formulation of what are to an important degree social variables, giving rise to the hypothesis that there are psychodynamic and sociodynamic processes at work even in this relatively 'self-conscious' area of knowledge production.

Guntrip's account of the development of object relations theory will be used to trace its central theme, although I hasten to add that this carries no strong implications as to its objectivity. He integrates its various strands to his own purpose, providing yet another example of the reworking of knowledge in process of transmission. It is, however, interesting to see that his approach presupposes a sociology of knowledge.

All theories, especially those about human nature, are conditioned by the cultural era, the prevailing intellectual climate, and the dominant ideas of the time in which they are developed.[1]

He might have said *time and place*, but basically this adoption of a sociology of knowledge should by now bring no surprise since it has been shown that self and role theories are deeply enmeshed in psychological and social processes, so that even when theorists seek to limit the scope of their claims they are still engaged in negotiating a place for themselves and their work within a social context. One of the most powerful ways of moving beyond another theory is to show by explicit criticism why it took on its particular form, an activity which has been shown by reference to a range of personality theorists to be clearly distinguishable from attitudinal resistance to a threatening formulation.

Guntrip is a refreshingly bold writer who states his aims with great feeling and puts together disparate contributions with firm conviction.

> Psychoanalysis has, now I believe, uncovered the deepest and most awe-inspiring problem from which human beings can suffer; the secret core of total schizoid isolation. [2]

He sets out to demonstrate this with the clearest possible acknowledgement to Freud. However, Freud failed to integrate the two strands in his thought: one an emphasis on instinctive physiological phenomena, the second a concern for ego and personal self. But then Freud was a child of his scientific time, working with a determinist, reductionist model into which he forced the intuitive and imaginative insights of his therapeutic practice and investigation. Such structural accounts are inherently dualistic.

> The only escape from a dualism of radically opposed structures is to banish the term 'id', and reserve 'ego' to denote the whole basically unitary psyche with its innate potential for developing into a true self, a whole person, using his psychosomatic energies for self-expression and self-realization in interpersonal relationships. [3]

It seems a rather clumsy, little argued, integration of his own extreme polarisation of the subject matter to recommend that one pole should be banished and the other read in a preferred way, although this style of argument is familiar enough. Thus it seems that Guntrip's self-concept with its optimistically integrative stance is likely to produce an account which moves in the same direction as many other American personality theorists. Later some explanation of this characteristic world view will be sought, but for the moment let Guntrip lead the way through object relations theory.

Melanie Klein's work is valued because although she bases the whole of her metapsychology on Freud's death instinct, retaining all the Freudian terminology and models, it does show a development, namely, the recognition of an inner fantasy life in very young children based upon the relations between objects created by complementary processes of projection and introjection. For example, the child's relation to itself compels awareness of a death instinct which may destroy it. The only relief is to project this feeling out onto an external object—inevitably at this dependent primitive stage onto the breast or source of food. And then a way of dealing with the threatening object so created is to take it back, by identification, into the ego where it can be to some extent controlled.

For Guntrip a development of very great importance is Klein's conceptualisation of 'positions' the growing child must pass through: the paranoid–schizoid position in which the child is persecuted by its objects, and the depressive position which follows from the child's discovery that it can hurt the ones it loves. He prefers to separate out the paranoid and the schizoid, conjoined in Klein's concept, into separate positions thus making three in all, but the most important thing is that Freud's developmental stages give way in this theory to positions characterised by typical relations to objects.

Guntrip regrets Klein's acceptance of Freud's 'biological mysticism', seeing it as 'more like a revealed religious belief than a scientific theory'.[4] The contradiction is that he does not see his own view of the unitary personal self in a similar critical light even though, as was indicated earlier, one of his philosophical sources, Macmurray, derives 'the personal' from God. As Masud Khan says

> There is a distinct danger of romanticization of a pure self-system. Guntrip . . . betrays this tendency very clearly when he says the aim of psychotherapy is to sponsor 'an original unique person with creative capacities to produce the unexpected'.[5]

I conclude that Guntrip's sociology of knowledge works only in one direction: he shows how others are limited by their time and place but fails to complete the circle of reflexivity that would entail radical self-criticism. This stance is of some importance to Guntrip providing the basis for his rejection of the death instinct, that element of

Freud's theory which excites the greatest resistance for followers and critics alike. Of Klein he says

> Bad object experience is overwhelmingly primary for Klein who has then to say that the baby urgently needs to internalize a good breast to counteract it. I cannot see how, on Klein's assumptions, a baby can ever experience a really good breast at all. [6]

I cannot see on the basis of any argument presented by Guntrip why the really good breast should take precedence over the bad breast. To argue in terms of the 'really good' in the context of the infant's many-faceted and at least partly phantasised world seems beside the point. At most I can respect his attitudinal preference for a psycho-dynamic theory without a death instinct. As I see it there is no more real a goodness than there is a badness, either in the world of the child or in a therapeutic relationship: is not learning the nature of this ambivalence a more important step in therapy than the idea of 'really good' experience?

Having laid the foundation of object relations theory, Guntrip seeks to widen its theoretical scope by drawing on the contributions of Erikson and Fairbairn. Erikson overestimated the extent to which Freud left behind his physiobiological conceptions, but does at least move towards a more holistic concept of the person. Somatic, inter-personal and social levels are distinguishable, all as parts of the integrated whole that is drawn together by the ego. Freud's organ-modes give way to psychogenetic stages, each with a typical way of relating to objects, enabling us

> . . . to think in terms of a developing psyche as the vital stimulating factor evolving a body to meet its needs. [7]

Guntrip regrets that Erikson retains the id in his theory because this creates a Centaur model in which the life of the object-relating ego is tied to a primitive foundation. Such dualism does not accord with Guntrip's completely unitary model. He therefore turns 'with relief' to Fairbairn, 'who clearly saw this problem of making theory consistent. He totally rejected the id concept. [8] Fairbairn was able to see his way through to the new position because, unlike Freud, he had the benefit of modern scientific conceptions of structure and energy in the physical world.

> The inert and indivisible particles or atoms, of which the physical universe was formerly thought to be composed, are now known to

be structures of the greatest complexity embodying almost incredible quantities of energy—energy in the absence of which the structures themselves would be unintelligible, but which is equally difficult to explain in the absence of the structures.[9]

The new metaphor which does not split energy and structure allows Fairbairn to concentrate on the formulation of dynamic ego structures.

> The pristine personality of the child consists of a unitary dynamic ego.[10]

Thereafter the unity is split by experience of the 'exciting object' and the 'rejecting object'. These two objects give rise to the formation of the 'libidinal ego' and the 'anti-libidinal ego' respectively. The 'central ego is what remains of the internalised parents after the libidinal and anti-libidinal egos have been separated off. Thus with a complex set of five egos and objects over all, the theory is capable of dealing with a very wide range of psychological and psychopathological phenomena.

Having cleared away the specifically Freudian biological and instinctual impediments to the emergence of a theory of dynamically structured object relations, Guntrip explores the modern and partly biological ego theories of Hartmann and Jacobson. Hartmann is so limited by his concern for the biologically adaptive qualities of the ego that he can be set aside. Jacobson retains some elements of biologically given aggression in her theory but also sees some drives arising out of ego reactions to objects. Guntrip would take this even further and says that in twenty-five years he has not seen a single case where aggression could not be accounted for in relation to defensive reactions of some kind. He therefore goes all the way and posits

> . . . one basic psychophysiological life-drive toward the object world, which generates fear and aggression when thwarted.[11]

Alternatives to this are, as he repeats frequently, 'purely speculative'. He is reinforced in this by the work of Winnicott, which shows out of a lifetime of therapeutic practice with children and adults the importance of 'basic ego relatedness', a condition which depends on 'good-enough mothering'; the kind of relationship which draws the true self out of its potentially schizoid isolation and provides a foundation for identity.

... the identity problem, is the biggest single issue that can be raised about human existence.[12]

There are some interesting themes in this all too brief and partial account of the development of British psychoanalysis. In Guntrip's 'integration' of the various theoretical positions there seems to be the possibility of a new split occurring. Not this time into the Centaur model of a human ego attached to a primitive base (Erikson) but of a dynamic structure of object relations, modelled on energy and structure in the physical world, and a true self emerging into secure identity. Masud Khan, who criticised Guntrip for idealising the self-system still detects two distinct kinds of activity in therapy.

One type of relating is covered by interpretative work, which helps the patient to gain insight into his internal conflicts and thus resolve them. The other sort of relating, which is harder to define, is more in the nature of providing coverage of the patient's self-experience in the clinical situation.[13]

A further point is that there is a tendency in object relations theory to concentrate on the basic forms of relationships to objects without exploring the social context within which many qualities of the objects are created. This could be regarded as nothing more than rigorous specialisation which usefully enables scientists to focus on one kind of phenomenon at a time, except that it goes along with a tendency to extend inferences far beyond the phenomena under investigation. For example, Fairbairn's early discussion of communism,[14] and more importantly his view that

... if modern psychoanalytical theory is capable of ameliorative clinical application in the case of psychological disorders, it is also capable of ameliorative clinical application in the case of sociological disorders which are only psychological disorders writ large.[15]

In short, what psychoanalysis still needs to develop is a sense of the social context of its own theory and practice, for if it has anything to offer the wider society rather than the relatively prosperous middle classes who presently form its clientele it must cease to take society as given and notice how very much the social structure sends in—sometimes literally forces in—to ego structures.

REFERENCES

1 H. J. S. Guntrip. *Psychoanalytic Theory, Therapy and the Self,* Hogarth, London (1971), p. 10
2 ibid., p. 195
3 ibid., p. 41
4 ibid., p. 58
5 M. M. R. Khan. *The Privacy of the Self,* Hogarth, London (1974), p 304
6 H. J. S. Guntrip. *Psychoanalytic Theory, Therapy and the Self,* Hogarth, London (1971), p. 67
7 ibid., p. 87
8 ibid., p. 91
9 W. R. D. Fairbairn. *Psychoanalytic Studies of the Personality,* Routledge, London (1952), p. 127
10 W. R. D. Fairbairn. Quoted in H. J. S. Guntrip, *Psychoanalytic Theory, Therapy and the Self,* Hogarth, London (1971), p. 92
11 H. J. S. Guntrip. op. cit., p. 133
12 ibid., p. 119
13 M. M. R. Khan. *The Privacy of the Self,* Hogarth, London (1974), p. 305
14 W. R. D. Fairbairn. *Psychoanalytic Studies of the Personality,* Routledge, London (1952), p. 233
15 ibid., p. 255

8
Reading and Revisionism

It has been shown that the field of personality theories is particularly vulnerable to distorted perception and tendentious theorising because of the inescapably dynamic relationship between theorists' self-structures and the theories they are trying to produce. Since some aspects of self-structure come in from a social context of which social roles are an integral part, it has further been possible to show that theories often take some of their form from the roles made available by social contexts: here it is the effect of role exigencies on role theories which is most dynamic and reflexive. Critical analysis using all the resources and techniques available to the human sciences for reading deeper levels of personal and social process and praxis (textual criticism, psychoanalytic interpretation and social criticism) has shown up flaws and weaknesses, as well as a few strengths, in these bodies of knowledge, laying a sounder, more sceptical, foundation for future work.

Although there can be no pretence that all areas of the human sciences have been fairly represented and that the emergent patterns have general or exclusive validity it is useful to see certain consistencies in relation to social and psychological phenomena, which help to explain forms of knowledge and the delineation of specialities within sociology and psychology, as well as the relation between the disciplines and the condition of areas common to the two disciplines now occupied by the curiously split discipline of social psychology.

The most consistent patterns of reaction have appeared in relation to Freud, Marx, Husserl and behaviourism: 'there has been an immense attempt to rework Freud into a more personally and socially acceptable form; there has been an equally strenuous effort to ignore or minimise class conflict and the many consequences that Marx held to follow from it; there has been a serious failure of understanding in relation to phenomenology and existentialism including ignorance of its roots in Husserl, adoption of its most superficial aspects, and rejection of it in parodied versions; behaviourism has been criticised for pretensions it never had. Reactions of this kind should, however, cause little surprise when it is appreciated that each of these theories or programmes is a threat to groups of people identified with alternative viewpoints. Freud insists on bringing to the forefront an aspect of human relationships normally repressed both in society and in the sciences.[1] Marx threatened to reveal the oppressive nature of social relationships in capitalist society and undermine knowledge in almost every field by unmasking ideologies. Husserl offered a view of human science which would make redundant the more positivistic kinds of social and behavioural sciences. Behaviourism, working in the opposite direction to Husserl, sought to limit the subject matter of the human sciences by rejecting experiential phenomena in favour of more publicly observable behaviours.

Does this mean that behind all the smokescreen of rejection and modification strategies there is a true Freud, a true Marx, a true Husserl and even a true behaviourism to which we can now turn for enlightenment? In one sense, yes, because the misreading and rejection of sources carried on by the people whose work has been examined is usually so crude that in some cases it is doubtful whether they have consulted the original works; in other cases it is clear that any reading has been extremely selective. Any stronger sense in which the sources might be called true is ruled out by the fact that anyway they are not fully compatible and cannot all be true. What can be distinguished is rejection or modification on the basis of mistakes, misreadings or an unfavourable attitude and the presentation of arguments against a correctly seen position. Marcuse's term 'revisionism' might be used for the former activity although it is bound to cause some difficulty in relatively liberal contexts where it tends to be confused with the desirable freedom to reinterpret earlier viewpoints and is confused with a doctrinaire attitude. But whatever term is finally used it is possible to distinguish, relatively, between irrational socially determined reactions to earlier work and the attempt to develop and explore alternatives to a position properly comprehended. Where proper comprehension turns on finer points of interpretation than those dealt with above it will be less easy to draw a boundary but the existence of finer points will make it less essential for a line to be drawn since it is likely that 'finer points' presuppose more rational appraisal and debate.

So the objective is not to reassert a dogmatic Marx, Freud or Husserl but to reject false alternatives which bar the way to critical appraisal of the resources of the human sciences and fill the literature with alienated knowledge.

There is one particular kind of return to the sources of theory which must be noticed. This consists of a quite conscious attempt to read the sources through the lenses of a newer theory, the clearest relevant examples being Louis Althusser in relation to Marx and Jacques Lacan in relation to Freud. Both take some of their inspiration from 'structuralism' which provides a method for the crystallisation of texts—verbal or written, myth or science—into relatively few oppositionally defined elements which in combination order their meaning. This is not to overlook Althusser's unwillingness to be assimilated to the structuralist *ideology* and it will become clear how he achieves a separate identity. Another form of interpretation, related to structuralism but drawing on information theory, exists in the work of Anthony Wilden[2] who brings back into the debate Gregory Bateson's ecological theory of mind, a development of ideas that gave rise to the double-bind hypothesis, once used by the British existentialists. These contributions will now be reviewed, beginning with Althusser.

8.1 L. ALTHUSSER

The central theme of Louis Althusser's work is a proposal that we should read *Capital* by Karl Marx, and should study Lenin both as a principal source of information on the history of class struggle in which he was deeply involved, and as a philosopher who has helped to bring out distinctions of the most fundamental kind between ideology, science and philosophy. His relevance for the present study is then clear: to the extent that the bodies of knowledge criticised herein are *ideologies*, that there is a possibility of criticising them from or towards a more *scientific* standpoint, and that *philosophical* methods of analysis have been employed, all three terms of his theory come into consideration.

But first what is it to 'read' the great originators of theories in the human sciences? Certainly a problem, as I suggested at the outset, and a problem which may be roughly described in terms of levels and depth. Althusser's aim is to read Marx in the way that Marx read his predecessors in clasical economics

> . . . a reading which might well be called 'symptomatic' (symptomale) in so far as it divulges the undivulged event in the text it

reads, and in the same movement relates it to a *different text*, present as a necessary absence in the first.[3]

Using this particular kind of sensitivity both to texts and contexts Althusser claims to have detected in the work of Marx an epistemological break[4] or a period during which Marx gradually works himself free from the language, concepts and limitations of the philosophers, without whom he could not have begun but who must be shaken off if Marx is to open up to scientific study the 'Continent of History'. The early works of Marx are 'humanist' in their concern for overcoming the alienation of man, the species-being. Gradually, and partly as a result of his revolutionary practice, Marx moves towards the writing of his *Capital*, a work which contains some remnants of the early formulations but has quite distinctively gone over to a view so radically different that it founds a new science. From humanism, an *ideological* conception, he passes to a *science* of history, of which the *philosophy* is dialectical materialism. An implication of this view is that when successors attempt to rescue this humanistic aspect of Marx's theory, be they revolutionaries, neo-Freudian theorists, sociologists or whatever, they are trying no less than to destroy the singular achievement of a man whose importance is to be judged by the fact that very few similar breakthroughs are available in our history: mathematics (by the Greeks) and physics (by Galileo), the unconscious (by Freud). Being steeped in the ideologies of their time these revisionists may not consciously with to bring about a regression in knowledge, but that is the effect of their action.

Science is a rigorous system of concepts adequate to the object of study: ideologies are linked to more practical purposes, in this case the exclusion of Marx's radically subversive—both for ideologically distorted knowledges and for social relations—theory of historical materialism. Since most existing human sciences either remain studiously ignorant of this one possible basis for scientific work, or admit only a 'humanised' and therefore disabled Marx, they are all ideologically distorted.

Needless to say there have been many critical responses to Althusser who seems on the one hand willing to alter Marx's theory and on the other to be ruling out humanist and existentialist readings. Paradoxically, it is the humanists and existentialists, now quite widespread in their influence, who can make the most demonstrable

claim to have seen more *of* Marx's work with the successive discoveries of his early and middle period writings, the *Economic and
Philosophical Manuscripts* in the nineteen-thirties and *The Grundrisse*
(English translation 1971). Against them Althusser could argue that
he has seen so much more *in* the mature works that the early works
take their place not as worthless *juvenilia* of the Stalinist evaluation,
but as early steps in a long theoretical development: a beginning with
concepts which come to Marx as little more than rough direction
indicators which will take him into the right problem area, needing
then to be reworked into a rigorous system which, without casting
them off, gives them new meaning. Thus it is not the presence or
absence of particular words such as 'alienation' in late texts that
decides the question of continuity in Marx's thought but the precise
meaning taken on by concepts ordered according to a new, more
rigorous, scientific theory. What Althusser seems to be arguing in
relation to Marx is, according to Kuhn the philosopher of science,
one possible line of development in knowledge. Objects normally
grouped together in similarity sets may change their relationships
following a revolution in science.

> Think of the sun, moon, Mars and Earth before and after
> Copernicus; of free fall, pendular and planetary motion before and
> after Galileo; or of salts, alloys, and a sulphur–iron filing mix
> before and after Dalton. Since most objects within even the
> altered sets continue to be grouped together, the names of the sets
> are preserved. Nevertheless, the transfer of a subset is ordinarily
> part of a critical change in the network of interrelations among
> them. Transferring the metals from the set of compounds to the
> set of elements played an essential role in the emergence of a new
> theory of combustion, of acidity, and of physical and chemical
> combination. In short order those changes had spread through
> all of chemistry. Not surprisingly, therefore, when two men
> whose discourse had previously proceeded with apparently full
> understanding may suddenly find themselves responding to the
> same stimulus with incompatible descriptions and generalizations.[5]

In the light of the above considerations I find it difficult to accept
McLellan's exaggeration of Althusser's thesis and sharp dismissal
of its relevance.

  ... Althusser's search for a timeless rationality reminiscent of
Comte (for whom Marx himself had no time) involves the banish-

ment of both history and philosophy. When applied to Marx this involves cutting his work into two separate conceptual structures with the dividing point around 1845.[6]

McLellan sees *The Grundrisse* (which he translated) as helping to establish that there are humanist and Hegelian elements in the later Marx as well as confirming that his work is incomplete. But Althusser has never denied the presence of such elements.

In the grip of a Hegelian conception of science (for Hegel, all science is philosophical and therefore every true science *has to found its own beginnings*), Marx then thought that the principle that 'every beginning is difficult . . . holds of all sciences'. In fact, Volume One, Part I, follows a method of presentation whose difficultly largely derives from this Hegelian prejudice.[7]

The point is that in a new context these old elements play a different role, perhaps of such complexity that even when Marx himself thought he was depending on Hegel he was actually surpassing him.[8]

It is the conceptual sophistication of Althusser (admitted by McLellan) that makes him interesting. Most directly for purposes of this study the interest lies in his challenge to its presuppositions, for it began as a search for a satisfactory self theory and, if Althusser is followed, the person or individual who formed its naive starting point seems about to disappear in favour of a social process, much in the way that the early Marx's species-being has been overtaken by the economic forces of capitalist society. What then is the core of Althusser's assertions on the relation between society and the person?

Althusser seeks to establish that the philosophical ideas Marx used in order to locate, and relate, economic phenomena are ideologically distorted; they can therefore be removed to leave a space in which a more scientific conception may be arrived at. A more scientific conception will construct the concept of the relevant object (not repeating the philosophical mistake of searching for its essence— idealism, or assuming that it is given—empiricism). Rather than a planar space we must conceive

. . . a complex and deep space, itself inscribed in another complex and deep space.[9]

But then even this metaphor breaks down and the nature of this kind of *complexity* must be conceived as

. . . the (global) *structure* of the mode of production, in so far as it determines the (regional) *structure* which constitutes as economic objects and determines the phenomena of this defined region, located in a defined site in the structure of the whole.[10]

Two consequences are that we can only measure phenomena of which the concept has been constructed, and that causal relations so discovered will involve not linear causality but the causality of determination by a structure.

So far we have been dealing with matters which are possibly familiar under other descriptions within existing disciplines. For example, sociologists have been forced to consider the inadequacies of idealism by the failure of formalism[11] and the shortcomings of empiricism by the lack of integration between empiricist data collection and the body of sociological theory.[12] This has led to a reassessment of causality and differentiation of certain forms of causality.[13] Determination by a structure has arisen in relation to Chomsky's linguistics, and anthropologists have attempted to conceptualise the structure of a society in terms of inclusiveness and the dominance of certain phenomena.[14] So far then we have been given a sophisticated concept of the social structure of a society.

Within the structure can be distinguished four types of production: economic, political, ideological and theoretical. The economic is determinate 'in the last instance'. However, time is not the unitary inflexible time of the naive empiricist historian or the historicist: the different regions may move at different rates of development so that it is possible to speak of 'backwardness', 'underdevelopment' and similar time-embedded situations. Presumably this is intended, like the concept of structure, to create what might be called a 'space in time' within which complex relationships may work themselves through. An extremely crude counterpart might be the sociological concept of 'culture-lag'.[15]

The next step is most revolutionary since it seeks to show how in the region of theory Marx achieved his epistemological break with earlier ideological forms of explanation, thus opening up the science of history. It will be necessary to outline the multiple tasks undertaken by Althusser in this crucial step which creates and exemplifies his key term—theoretical practice. He has before him the immense written output of Marx, possibly incomplete but nevertheless a substantial record of a life's intellectual endeavour. To this work he brings a philosopher's 'guilty' reading;[16] guilty in that it knows much of what has gone before Marx as philosophy and also what has transpired since, especially what Lenin managed to make of Marx in both thought and social action. Using Lenin's reading of Marx and also Lenin's interpretation of Marx's relationship to Kant and Hegel, Althusser believes he has recognised the point at which the relationship between a group of disciplines becomes transparent—philosophy, historical materialism and dialectical materialism.

It appears to Althusser that philosophy has no history, merely the repetition in various guises of the polarisation—materialism versus idealism; thus accounted for, philosophy cannot be regarded as the core of Marx's work, although it comes in as one element to be dealt with. Historical materialism is the science that Marx created by constructing (through his reading and critique of the classical economists) the concept of its object, crucially labour *power* and surplus value, giving rise in Althusser's interpretation to the extremely complex and sophisticated conceptions of socioeconomic structure ('a structure in dominance') and of historical time. Remembering that the structure holds four regions—the economic, the political, the ideological and the theoretical—we can see that Althusser is working in the *theoretical* region to explicate Marx's achievement. Dialectical materialism is the philosophy which gives expression to historical materialism, but it was not Marx who gave it such expression. Lenin did this, and in doing so brought to realisation *dialectical materialism*, the most useful approach to constructing the concept of the object of socioeconomic processes. This shows that economically determined social structures are best conceived as *a process without a subject.*

The exact point at which Althusser detects this dramatic change is in Lenin's reading of Hegel, recorded in his notebooks: from a study of these it is possible to see that Lenin followed Hegel's criticism of Kant to reject Kant's subjectivism. However, Lenin's criticism took its stand on scientific objectivity rather than on Hegel's criterion of truth represented by the Absolute Idea. And yet, whilst rejecting Hegel's Absolute Idea by means of a materialist and proletarian reading of it, Lenin was able to gather from it the dialectical method.

The sum total, the last word and essence of Hegel's logic is *the dialectical method*—this is extremely noteworthy. And one thing more: in this *most idealistic* of Hegel's works there is the least idealism and the most materialism. 'Contradictory', but a fact.[17]

Thus Althusser sees in Lenin's ability to bring together philosophical criticism and sensitivity to proletarian experience the achievement of a particular understanding which creates

> ... the Marxist–Leninist concept of the materialist dialectic, of the absoluteness of movement, of the absolute process of the reality of the method: to be precise, the concept of the fundamental scientific validity of the concept of a *process without a subject*, as it is to be found in Capital, and elsewhere, too, in Freud, for example.[18]

We can appreciate now the criticisms which McLellan and others bring against this 'timeless rationality'. Nevertheless, another central theme has emerged. Althusser's attempt to recover Marx from a hundred years of misreading suggests the possibility that all existing concepts of personality, self and role may be not only ideologically distorted but also misconceived in a more fundamental way: they may be redundant, or their understanding may depend on a transformation of the order contained in the idea of an epistemological break; their scientific usefulness may not yet have been achieved. We must hold this radical thesis in abeyance, accepting Althusser's indication that Lacan's reading of Freud has important relevance, and turn now to Lacan's attempt to recover Freud from those who have buried him.

8.2 J. LACAN

The problem of reading now becomes very complex. I am dependent on Anthony Wilden for his translation of the work of Lacan and for his extensive commentary on Lacan's 'dense and allusive' text. But Lacan's work in turn consists of a very particular reading of Freud, a reading which is peculiarly French in that it rests on the complex of disciplines and personal influences which surround Lacan's development and which define more fully than heretofore the intellectual climate of this part of Europe. According to Wilden, comprehension of Lacan's text depends on

> ... a more than usual intimacy with the texts of Freud ... upon an acquaintance with Hegel and his French commentators, upon a familiarity with the early Heidegger and the early Sartre, and upon a knowledge of the concepts of structural linguistics (Saussure, Jakobson) and structural anthropology (Mauss, Levi-Strauss).[19]

Wilden displays, in his study of Lacan, all the above attributes together with such a fine ability for 'patient communication'[20] with the subject matter that dependence on his reading is no substantial hazard, for his method is to make transparent his own response and then further clarify the situation by bold and scholarly cross-reference. Even as he struggles for a very deep understanding of Lacan he becomes aware of further possibilities for developing a new position made available by the interaction of psychology with communications theory in America.[21] He will later be seen to move firmly in this direction, but for the moment let his choice of a quotation to acknowledge a great debt to Lacan refer back to Althusser, who wrote

> It is to the intransigent, lucid, and for many years solitary, theoretical efforts of Jacques Lacan that we owe today the result which has drastically modified our *reading* of Freud. At a time when what Lacan has given us which is radically new is beginning to pass into the public domain, where anyone may make use of and draw advantage from it in his own way, I must insist on recognizing our debt to an exemplary lesson in reading, which in some of its effects, as will be seen, goes far beyond its original object.[22]

The source is, of course, Althusser's *Reading 'Capital'* where he makes use of concepts provided by Lacan's reading of Freud. These concepts will provide a useful point of entry to the work of Lacan.

Althusser acknowledges that Lacan enables him to see Freud's real achievement, and as the detail of this achievement is set out there appears a striking parallel with Marx. Freud founded a new science. Like all such epistemological breaks the central problem is to develop the concept of the object of the science, in Freud's case the unconscious. As with any science worth the name, there is a practice connected rigorously to a theory and since no science begins in pristine innocence (although George Kelly may have wished it so[23]) it is possible to see Freud pass from an ideological stage in which he struggled with inherited, psychobiological concepts, to a mature stage in which the relation of concept to object is more adequate. What Lacan recovers then is Freud's *science* and it is necessary to speak of recovery because, like Marx, he has suffered rejection and vilification, followed by voracious acceptance in ideologically reworked form. The fate of psychoanalysis has been to suffer dissection into pieces that fit easily into the framework of other disciplines—psychology, bioneurology, anthropology, sociology and philosophy. The most serious injury is that of separating off the practice of psychoanalysis to institutionalise it as one technique of therapy among others. Now that the case studies of personality theorists presented earlier are available, this history of reactions to Freud takes on substance and seems all too familiar.

Althusser found the concept of 'overdetermination' very useful at a certain point in his attempt to understand how Marx moved from an Hegelian starting point toward a mature theory. Reflecting upon the vulgar statement that Marx inverted Hegel's idealism to establish the materialist theory, he suggests that it was no simple inversion. The Hegelian principle of determination by consciousness of self gives way to a different relationship.

> . . . on the one hand *determination in the last instance by the* (*economic*) *mode of production*; on the other, *the relative autonomy of the superstructures and their specific effectivity.*[24]

This new concept of structure (structure in dominance) is adequate to the object in that it leaves room for a complex set of determinations—it is overdetermined. More concretely, the contradictions of a capitalist society are carried in its political structure, its dominant ideologies, its history, traditions, the world context, and so on, all operating simultaneously and with some limited degree of autonomy.

The source of this in Lacan can be discovered by considering the relation between three orders of existence—the Symbolic, the Imaginary, and the Real. Lacan contends that this distinction, never previously made in psychoanalysis, provides the key to understanding the coexistent determinants of a person's action. According to Wilden

> The Symbolic is the primary order, since it represents and structures both of the others; moreover, since it is ultimately only in language (or in judgement) that synonyms, ambiguities and interpretations can operate, Lacan avers that it is not possible to view the Freudian concept of overdetermination (of the symptom) as originating outside the Symbolic order.[25]

Postponing for a moment the need to clarify many of these terms, it can be seen that here is something like Althusser's 'structure in dominance': the Symbolic is determinant in the last instance but it is an overdetermined structure. Leaving aside now Althusser's relation to Lacan, what are the essential gains made by Lacan in his reading of Freud? Can his central theme be given expression?

Beginning with the quotation from Wilden, it seems that one element must be the *primacy of the Symbolic*. If it is indeed primary then it should lead on to other elements in Lacan's theory. Its primacy is in relation to two other orders, the Imaginary and the Real. These various orders may be seen as necessities of human existence: the environmental and organismic level can be related to the most basic *needs* of the person which, within certain broad limits, are given. Lacan's term for this is the 'Real'. But human wants refer also to other human beings (or parts; for example, the breast) on whom the child is totally dependent during early life: these are *demands* for love, directed to others in the person's world, originating in the prelinguistic and primitive stages of early childhood. Lacan's term for this field of experience is the Imaginary. Finally, there is the level at which the Symbolic qualities of human action are apparent, the interactions are meaningful, as is so obvious in the case of verbal activity and interchange, but which can be interpreted into other kinds of interaction provided the appropriate code is known. In Symbolic interaction the primary motivation is *desire* for recognition. Thus three kinds of motivation—need, demand and desire—correspond to three orders of existence: the Real, the Imaginary and the Symbolic.

Set out in this way as a progression through levels of existence it appears that the development of a child from organism to self-conscious subject is being described. The formulation may serve this purpose provided it is remembered that during socialisation the Symbolic operates on the child through the parents right from conception. For example, the Phallus—as a symbol of patriarchy, not to be reduced to a physiological fact—is the signifier of signifiers; literally a 'master' symbol which determines the course of the Oedipus stage and with it family relationships. It becomes clear that the spatial metaphor of 'levels' is misleading: since the Symbolic represents and structures the other levels, it would be better to adopt something like Althusser's concept of interpenetrating regions within an over-all 'structure in dominance'. It hardly matters what models or metaphors are used along the way as long as the resultant conception captures the sense of cumulative co-presence of distinguishable influences in the human situation, which in its most important characteristics is interwoven with language and communication. Nowhere is this more apparent than in the primarily verbal interchanges of psychoanalytic theorapy.

Lacan's position may now be hinted at, since it is too complex to be addressed more directly at this stage. He is a psychoanalyst who believes that the orthodox psychoanalytic movement has lost sight of Freud; in America, for example, because of the lack of any sense of history and because of the dominance of behaviourism. He attempts the kind of reflexive critique which turns a theory around upon its users.

> In order to get at the roots of this deterioration of the analytic discourse, one may legitimately apply the psychoanalytic method to the collectivity which sustains it.[26]

Such an approach is made necessary by the various forms of resistance, denial and misrecognition the orthodox movement has overlaid on the original Freud. Because of these views he left the official psychoanalytic organisation, determined to recover Freud from the Freudians.

At the centre of his effort to return to Freud is a concern with the functions of language in psychoanalysis, a special kind of discourse embedded in the more inclusive structure of societal interaction, considered for these purposes as a symbolically structured social discourse. At first sight nothing would seem more obvious than the dominant role of language in therapy—the talking cure—and in society at large. However, the elaboration of a conceptual structure designed to describe and relate instinctual conflicts diverted attention from the discourse toward the possible sites and processes of which language was merely a kind of indicator or reflection. To propose a shift of attention to language itself is the kind of 'Gestalt-switch' which constitutes in Kuhn's terminology a revolution, or in Althusser's, an epistemological break. It is easy to see what European resources of knowledge help Lacan towards new views: principally Saussure's linguistics, the structuralism of Mauss and Levi-Strauss, the phenomenology of Hegel, Husserl, Heidegger and Sartre. Saussure provides an abstract conception of language as a system of diacritical distinctions to which various objects, experiences and relationships can be attached. Mauss and Levi-Strauss conceive society as a system of oppositional distinctions worked up into symbolic structures such as the myths which are used to regulate and make sense of social relationships. Phenomenology provides access to human experience which, in Heidegger particularly, consists of a self in discourse.

Within this central theme of the Symbolic certain episodes take their place. For example, Lacan's original and possibly most famous concept of a 'mirror-phase' in human development. This is addressed to the question of how the human subject comes to selfhood which is answered by recourse to the Symbolic.

> . . . the child begins outside the Symbolic. He is confronted by it, and the significant question—ultimately the 'Who (or what) am I?' is articulated on the problem of entry into it. [27]

According to Laplanche and Pontalis, the mirror-phase occurs at between six and eighteen months when the infant is still lacking co-ordination. The child experiences an imaginary sense of unity.

> This imaginary unification comes about by means of identification with the image of the counterpart as total Gestalt; it is exemplified concretely by the experience in which the child perceives its own reflection in a mirror. [28]

The phase can be related to Freud's hypotheses on development of the ego; at the same time it must be seen to include the Sartrean notion (traceable to Hegel) of identification in relation to the opposing, alienating other, and it goes beyond Freud by giving such unequivocal importance, for later identifications, to this early stage of childhood. It is derived by Lacan in a way which recalls the diacritical differences of a Saussurean language system and also the oppositional terms of Levi-Strauss' structural analysis: he discovered it in Freud's story of a child playing with a reel of cotton to make it disappear and return—Here! and Gone! For the child such experiences introduce the binary opposition of presence/absence, which can be extended to the relation between part-object and a totality; the lack of object (or lack of wholeness) is an absence like the gap in a chain of signifiers which the subject seeks to fill by his discourse. Without going into the linguistic technicalities of the signifier let it suffice to say that motivation, the onward movement of the human subject, is here not an instinct or drive considered out of relation to its meaning or significance within a never-to-be-completed discourse. All this may help to convey the importance of Lacan's idea that psychoanalysis, at best, consists of movement towards full discourse (*la parole pleine*) against all the gaps, absences and distortions introduced by phantasy relationships operating in the Imaginary mode. It may now also be apparent why 'cure' consists of the realisation that the discourse could go on forever.

It follows from the shift in focus onto language that the unconscious takes on a new definition.

> The unconscious is that part of the concrete discourse in so far as it is transindividual, which is not at the disposition of the subject to re-establish the continuity of his conscious discourse.[29]

And as a consequence of Lacan's view that 'the symptom itself is structured like a language' it follows that

> The unconscious is structured like a language.[30]

Some implications of the new definition will be explored later in relation to Wilden's own development of Lacan's view.

With regard to the Self, it has been seen that this comes into being in an Imaginary and alienated form through the mirror-phase, later gaining its most distinctively human chacacteristics when it moves into the Symbolic order of existence. The Imaginary self is never completely shaken off but remains as one kind of influence on the Symbolic self. For this reason self-consciousness or self-concepts cannot be reduced to 'attitudes toward the self', the usual over-simplification of the social and behavioural sciences: the self is just not as accessible as this would imply. The self-concept is not the self of discourse because

> One of the prime functions of speech, like Orwell's Newspeak, is not to reveal thoughts, but to conceal them, especially from ourselves.[31]

Nor is it the self of Imagination because this is by definition the realm of unconscious phantasy. Neither is there any original, true or real self available as an anchorage for subjectivity because subjectivity is gained only after the Real (organismic) and Imaginary phases have been passed through, though remaining as life history. It is this sense of the elusiveness of self which brings out the value to Lacan of Husserl's phenomenology, as a method of gaining access to this complex structure of human experience, with the qualification that Lacan turns it towards a phenomenology of language (Heidegger's emphasis) rather than of consciousness.[32]

The other major source for Lacan's concept of self is quite explicitly Hegel. Hegel's self comes into being only in relation to the Other: this immediately places the site of self-discovery outside the self, and Lacan uses this idea as part of his return to 'the principles which govern Freud's Word'.

These principles are none other than the dialectic of the consciousness of self, as it is brought into realization from Socrates to Hegel, starting from the ironic presupposition that all that is rational is real, eventually to be precipitated into the scientific judgement that all that is real is rational. But Freud's discovery was to demonstrate that this verifying process authentically attains the subject only by decentering him from the consciousness of self, in the axis of which the Hegelian reconstruction of the phenomenology of the spirit maintained it . . .[33]

To condense the process somewhat, it can be said that in coming to self-consciousness the self first knows the Other as an object (there is, of course, a reciprocal process going on). The relationship is therefore a competitive and aggressive one usually involving unequal power, as in Hegel's parable of lordship and bondage, and it is only when the self risks all to negate the Other that it may come fully into its own self—knowledge and subjectivity. Sartre's primary alienation is also recognisable here.

In reflecting on my own text at this point I realise how inadequate it is to convey the range and subtlety of either Lacan or Wilden; it is a poor substitute for reading the original works. The only possible justification may be that Lacan's central theme has been well enough treated to bring it into contact with other lines of work. Sociologists will have been alert to the fact that Lacan's subject is at least an interactional self, and if the dominant symbol structures of society embodied in language and in all the other institutionalised systems of signification are taken as the effective social structure, it is a 'social self'. Similarities between Lacan's and Mead's concepts of symbolic interaction and their concepts of the social creation of self are apparent. Mead's 'generalised other' based on an internalised conversion of gestures seems highly relevant, and so too does Cooley's dependence on a 'looking-glass self'. A digression into this parallel stream of American work will sharpen the contrasts already referred to between American and European work as well as providing additional evidence on the peculiar boundary conditions which tend to keep apart American and European bodies of knowledge.

Cooley and Mead have had such a long-standing influence on the development of American sociology and social psychology that an examination of their most fundamental ideas will help to characterise these disciplines and therefore throw light on their relation to each other. Both theorists have something to say on the concept of role which has here been used to test the limitations of separate disciplines. My reasons for asserting that Mead in particular is an important and continuing influence are the frequency with which he is cited as the originator of the concept of a social-self and the fact that his work has increased in popularity over the past decade, no doubt in part because of the rise of interpretive, phenomenological and ethnomethodological specialities within sociology. Not only does he gain adherents in the United States, together with new presentations and reprints of his work,[34] it is also suggested that European theorists have neglected Mead to their own disadvantage and that they should embrace him.

> . . . just as the indifference to the sociology of knowledge on the part of American social psychologists has prevented the latter from relating their perspectives to a macrosociological theory, so is the total ignorance of Mead a severe theoretical defect of neo-Marxist social thought in Europe today. There is considerable irony in the fact that, of late, neo-Marxist theoreticians have been seeking a liaison with Freudian psychology (which is fundamentally incompatible with the anthropological presuppositions of Marxism) completely oblivious of the existence of a Meadian theory of the dialectic between society and the individual that would be immeasurably more congenial to their approach. For a recent example of this ironic phenomenon, cf. Georges Lapassade, *L'Entree dans la vie* (Paris, Editions de Minuit, 1963), an otherwise highly suggestive book that, as it were, cries out for Mead on every page.[35]

The irony in this is much greater than Berger and Luckmann suspect. The idea that Mead, whose blindness to conflict in the social structure is exceeded only by his inability to recognise the individualism of his 'I'/'me' dichotomy, could be integrated with Marx seems like a fantasy that opposites can be put together and reconciled. What Mead could offer is only some adulterated Hegel, a position that

Marx had to go beyond by 'inverting' Hegel (to use the popular but, as Althusser shows, inadequate term for Marx's progress beyond him). By adulteration I mean that Mead used the Hegelian notion of totality to cover his reworking of the social whole into harmonious form and then tried to support this unadmittedly metaphysical notion by a rock-hard foundation of behaviourism. In this way he matched an idealised model of American democratic society to the very practical and empirical concerns of American pragmatism. Presumably this mood of practicality is what Philip Rieff means when he says

> Like the philosophers Mead and James, the sociologist Cooley was too hard-headed an American to be interested in the European shadow play of the dialectic between essence and existence.[36]

Strangely it is precisely as a shadow play that Mead and others interested themselves in European thought. Mead was interested in it for what he could turn it into, so that it might fit his own self-concept and his benign view of his own social context.

> Trained in the Hegelian tradition, he soon transformed that idealism into a pragmatic 'social idealism' which included reliance upon experimental science, the moral values of democracy, empirical naturalism, historical and psychological relativism, the primacy of experience, and the employment of biological and sociological categories in the consideration of philosophical and psychological problems.[37]

In short, Marx went beyond Hegel by asserting materialism; Mead left behind Hegel to become 'hard-headed'.

Cooley's concept of a 'looking-glass self' appears in *Human Nature and the Social Order*, originally published in 1902. The 1964 Schocken edition carries a foreword by Mead reprinted from an article on Cooley originally published in 1930. It is possible to read together Cooley's concept and its significance for Mead. Cooley's attitude is even more down to earth than Mead's.

> It is well to say at the outset that by the word 'self' in this discussion is meant simply that which is designated in common speech by the pronouns of the first person singular, 'I', 'me', 'my', 'mine', and 'myself'. 'Self' and 'ego' are used by metaphysicians and moralists in many other senses, more or less remote from the

'I' of daily speech and thought and with these I wish to have as little to do as possible.[38]

Although I have now seen this peculiarly American kind of wish to shake off tradition and start again in a more practical, common-sense way many times, I confess that I still cannot understand its pervasiveness and power as a cultural value. Of course I can say the word 'pragmatism' and appreciate that in seeking knowledge these sociologists are trying to make, and speak for, American ideals of a democratic society, but I am continually surprised at the innocence of the world view. As Mead said

> The community that he discovered so to speak from the inside, was a democracy, and inevitably an American democracy.[39]

And again, of Cooley's purpose

> His undertaking is to locate and define the 'solid facts of society'. Ignoring the philosophical problem does give him elbow room.[40]

Thus Cooley proceeds to regard society as an organism or 'living whole made up of differentiated members, each of which has a special function',[41] and the solid facts are 'the imaginations which people have of one another'.[42] And so society is to be found in the mind: the looking-glass selves are tied together by reflected appraisals which together make up 'a group state of mind which is more or less distinctly aware of itself'.[43] All this is so much of a surface account that any ground of comparison with Lacan's mirror-phase simply disappears.

Mead's further comments on Cooley criticise the fact that he looked in the mind for a self. He might better have considered the process by which the self comes into being by emergence from relationships between organisms, and with self, mind. Cooley simply gave 'an account of the American community to which he belonged, and presupposed its normal healthful process.'[44] Mead believed his own account to be more realistic in that it looked at 'the dim beginnings of human behaviour'.[45] It will be clear already that I do not find Mead's concept of the social-self, which never clarifies the relation between species-evolution and individual development, any more realistic or useful than Cooley's. I would say rather that both their approaches, together with the significance others decided to give to them, pushed American sociology and psychology into a long retreat from which it has never properly recovered.

Consider for example the attempt by Hans Gerth and C. Wright Mills to develop symbolic interactionism in their *Character and Social Structure*. They escape from Mead's concept of a 'generalised other' by substituting the concept of 'significant others'; this opens up the concept of the social process to include different and possibly conflicting influences upon the self. They posit the division of society into 'symbol spheres', each relating to an institution: the political, economic, military, religious, kinship and the educational. 'Master symbols' control and co-ordinate the roles which make up these institutions, supplying the 'vocabulary of motives' a person may use to explain and justify actions. But the master symbols are particular to their separate symbol spheres and there is no signifier of signifiers —the Phallus (Lacan)—which orders all social discourse. Nor do they relate the symbol spheres to a 'structure in dominance' such as that of Althusser where the economy is determinant 'in the last instance'; institutional relationships, though now more differentiated than in Mead, remain in a typically American state of pluralism.

> The institutional patterns of different orders are not equally or evenly implemented by means of symbols. The dominant symbols of a whole social structure will tend to be in the symbol sphere of its dominant institutional order. These symbols will legitimate the symbols and practices of other orders as well as those of its own. If the economic order is the weightiest one within a social structure, the legitimating symbols of the whole structure will likely be related to the economic order.[46]

Gerth and Mills polarise vulgar Marxism and *'principled and dogmatic pluralism'*, taking up a position between them.

It is a very similar strategy which underlies their wish to integrate Mead and Freud, although the consequences for Freud's work indicate something of what Lacan called 'voracious acceptance'.

> Various philosophical assumptions that had crept into Freud's work have been torn out with little or no damage to what remains.[47]

They will therefore accept the revisions of cultural anthropology and the neo-Freudians.

Perhaps this glimpse of the looking-glass self and symbolic interactionism is enough to show that in spite of their homonymy with the mirror-phase and the Symbolic there is a very great difference between the American and the European approaches: a boundary so strong that it turns upside down, or tears something out of, the knowledge which crosses it.

I turn now to the work of the only theorist I know who has taken European and American ideas in all their force and made something new by situated critical reading: Anthony Wilden.

8.3 A. WILDEN

Towards the end of his virtuoso exposition of Lacan, it is apparent that Anthony Wilden has come through to an understanding of Lacan so complete that it is able to comprehend the limitations of Lacan's position and is ready to go beyond it. Since it is so close to the core of the intellectual material at issue one could speak in Hegelian/Lacanian terms of Wilden's relationship to Lacan. At first his attention to the Other (Lacan) is so total and so patient that Wilden seems captivated: his voice is not heard except in speaking Lacan, which he does so faithfully that he is sometimes seen as a disciple. And then by the very risk of this submergence in another's Word he finds the resources to say more; he finds his voice and his self, a return from the Other into himself and into triumphant self-consciousness which bursts out of the urgently episodic pages of *System and Structure*.

The point of departure seems very simple. It is that within Lacan's idea of the *levels of language* there is room to see the symptom not merely as structured like a language, a view which emerges from Lacan's deep reading of Freud, but as '*a statement in a meta-language about an object language*'.[48] The direction of search indicated by this new interpretation is toward 'analyses of relationships, dialectical opposition and communication'.

The number of influences pouring in to Wilden is even greater than for Lacan. In addition to those which come in with Lacan there are Gregory Bateson, whose ecological theory of mind based on a study of animal and human behaviour looms very large, and Marx, whose historical materialism can be read at many levels and to many purposes. Fortunately, these and many other minor contributions can be gathered together under the theme of language and communication in open systems. The first problem is to understand what it means in this context for a metalanguage to comment on an object language.

Wilden shows that there are two theories of symbolism in psychoanalysis. One sees the symbol as naturally connected to what it stands for; for example, in a dream which contains a house that is urgently being repaired by the dreamer, the element, house, is connected to the object, house, by the anxiety caused by a threatened intrusion of unbearable experience which the dreamer cannot express more directly. The house dreamed about may come from childhood or other experience of houses. This may be called the Atomistic theory because of its concentration on tracing back the underlying cause of this single element. The second theory is concerned not so much with single elements and their causation but with the relations between any particular symbol and the others which are implicit in its use; that is to say, with *the symbol system* which enables, among other things, reference to be made to a very wide range of objects, situations and experiences. For example, the 'house' might be a reference to the work needed for its repair, to the environment, to reparation toward another, and so on, depending on the context of symbolisation. Here we pick up the Saussure/Jakobson emphasis on language as a system of diacritical distinctions and must register the structuralist assertion that when gifts are exchanged, even though they may symbolise something (as when flowers are given meanings), they are most importantly 'symbols of the act of exchange itself.'[49] Lacan calls this second approach in Freud 'the Symbolic', which is to be distinguished from the first approach—'Symbolism'. Wilden notes that Freud himself was not always consistent here because of his own struggle to follow his subject matter through naturalistic to symbolic interpretations.

Building gradually on such insights and bringing in material from Bateson, Wilden works his way towards a distinction that is essential to his whole position, the distinction between analog and digital relationships. Analogical interpretation depends on the existence of phenomena which can be accurately represented by a continuum; for example, the quantity of a liquid. Such a variable could be programmed into an analog computer and related to other variables for some purpose. Digital interpretation is based on the occurrence of phenomena which can be accurately represented as in one of two alternative conditions—on/off, yes/no, present/absent—the kinds of relationships that a digital computer is designed to handle. We recall that Levi-Strauss assumes the human brain to operate in this way, and that he accounts for the universality of binary oppositions in the structure of myth by this assumption. It has already been shown that analog variables can be reduced to digital relationships by introducing boundaries (Kelly's personal constructs), and it is this kind of relationship between the analog and the digital which greatly interests Wilden, for its consequences in relation to communication are many.

He shows first that, contra Levi-Strauss, the human brain functions as a system of analog *and* digital processes, each performing a distinct and integrated role. There is both quantitative build-up and digital 'triggering' or 'firing' so that concentration on any one is an oversimplification. Such systems are common in organismic processes. The important question is, then, the relation between the analog and the digital, particularly if that will clarify the relation between an object language and a metalanguage.

Wilden notes that Carnap tried to solve certain philosophical problems in logical positivism by recognising two kinds of language: Language I, an object language, contains words referring directly or indirectly to empirical phenomena; Language II is a metalanguage devised for the purpose of commenting on the structure of the language in which empirical references are made. Wilden draws again on philosophy by introducing Russell's theory of logical types which deals with the relations between objects and classes. Russell came to consider classes that were not members of themselves.

> When he asked whether the class of all such classes was a member of itself, he was easily able to demonstrate that it *was* a member of itself if and only if it *was not*.[50]

There are many interesting elaborations of this paradox, the one of greatest interest to Wilden being the conclusion that not all objects belong to one level. Thus there appears to be some philosophical support for the notion of *levels of language* and *levels of objects*.

The famous double-bind phenomenon, noticed by the Bateson group and Laing and Esterson as similar in some respects to schizophrenogenic interaction, can be understood as contradictory injunctions at different levels which, in some situations, make it impossible to avoid unbearable consequences using the responses apparently available. It is only when communication about the communication process—metacommunication—can be achieved that the bind may be broken. But this is just what the relation between the analog and digital does allow: the digital can comment upon the analog because it possesses greater semiotic freedom.

. . . the transcendence of any paradox or double bind, in logic or in life, involves some form of metacommunication, and (2) . . . the transcendence itself engenders paradox at the metacommunicative level—or at the level of the next higher logical type. In other words, Russell's theory of logical types, Carnap's levels of language, and the double bind theory of schizophrenia are all paradoxical in themselves. It is easy to see why. On the one hand, all such theories correspond to the necessity of digitalizing analog continuums by introducing discrete boundaries into the non-discrete. On the other hand, in logic and in language they involve the use of 'not'.[51]

So the power of the digital depends on its capacity for dealing with absence and negation (there is no negation in the analog since it is only a matter of more or less presence).

Returning to the assertion which provided a transition from Lacan to Wilden, can it now be shown how the sympton is a metacommunication about an object language? A sympton, by definition, is not in itself the illness to be cured; it stands in relation to it as an indication of the source of the difficulty. In psychoanalysis the source of any difficulty is to some degree unconscious; in other words, it cannot be reported on or responded to directly, and yet the symptom in some way represents the difficulty. But since it is an alternative to direct encounter with the difficulty it could be said to systematically *mis*represent it by blocking its accurate expression. Misrepresentation may occur because of the unavailability of a word (as in Freud's own experience of forgetting the name of 'Signorelli' whose face was nevertheless present as a 'thing presentation'), or because of the availability of persistently misleading alternative words ('Botticelli' and 'Boltraffio' instead of 'Signorelli'). Now these kinds of transformations involving absence and negation are characteristically digital and can easily be managed in a digital language. But no matter how perfectly the sympton is handled in digital language, it cannot by itself transcend the contradictions and oppositional fluctuations of the digital (Imaginary) mode. It is only as analysis proceeds and the gaps and negations are filled in—movement from the empty word to the full word—that continuity of the discourse (dependent on analog relationships) be can achieved. What could not be addressed can now be expressed, with the prospect that it may be overcome as an unconscious determinant of a person's behaviour and experience.

It may not yet be clear what Wilden is moving towards through this apparently technical involvement in language and communication, or what relevance it has to a study of the self/society relation. The next few steps in the argument will show a common goal, being concerned with epistemological questions—what it is to know something—including the problem of locating the knowing mind and the human subject.

Bateson derived from a long study of human and animal life patterns a perspective which attempts to delineate the unit of survival for humankind. Going beyond the naive polarisation of organism and environment he argues that the relevant unit is an ecosystem. Complex chains of dependency control the survival of various species, making it difficult to define the effective unit.[52] A factor of some importance is the flexibility or adaptiveness of species, but even here there is always the risk of counteradaptive consequences, when short-run beneficial changes lead in the long run to destruction. For example, the species which expands and improves its ability to catch a prey may wipe out both the prey and, in consequence, itself. Advanced industrial societies are already well into counteradaptive consequences.

> Every system involving life or mind, or simulating life or mind, is an open system.
>
> An open system is such that its relationship to a supersystem (which may be referred to methodologically as its 'environment' or as its 'context') is indispensable to its survival. There is an on-going exchange of matter—energy and information between them.[53]

In contrast to the negative feedback within natural systems which aids their survival, industrial societies induce positive feedback which multiplies their speed towards disaster. But why does wo/ mankind seem so incapable of correcting the runaway processes? Because of a prevailing epistemology which is unable to know what is happening.

Descartes' philosophy contributed to our epistemological inadequacies by equating self with substance ('I think, therefore I am') such that the notion of self as property is 'embedded in our culture'.[54]

The human 'I' is not the body but a 'LOCUS in the system (perhaps similar to what G. H. Mead would call a role)'.[55] Although Wilden does not pursue this reference to G. H. Mead it does raise a point which can be read back towards the starting point of this study. Mead, correctly, looked outside the body for the locus of self. Having located it in role—though misconceived as a unitary 'generalised other'—he continued to search for the 'I' which corresponded to his own culturally reinforced sense of separate individuality, preserving in the concept of self the duality he had set out to overcome.

As Wilden puts it

> . . . the self as SUBJECT (not as entity) is neither transcendent to nor immanent in the subsystem which thinks it. The subject is immanent in the UNIT OF MIND (Bateson), which, isomorphic with the unit of survival, includes the rest of the system in which the appropriate transformations of difference (information) are transmitted. The unit of mind is not either sender or receiver: it is both–and.[56]

So this central theme of language and communication leads back eventually to self, knowledge and society. Reflecting again on the personality theories which opened this study, it does seem as though their most common failing is the inability of their authors to think in 'both–and' terms about the person and society. Such 'integrations' as they do produce are managed in the Imaginary mode by creating gaps and absences in their discourse. I will return to this point, simply noting for the moment that Wilden comes by an independent route and from a different starting point to conclusions which agree with my own in relation to the production of knowledge.

Wilden carries through some of the many implications of his theory to describe and explain the condition of modern societies. He sees them beset by crises of oppression, violence, madness and destruction of the human environment, all capable of being analysed in terms of communication: not the over-used diagnosis of 'failures of communication' for the ills of conflict, but as relationships in which certain kinds of communication—positive and negative feedback, analog and digital messages—have become incoherent or gone out of control. The knowledge which could potentially arise *at its appropriate point in the open system*, to change goals, to achieve a metasystemic adaptation to new conditions is stifled by an inability to understand communication processes. Some of the most dangerous distortions are, paradoxically, systems of knowledge, strangled by their incapacity to comprehend the most basic condition of existence —communication—and therefore captured in their own circles of misunderstanding.

Typical destructive patterns of the modern situation are sexism, racism, economic exploitation and colonialism, each one traceable to the use of digital either/or conceptions which run permutations on oppositional categories without the opportunity of moving to a different kind of discourse. Even those theories which have helped to show something of the nature of communication are not free from misconceptions and constraints; however, it is possible to turn theories around on themselves and achieve a reflexive critique. Such is Wilden's critique of Lacan, whose valuable exposition of the Imaginary does not allow him to escape its vicissitudes, as can be seen by his phallocentrism and his elitist conceptual violence. For the person who seeks to comprehend the human situation there are great obstacles and, inherent in the prevailing epistemology, many invitations to retreat into that fullness of false knowledge which is provided by the oppositional terms of the Imaginary and the digital. By learning more about the open system that Wilden describes as his 'privileged model' there might be some useful result, but

> ... so long as, in a real world of oppressive relations, the question of subjectivity is necessarily posed for the INDIVIDUAL—rather than for the collective—then the subject's quest for identity will remain a quest for a justification of his alienation: a quest for a name in an Imaginary discourse, an empty word.[57]

For Wilden, only Marx understood symbolic communication and exchange well enough to envisage a situation in which 'man does not reproduce himself in any determined form but produces his totality'.[58]

REFERENCES

1 S. Marcus. *The Other Victorians*, Wiedenfeld & Nicolson, London (1966)
2 A. Wilden. *System and Structure*, Tavistock, London (1972)
3 L. Althusser and E. Balibar. *Reading 'Capital'*, New Left Books, London (1970), p. 28

4 ibid., p. 44
5 T. S. Kuhn. *The Structure of Scientific Revolutions*, University of Chicago Press, Chicago and London (1970), p. 200
6 D. McLellan. *Marx*, Fontana, London (1975), p. 82
7 L. Althusser. *Lenin and Philosophy*, New Left Books, London (1971), p. 87
8 L. Althusser and E. Balibar. *Reading 'Capital'*, New Left Books, London (1970), p. 51
9 ibid., p. 182
10 ibid., p. 182
11 T. B. Bottomore. *Sociology*, Allen & Unwin, London (1962), p. 53 (2nd edn, 1971)
12 N. Birnbaum. *Toward a Critical Sociology*, Oxford University Press, Oxford (1971), p. 215
13 W. W. Isajiw. *Causation and Functionalism in Sociology*, Routledge, London (1968)
14 S. F. Nadel. *The Theory of Social Structure*, Cohen West, London (1957)
15 W. F. Ogburn. *Social Change with Respect to Culture and Original Nature*, Viking, New York (1950)
16 L. Althusser and E. Balibar. *Reading 'Capital'*, New Left Books, London (1970), p. 15
17 V. I. Lenin. Quoted in L. Althusser, *Lenin and Philosophy*, New Left Books, London (1971), p. 116
18 L. Althusser. ibid., p. 119
19 A. Wilden. *The Language of the Self*, Johns Hopkins. Baltimore, Md (1968), p. viii
20 M. Merleau-Ponty. *Signs*, Northwestern University Press, Evanston, Ill (1964), p. 115
21 A. Wilden. *The Language of the Self*, Johns Hopkins, Baltimore, Md (1968), p. 310
22 L. Althusser. Quoted in A. Wilden, *The Language of the Self*, Johns Hopkins, Baltimore, Md (1968), p. 311
23 G. A. Kelly. *The Psychology of Personal Constructs*, Norton, New York (1955)
24 L. Althusser. *For Marx* (Transl. Ben Brewster), Penguin, Harmondsworth, Middx (1969)
25 A. Wilden. *The Language of the Self*, Johns Hopkins, Baltimore, Md (1968), p. 161
26 J. Lacan. The function of language in psychoanalysis. In A.

Wilden, *The Language of the Self*, Johns Hopkins, Baltimore, Md (1968), p. 6

27 A. Wilden, op. cit., p. 177

28 J. Laplanche and J. B. Pontalis. *The Language of Psychoanalysis*, Hogarth, London (1973), p. 251

29 J. Lacan. The function of language in psychoanalysis. In A. Wilden, *The Language of the Self*, Johns Hopkins, Baltimore, Md (1968), p. 20

30 A. Wilden. Quoting J. Lacan (1953). *System and Structure*, Tavistock, London (1972)

31 A. Wilden. *The Language of the Self*, Johns Hopkins, Baltimore, Md (1968), p. 241

32 ibid., p. 179

33 J. Lacan. The function of language in psychoanalysis. In A. Wilden, *The Language of the Self*, Johns Hopkins, Baltimore, Md (1968), p. 55

34 J. P. Hewitt. *Self and Society*, Allyn & Bacon, Boston, Mass. (1976)

35 P. Berger and T. Luckmann. *The Social Construction of Reality*, Penguin, Harmondsworth, Middx (1967), p. 218 (Doubleday, New York, 1966)

36 P. Rieff. In C. H. Cooley, *Human Nature and the Social Order*, Schocken, New York (1964), p. xvi (first published 1902)

37 P. Pfuetze. *The Social Self*, Bookman Associates, Copenhagen (1954), p. 39

38 C. H. Cooley, *Human Nature and the Social Order*, Schocken, New York (1964), p. 168

39. G. H. Mead. In C. H. Cooley, *Human Nature and the Social Order*, Schocken, New York (1964), p. xxii

40 ibid., p. xxv

41 ibid., p. xxii

42 ibid., p. xxii

43 ibid., p. xxiii

44 ibid., p. xxxvi

45 ibid., p. xxxvi

46 H. Gerth and C. W. Mills. *Character and Social Structure*, Routledge, London (1954), p. 302

47 ibid., p. 20

48 A. Wilden. *The Language of the Self*, Johns Hopkins, Baltimore, Md (1968), p. 30

49 ibid., p. 32
50 P. Edwards (ed.). *The Encyclopedia of Philosophy*, Vol. 8, Collier-Macmillan, New York and London (1967), p. 168
51 A. Wilden. *The Language of the Self*, Johns Hopkins, Baltimore Md (1968), p. 122
52 ibid., p. 205
53 ibid., p. 203
54 ibid., p. 210
55 ibid., p. 222
56 ibid., p. 223
57 ibid., p. 473
58 K. Marx. *Pre-Capitalist Economic Formations* (transl. J. Cohen) (ed. E. J. Hobsbawm), International Publishers, New York (1965). Quoted in A. Wilden, *The Language of the Self*, Johns Hopkins, Baltimore, Md (1968), p. 476

9
A Human Science of Self in Social Context

9.1 NOTES TOWARD REFLEXIVITY

It has been a recurring theme of this investigation that many failures in the human sciences result from the incapacity of certain theories to account for their own existence. When turned around upon themselves they fall into inconsistencies and contradictions which show up quite dramatically their limitations. With this in mind I offer some brief notes on my personal history which may account for and clarify my attitude to knowledge in the human sciences.

What has gone before is a record of an intellectual journey written over a period of several years although gathering together experience gained over the twenty years since I went to university as a misleadingly described mature student. At first, knowledge seemed so attractive and filled with the promise of personal integration and power that I believed everything and drank it in. The three subjects of psychology, sociology and philosophy offered, or so I thought, knowledge of the person (myself of course) in his most individual and private aspects, in his group and social interactions, and in his ethical, political and philosophical aspirations. I can hardly describe the wonder and innocence of this first encounter with academic knowledge. Not having been 'prepared' for university I knew nothing of the tacit criteria which govern academic work: an essay question set me to explaining the whole world, and subject boundaries meant little. The criterion for me was not whether a piece of work fell within my honours subject, sociology, but whether it interested me. And 'interest' is hardly strong enough a word to describe the sheer fascination that led me freely over the fields of psychology, sociology and philosophy, sustained by the illusion that all this knowledge would fit together. But of course it never did fit together and the wide-ranging search for integrating principles left me rather short on specialised achievements such that I was unable to write examinations with any more than moderate success.

The search for a comprehensive theory accompanied me through periods of teaching in further education, adult education and into a university, newly elevated from its previous status as a college of advanced technology. As a lecturer in modern cultural studies I enjoyed teaching a wide range of science students, extending my interests in the direction of film studies. Then came two experiences which finally shattered the fantasy of peaceful integration of different kinds of knowledge. Firstly, I attended the London School of Economics as a part-time student and became aware of such a strong barrier between psychology and sociology, and such firm institutional discouragement from mixing the two subjects freely, that I began to look for explanations of this tendency to compartmentalise knowledge.

Secondly, I became involved in designing and teaching a postgraduate interdisciplinary course in modern social and cultural studies where the resulting clash between disciplines was so fundamental and conflictual that some part-time teachers lost their jobs, the students took over responsibility for their own teaching programme and staff were called into seminars only by invitation. The conflict was never worked through but side-stepped by the institutional solution of moving the course towards literary studies, leaving some token coverage of social and psychological issues mostly by non-specialists. My own role as a human sciences teacher became very difficult, particularly since I had incurred wrath by trying to mediate between opposing factions. I had never experienced quite such violent misunderstanding, so I took sociology and psychology out of that department into a separate unit which later became a department in its own right.

With the freedom that comes from being the only full-time teacher in a field I set up an interdisciplinary first-year course for science students which now takes in over a hundred students each year: other course units of a unidisciplinary kind were developed and more recently some advanced undergraduate interdisciplinary courses have been added; for example, Science and Society, and Women in Society.

In 1972, largely as a result of the Todd Report recommendations, it was decided that the college would unite with a hospital and a dental school to form a multifaculty institution on a new site a few miles away. This implied something like a tenfold expansion of social and behavioural sciences to roughly three hundred students and thirty staff, so the college decided to appoint a new professor to lead this development. There was much talk of 'building upon existing strengths' but in practice every new proposal by existing staff to move towards new work was blocked on grounds that the new professor would have to be consulted, until it seemed that we were waiting not for a professor but for Godot.

The most inexplicable fact seemed to be that although the college was unable to recruit enough science students it was willing to continue its resistance to allowing any intake of social and behavioural scientists. It soon became obvious that in spite of their contributions to the liberalisation of science degrees (prompted by the Dainton Report findings[1]) and to successful new fields of study such as human biology, any development of the two disciplines in their own right (but most particularly sociology) was actually feared by the college authorities, who claimed that they were supported in this by the University Grants Committee: the UGC had indicated privately that they would not fund such a proposal. Reasons given were the 'abstract' quality of sociology (a peculiar criticism from scientists) and the need for 'more useful applied studies'.

For me this came as the most complete realisation yet achieved of the many psychological, sociological and political factors which bear on the institutionalisation of research and teaching. That a college would seek to develop 'applied' studies without accepting the duty of contributing to the source disciplines; that a subject which had proved its attractiveness and usefulness to the main body of science students and to new fields of study would be blocked by prejudice based on a layman's stereotype of a discipline; that a college would rather fall below its intake targets and lose revenue than take in sociology students; all this made sense only within some very strong conception of the sociology of knowledge and crystallised for me an approach to knowledge in the human sciences that had been growing over several years. Actual involvement in the institutionalisation of knowledge—the sociology of knowledge—and experience of the consequences for relations between disciplines had therefore, in a splendid union of theory and practice, given rise to a need for further theoretical understanding of these processes.

After continual pressure, steps were taken to form an advisory committee which might offer guidance on a new appointment. Because existing staff asked for consultation they were invited to submit written suggestions for membership of the committee and for priorities in development. Predictably, and against the recommendations of existing staff, the committee was overweighted towards social administration and a social administration specialist was appointed. The first set of proposals placed sociology and psychology in a very subservient role to social administration, with first priority going to a postgraduate social work course. After two years of planning and negotiation under mounting pressure of financial restrictions, proposals for a combined honours programme involving social administration, sociology and psychology were agreed. Almost at the moment of approval for these very detailed and thoroughly documented plans, further cuts in resources virtually wiped out the possibility of going ahead, as economic and political forces stronger again than those already encountered took their toll. It is now most unlikely that the college will become a multifaculty university in the forseeable future.

In a strange way the outcome of all this has a powerful logic of its own. Sociology and psychology, the fundamental disciplines of personal and social understanding and potentially the roots for a radical science of the human, have been prevented from either establishing themselves as disciplines or meeting to explore their deep transdisciplinary problems. Instead they will continue to contribute very substantially to 'useful' applied, vocational courses such as social work, nursing, speech sciences, human biology, medical studies, and will form subsidiary units within other fields of study including the natural sciences. In short, their very usefulness as social contextual studies for many other specialists will draw them away from deep *intra*disciplinary problems so that the only points of contact for *inter*disciplinary exploration will be within the framework of other specialisms, where professional and subject needs will militate against radical exploration of transdisciplinary questions in the human sciences. Once again it is obvious that what powerful interests demand—uncritical, useful, serviceable knowledge—is being created by a mixture of crude economic controls and subtle, tacit and informal pressures, bringing the danger that disciplines already underdeveloped theoretically will have their core resources further eroded. The liberal model of the institutionalisation of knowledge virtually disappears. Thus the sociology of knowledge, the least practically useful area of the discipline, but site of the most profound recent discoveries, comes into its own only when under attack for reasons which it alone can explain—a reflexive moment with a vengeance.

9.2 RECAPITULATION OF THE CRITIQUE

The present study had a simple beginning—the desire to understand self-theories. Careful reading soon led to the feeling that there was something very strange about their construction. Although some of the theories were set out in apparently rigorous 'scientific' form they seemed to reveal the very personal concerns of their authors, at work in the social process of putting forward, and gaining acceptance for, claims to knowledge. It was relatively easy to see that a theory of self necessarily includes its author's self and that this kind of theory is most vulnerable to projection of the author's self into the content of a theory. The only safeguard against this projection is a very high degree of critical self-reflection, and since this was evidently lacking in some theorists it offered the opportunity to examine limitations on personality theories dictated by the self-concepts of their authors. Such a study is then both a critique of knowledge and an explanation of the form it takes. It is, further, a study of *failed reflexivity*; that is to say, of the ways in which theorists faced with a necessarily self-reflective activity have failed to see what they were doing and so produced contradictory or false theories.

For the sake of clarity, and in order to capture the sense of flight from unwelcome views of the human being, I set up the theme of a 'retreat into positive generality', showing what form this took through the work of Mead, Sullivan, Erikson, Jourard, Allport, Maslow, Rogers and Kelly. Mead has been the major influence on sociological and social psychological approaches, Sullivan and Erikson on neo-Freudian theories. Allport is the supreme individualist and 'collector' of theories. Jourard, Maslow, Rogers and Kelly speak for humanistic psychology. They provide a catalogue of *reactions* to other viewpoints which run amazing variations on one or two common themes. Most outstanding is the debate they have carried on with the ghost of Freud: with a ghost because they have failed to read, or have misread, Freud so that their debate has been with a shadow or a stereotype; and yet Freud reappears in their theories in a peculiarly benign transformation which is consistent with their self-concepts. Here it is possible to see in some detail just how Freud's revolutionary and seminal contributions to knowledge have been reworked to other purposes.

The second great need among these personality theorists was for a method of gaining access to human experience and to aspects of human striving and creativity not easily dealt with by means of a simple scientific method. Husserl, the great contributor in this area, seems to have been unknown to them, and so a weakly phenomenological method had to be improvised. The anxiety that had to be managed was a fear of being identified with existentialism but, not knowing Husserl, they directed most of their distancing techniques toward the better-known, 'pessimistic' or 'negative' Sartre.

With the exception of Mead, who retained some allegiance to behaviourism whilst trying to build upon it a theory of the social creation of self, these personality theorists were in reaction to behaviourism which by its self-denying ordinance of concentrating on publicly observable behaviour seemed to work in the opposite direction to their concern for the whole person in all his richness of experience. Their dissatisfaction propelled them towards the psychoanalytic and existentialist alternatives but when faced with the potentially radical consequences their nerve failed and they struggled to remake these alternatives into an acceptable form.

The most serious lack in all these theories is sensitivity to a social context. This is a matter of degree: Maslow, Rogers, Allport and Jourard stand towards extreme individualism; Mead, Sullivan and Erikson towards social versions of the self. But even the theorists with greatest concern for the social produce terribly inadequate conceptualisations of social structure. Paradoxically, Mead, sociologically the most influential, offers the most fantastic view of a unified co-operative society. Erikson, whose language is quite radical at times, spoils a promising analysis of social roles and 'identity' by excessive use of integrative conceptualisations.

The work up to this point needed only some determination to read the theories in a thoroughly critical spirit, together with a general conception, taken from the sociology of knowledge, that knowledge is frequently given some significant part of its shape by the sociohistorical conditions within which it is created. This brought together the two disciplines of sociology and psychology and raised questions at another more sociological level: are there consequences for knowledge—production of the separation into disciplines?; what are the relations between disciplines in the human sciences?; and does the division of labour in intellectual work have implications for research (or the lack of it) into certain phenomena? The point of entry to this field was through the concept of role, a concept which

264 Self and Social Context

is used in psychology, sociology and several related disciplines such as philosophy and literary criticism.

Sociology and psychology were found to be substantially separate in their treatment of role, each operating a role-concept suited to its own purposes, each knowing the other's concept superficially and somewhat as a stereotype. The split between disciplines appeared also as a split within each discipline such that phenomena occurring at the meeting point of the personal and the social were consigned to separate specialities, thus avoiding the difficult problem of psychosocial mediations. Short explorations into some neighbouring disciplines—philosophy, literary criticism and anthropology—turned up some points of great interest but no general solution.

'Splitting', which as a psychoanalytic phenomenon appeared in relation to the reading of personality theories seemed to be mirrored at the sociological level by 'polarisation' as competition between specialists, particularly where exacerbated by a clash of professional interests, led to irrational exchanges. It appeared that polarisation is not an integrally flawed method of analysis but one which offers constant temptation to exaggerate differences between positions, sometimes as a prelude to choosing the more 'rational' middle ground between caricatured extremes. Occasionally, polarisations serve to create an acceptable position by contrast with an alternative, real or imagined. The extreme form of this integrative use of oppositional schemes, most flagrant in Maslow, recalls the period in Greek thought when the mere naming of opposites provided a framework for rationalising fantasies about human phenomena. As Lloyd points out, polarities such as hot/cold, wet/dry, when applied to problems of sex differences, provided persuasive arguments at a time when experimental evidence was difficult to come by.[2] Binary analysis, a methodology common to structuralism and personal construct theory, was seen to lead Levi-Strauss towards cultural determinism and Kelly in the opposite direction towards individual autonomy (man, the scientist).

If Freud and Husserl were the absent antagonists with whom the personality theorists carried on a fragmentary and unproductive debate, here at the more sociological level of role and the relations between disciplines Marx provides the target for reaction and provokes 'retreat'. Sociology's rejection of Marx in the early days became in the work of Weber a 'dialogue with the ghost of Marx'.[3] Whether the relation to Marx is one of denial by avoidance or debate

with a phantasm it seems unlikely that this kind of defensive interaction can produce knowledge. This was nowhere more evident
than in Mannheim's sociology of knowledge which, though resting
on Marx's materialism, turned his ghost into an elitist liberal intellectual capable of integrating perspectives. At this point it was found
necessary to recover Marx in more material form and so enrich
sociology's impoverished specialism, the sociology of knowledge.
Since it had already been shown that psychology had avoided Freud
and Husserl or debated with their ghosts, the prospect of a major
parallel clarification appeared. Sociology might, by accepting a
strong form of the sociology of knowledge, become *reflexive* and
therefore radically self-critical as a discipline. Psychology, by
recovering its past, its subject matter and most powerful method-
ologies, might become a strong and reflexive human science whilst
rejecting the superficial approach of its humanistic apologists. The
way would then be open to something more than 'interdisciplinary'
studies which, from the studies of interdisciplinarity in British
universities were seen not to have transcended the limitations of
their separate viewpoints. It is here we recall Dagenais' important
insight that the idea of adding together the results of separate
disciplines is a quite inadequate solution. New knowledge in this
area is necessarily subversive of disciplinary positions because these
are not in the human sciences partial, accurate accounts but distorted viewpoints.

Some further examination of the relation between sociology and
psychology in the United States and Britain, both as disciplines and
as *professionalising* disciplines, raised questions at the yet higher
level of ideologies in relation to social power. Professionalisation
takes the division of labour in intellectual work to its most refined
stage revealing the crude, non-rational processes which provide
frameworks for knowledge creation—the irrationality which often
surrounds the institutionalisation of 'rationality' in societies.

Analysis at this level simply demands a strong sociology of knowledge and a radically self-critical psychology. What then emerges is
not an interdisciplinary strategy but a *transdisciplinary* one. This
entails the reopening of psychosocial problem areas by critical
appraisal strong enough to reject the forms of false knowledge which
presently occupy this space, giving rise to some awareness of crisis in
the human science disciplines but providing barriers to a more
general solution. The sheer difficulty of moving in this direction can

be estimated by the immense investment of personal professional and societal interests in existing forms of knowledge: such work is therefore subversive of existing interests and is in this sense revolutionary.

In order to carry through the radical implications of this position it became necessary to look at theories which promised revolutionary solutions (Esterson, Laing and Cooper), theories which had tried to remain true to Freud (British psychoanalysis), and theories which embodied an explicit attempt to recover, by *reading*, the radical origins of Marx, Freud and the European tradition (Althusser, Lacan and Wilden). Esterson, Laing and Cooper tried to integrate a revolutionary existentialist theory with their own grounding in British psychoanalysis. Although rich at the interpersonal level this body of work is in revolutionary terms a spectacular failure, not withstanding Esterson's thorough account of unconscious phantasy in one family and his attempt to give it a political and theoretical context which does at least put a dialectical human science firmly on the agenda.

British psychoanalysis, although highly specialised towards the internal phantasy world of object relations, has produced a theory of some rigour: this reopens the problem of selfhood in a fresh way without as yet being able to deal with the self's social context.

Althusser, Lacan and Wilden penetrate very deeply into the European tradition in its most radical form, raising questions which arose independently out of the earlier stages of the present study. When I came across them as the work moved in a radical direction they provided some kind of support and encouragement to push on with the analysis. If there is a single most important conclusion here it is that the relation between self and society has been, and is likely to be, misconceived by casting it in polarised form. Althusser's theory of society as a process without a subject and Wilden's theory of society as an open system within which mind and self arise at an appropriate point give some indication that a more collectivist concept of the person and self might be more productive. It is a reminder of Marx's view that

> The essence of man is no abstraction inhering in each single individual. In its actuality it is the ensemble of social relationships.[4]

The challenge here is to win back our consciousness from the invading abstractions (knowledge) and ideologies which distort our awareness of ourselves and of the social processes in which we are implicated.

9.3 A HUMAN SCIENCE OF SELF IN SOCIAL CONTEXT

I have explored the human sciences in breadth and in depth in order to clear the ground of false knowledge and make space for a better account of the relation between self and society. Points of strength in existing work which have withstood radical criticism now appear as the few resources with which to move on to this task. In addition, repeated failures in theorising stand as the lessons to be learned, or as the 'pitfalls'[5] of the human sciences. It is therefore possible to assert three promising criteria for new work: reflexivity, transdisciplinarity and the subversiveness of discovery. It is further necessary to state the risk involved in any attempt to learn and practice wider understanding—it is an attempt to 'think the unthinkable' in terms of existing professionalised disciplines. Finally it entails acceptance of the consequent marginality of the position taken up, together with the possibility of professional and institutional sanctions.

I will now try to elaborate the three criteria—reflexivity, transdisciplinarity and the subversiveness of knowledge—before going on to apply the new approach to two substantive problem areas in the human sciences: women's roles and class conflict.

Reflexivity applied as a criterion entails the requirement that any theory in the human sciences should be turned around upon the person or group producing it and must thereby account for the concurrently personal and social activity of producing the theory. It is probably sufficient to say that the activity of producing the theory must at least be consistent with the theory itself; that is, it should provide some understanding, not necessarily complete, of how it came to be produced in its particular time and place. If there is an inconsistency between the content of a theory and the conditions of its emergence it starts its career with a built-in implausibility or limitation. Recalling the many personal and social purposes of knowledge production, which was seen in many cases to be simultaneously a process of knowledge *avoidance*, it is not surprising that flawed theories come to be produced. At the same time it has been amply demonstrated that by forcing the issue, so to speak, and making a theory answer to itself, a critique of considerable power can be constructed; a critique which uses the rigorously drawn conclusions of a theory against the theory itself. I note that the virtuoso 'readers', Althusser, Lacan and Wilden, all use the resources of a theory to criticise and develop it: dialectical materialism is turned on Marx, Freud's theory is turned upon the psychoanalytic community, and Lacan's theory is turned around upon Lacan himself by Wilden.

In fact, the results of reflexive analysis of personality and role theories give a strong indication of certain kinds of approach so radical in their implications that they cannot be fitted into subsequent theories without undergoing considerable distortion. I refer to the three great contributors who appeared most frequently as absent or shadowy antagonists in the work here analysed: Freud, Marx and Husserl. Freud's theory is reflexive for it grew out of his own long and painful self-analysis. Marx's theory is reflexive because it accounts for the emergence of just such a theory as Marx produced at the time and place in which he worked. Husserl's theory is reflexive because its phenomenological method is based on, and shows the need for, radical self-reflection.

But assuming the lesson of failed reflexivity is now well learned and comes to be asserted as a criterion in future work, what has brought about this new possibility? Obviously this question must be asked in order to abide by the most elementary rule of reflexivity, which is that a new standpoint in the human sciences must *explain itself*. Dealing first with sociology, the development of the discipline must be related to the development of its subject matter—society. That the early history of sociology was dominated by the desire to emulate the successes and methods of the natural sciences I take to be beyond dispute. That it continues to develop substantially in this direction using organismic analogies and evolutionary models (no matter how transformed into concepts of development, modernisation and the like) is, I suggest a fair general description of the discipline, in spite of minor diversions into cultural sciences, symbolic interactionism and, more recently, interpretive sociologies. That sociology developed as an alternative to revolutionary thought and is a bastion against such disruption is I think a more debatable proposition. It has been described in exactly this way.

Sociology was born as the conservative answer to socialism. . . .

An image of society was presented which required respect for its wholeness, untouchability and integrity. At the same time, by appropriating the scientific method and pressing it into the service of the organismic theory, the teeth had been pulled from reformist, revolutionary and socialistic programs.[6]

Nisbet, too, has taken a similar view, seeing the sociological tradition as a nineteenth century 'reaction to individualism' which takes a polarised form, with Tocqueville at one extreme and Marx at the other.[7] Bottomore would draw attention to the liberal and radical contributions to the formation of sociology.[8]

As I see it there is a need to differentiate European, British and American sociological traditions because I think it has been clearly demonstrated that transformation processes operate at the boundaries of these separate systems, quite capable of giving greatly altered significance to a common source. The liberal and radical contributors were not British and the British tradition is strongly conservative, positivistic and evolutionary through the line of Spencer, Hobhouse and Ginsberg. Sociology as a theoretical discipline did not grow quickly in Britain although empirical work on the great social surveys took place. Social thought was dominated by the social philosophers who, from Burke through T. H. Green to Bosanquet, formulated the conservative and liberal idealist positions which although a 'reaction to individualism' resolve potential conflict by the powerful idea that self comes to full realisation in and through an organic whole-society or the State. Thus idealism has never disposed of individualism, merely rationalised it, and presumably this is because the economic and political holders of power have never been displaced, and still require an ideology of individualism.

Given this general direction of the discipline, what needs to be explained is the very recent change, occupying not much more time than the period over which this study has been gradually formulated: the change which opens up the possibility of a reflexive sociology. It is not, paradoxically, a consequence of current concern with interpretive, ethnomethodological or phenomenological paradigms of sociology, in spite of the concentration of these groups on reflexive aspects of human action. It is rather two other changes of a more economic and ideological character which have been decisive.

Firstly, sociology's recent acceleration of research into the social processes of the natural and physical sciences has shown what an inflated valuation sociologists had placed on these apparent exemplars of methods and criteria in scientific work. It is to David Bloor[9] that we owe the clearest expression of achievements along this line of work: his *Knowledge and Social Imagery* draws upon the philosophical writings of Wittgenstein,[10] the anthropology of Mary Douglas,[11] and is an attempt to realise a sociology of knowledge adumbrated but not developed in the later work of Durkheim. It is a strong sociology of knowledge in the sense that it shows the great scope for interpetation and negotiation even within the apparently most objective and pure disciplines. Although Mannheim excluded mathematics and the natural sciences from exploration by means of a sociology of knowledge, Bloor shows that no area of knowledge is immune to such analysis. One of Bloor's contributions is that he brings philosophy back into sociological analysis and shows by implication what a great loss it was that sociology moved away from philosophical questions, for the professional and historical reasons explained earlier.

Mary Douglas, whose study of meaning, ritual, symbolism and cosmologies is acknowledged by Bloor, returns to sociology its anthropological resources, showing again what a price has been paid for the division of labour into separate disciplines. The illogicality of this particular separation, already noted by MacIntyre and Emmet, may be seen as one of the factors underlying MacIntyre's view that the 'key point of our intellectual failure is in the human sciences'[12] and also that the

> ... absence of a central concept of human nature and the non-historical features of the social sciences continually invade other disciplines.[13]

My own approach to enrichment of the sociology of knowledge was to note the irrational and contradictory way in which Mannheim moved away from Marx by excluding the study of ideology whilst relying heavily on Marx's basic theory. So although I began from a weak sociology of knowledge I discovered at an early stage in the present study that a stronger thesis was essential to take account of discoveries relating to transdisciplinary questions surrounding personality and role theories.

All three approaches—the close study of scientific knowledge, the anthropological investigation of knowledge in relation to social structures, and the analysis of self, role and the relations between disciplines—seek to put back into sociological analysis theories, methods and insights which were excluded for reasons that can now be explained—the division of labour, professionalisation and their cognitive and ideological concomitants. And since the restoration of sociology's most powerful resources also results in the creation of a sociology of knowledge powerful enough to apply to sociology itself, this is a reflexive clarification of a major kind.

And now the second major reason for this move towards reflexivity may be set out. The great expansion of sociology in the nineteen-sixties threatened a widespread propagation of relativist (and therefore potentially subversive) views of society, a threat seemingly confirmed by the involvement of sociology students in campus and other disturbances. Whether or not sociology was revolutionary at this time it became a scapegoat and was treated as such by governments, mass media and the public. What better incentive to explore revolutionary theories than to be accused of holding them? This set the stage for a serious return to Marx and the neo-Marxists. Marx could now be taken back into the discipline without cost to professional and institutional status because the price had already been paid in prejudice directed at a stereotype.

A pendant economic point is that the expansion of sociology now made it commercially viable to translate and import the literature of the European revolutionary tradition.

In summary, sociology may now have overcome its 'imprinting' on mistaken parent figures—the natural and physical sciences—so enabling it to recover its history, its subject matter and most powerful analytic tools: it has come of age. The condition of this emergence is a strong sociology of knowledge capable of turning sociology upon itself in continuous criticism and collective self-reflection—reflexivity at last.

Turning now to the second criterion, transdisciplinarity, it may be possible to bring out the relation between sociology and psychology. Just as social theories are born in a particular social and historical location, so are theories of self and personality the product of a particular self-structure within a social context. But since the social context acts formatively on the self, radical self-reflection includes the need for a sociology of knowledge; this in addition to the more obviously psychological resources for self-reflection available in psychoanalysis and phenomenology. So the reflexivity of psychology is dependent on a transdisciplinary approach which uses an enriched sociology capable of clarifying both itself and psychology. But this is not quite all because, although it was left aside from the discussion of sociology to wait until psychology had been dealt with, it follows that any formative, social contextual influences operating on all theorists within the human sciences are located in self-concepts and include psychological variables. Thus it appears that the last thing we must do is leave psychology to the psychologists and sociology to the sociologists. And this programme of double-clarification based on the critical interaction of two disciplines now seems worthy of the term '*a human science*'.

The subversiveness of exploration at this level consists in its refusal to see a disciplinary boundary as anything more than a challenge to psychosocial explanation. As Wilden points out, drawing a boundary at a particular point on a continuum creates paradox, and it is only when we have learned to become aware of the consequences of these discontinuities that we are able to climb out of the maze of polarisations, mirror identifications, and endless repetitions of mistaken view.

9.4 A HUMAN SCIENCE IN ACTION

If the foundations of a new approach have been well and truly laid it should be possible to build something upon them. This is not to underestimate the difficulty of work in a new field or to think that problem areas will simply dissolve when set out in a new way. It is only to say at this stage that it should be possible to see the way through some problem areas, subject to detailed working out in the light of relevant and feasible investigations. For purposes of trying out a more transdisciplinary strategy I propose to work gradually towards the exploration of two problems which at the moment lie across the disciplinary boundaries of sociology and psychology: women's roles, and the possibility of a role theory of class conflict. Selection of the first problem probably needs no further justification since it is an urgent and pervasive issue of the present day. The second problem will cause little doubt as to the importance of class conflict but it may not be readily apparent why the relevance of role theory is an open question. The point is that if Worsley's estimation of the central importance of role[14] is set alongside Popitz's considered opinion that the concept has limited applicability to class conflict[15] (and both are theorists of some quality) then it may appear that the central concept of the human sciences is unable to deal with the central problem of human societies. All is lost before we begin. I propose therefore to draw together the resources necessary for exploration of the following hypotheses.

(1) *It is only the impoverished concept of role, lacking an inter-disciplinary base or transdisciplinary sensitivity that is unable to deal with class conflict.*

(2) *It is possible to devise a concept of role which is adequate to the subject matter of women's roles within the area of women's studies.*

The build-up to this will consist of recovering for role theory what has been excluded and separated by the social processes previously discussed: to this may then be added insights gained in the course of critical analysis and the results of other similar or relevant approaches.

A common objection to the concept of role is that since it comes into sociology as a metaphor derived from playing a role in the theatre it is not strongly applicable to the 'real life' of society. After all, actors drop their acting at the end of a performance and go back to their 'real life'. How can such a pretence as acting capture the serious business of social interaction. The objection is not well founded and attempts to erode the value of the concept by too literal an interpretation of the metaphor which brought it into the human sciences. It shows that a relatively superficial view of theatre as diverting entertainment is being used to separate play-acting from social-acting. Just a glance at the extent of dramatisation and enactment of social events will show that the drama takes its form from the social interaction of which it is a part. This is not to say that even the most realistic drama is only a re-enactment of a 'slice of life' because the fact that something is selected for re-enactment suggests that it has resonances and references beyond itself. It may be very literally a re-enactment of some event, like the recreation of a trial taken from a transcript, but the emphasis that is implicit in this choice says something more than is contained in the events of the play: it says something about the human condition, however particular or general. And the acting work that is put in by the role-players is quite as serious as any other kind of social occupation.

The same issue can be tackled by argument from another direction:

the extent to which society's 'real life' is endowed with the characteristics of enactment. Consider, for example, one of the crucial points of class-conflict theory; the thesis that a minority of the population can, by use of the political apparatus of the State which possesses a monopoly of the means of violent force, maintain its oppression of the majority. How often is this force actually used? In relation to its potential use the answer is virtually never. And yet it stands as a constant threat and reminder by very frequent enactment of its power through displays of many kinds. While the actual bodyguards are dressed in plain clothes, a guard of honour is paraded for inspection. In other words, the drama has many levels: the actual need for protection of a public figure is concealed at the same time as a symbolic enactment of the protective function is displayed.

Not only is power virtually never used, there is also a sense that when its stronger elements do have to be used something has been lost. When, for example, a police force can no longer keep control and the army has to be called in this shows what a serious threat has been posed. If strikers face troops, or even have their jobs done by troops, this is a sign that the situation has become serious: the forces of capital and labour face each other unmediated by the normal peace-keeping functions of police intermediaries.

On the other hand, consider the dramatistic qualities of strikes and demonstrations. A withdrawal of labour is most significant for the repercussions it causes, since this reveals interdependencies not normally appreciated and draws attention to, or dramatises, the striker's case, though filtered through a biased communication system. A demonstration hardly needs discussion, so evidently is it a display. Estimates of numbers, frequently discrepant by one hundred per cent, show the importance of the question as to whether this particular turn-out, with all that it represents, constitutes a threat to the ruling powers. So its relation to the dramatistic model of society does not so much disqualify the concept of role as support its application to social interaction; the metaphor is well drawn and rich in possibilities.

Lionel Trilling has used the work of Clifford Geertz, an anthropologist, to show that in some cultures the dramatistic metaphor is very directly related to the social reality.

Javanese culture has as one of its functions to induce its members to become as much as possible like works of art.[16]

And quoting Geertz

> ... that there is in Bali a persistent and systematic attempt to stylize all aspects of personal expression to the point where anything idiosyncratic, anything characteristic of the individual mainly because he is who he is physically, psychologically, or biographically, is muted in favour of his assigned place in the continued, and so it is thought, never changing pageant that is Balinese life. It is dramatis personae, not actors, that in the proper sense really exist.[17]

Trilling suggests that in the West, familiar as we are with the idea of playing our role in society, we still tend to look for the more essential reality, feeling that it would be morally wrong to arrange our social life in the manner of the changeless pageantry of the Javanese and Balinese. Our own ideal of the expressive, articulate self contrasts sharply with the self-effacing pattern of their lives. And yet the beautiful unchanging form of their social rites, seemingly touched with the changeless immobility of death, is fascinating to us. Do not we, in enjoying the working out of a tragedy or in contemplating the fixed forms of works of art, show that the idea of integrated perfection, or the idea simply of *being* is attractive and important? Trilling sees these alternations between the ideals of an individually articulate, expressive self and the frozen beauty of fixed life/art forms as a dialectic 'with all the dignity that inheres in that word . . .'[18] (and here his manuscript ends with the last act of writing before his death).

So the deeper qualities which give form to the dialectic of various self/society relationships are accessible to the humanistic critic. Given this, Trilling wonders whether Geertz needs to employ the difficult process of elucidation implicit in the 'hermeneutic spiral', a method frequently used by anthropologists to work out the meanings attached by participants to the unfamiliar life forms they seek to understand. The method involves repeated movement from general conceptions to the form of life under investigation to 'the vehicles in which that form is embodied'. In more familiar terms: movement between the society and the self. The interest of Trilling's contribution is that he exemplifies the humanistic critic, secure in his intuitive grasp of various forms of life and slightly impatient with the anthropologist who spells out his hermeneutic methodology as though to demonstrate the reliability and rigour of his approach. Moving further away from the humanities and Trilling, towards greater methodological rigour, the next discipline to be encountered would be sociology with its stress on causal relationships and generalisations. And yet they are all devoted to the same problem: the dialectical relationship between self and society. The most intuitive (Trilling) knows that he must draw reliable conclusions from the evidence of his experience; the most 'scientific' (the sociologist) knows that he must inject intuitive, conjectural insights into his scientific methods if they are to come alive. Differences of approach seem to be a matter of disciplinary convention, and of trivial importance compared with the interest in identical subject matter.

It can be shown that Trilling's concept of the articulate, expressive Western personality is somewhat class-bound in that it is more typical of the middle-class than of the working-class person.[19] On the other hand, it is easy to demonstrate by the paucity of the literature that sociology has not managed to cope with the arts and human expressivity. In short, their respective failures show how very much the disciplines need to be placed in critical interpenetration. It seems that for the sake of addressing the particular qualities of this subject matter one is entitled to reject subject boundaries, make strong use of the dramatistic model of society, and to notice that the concept of role directs attention to the site of significant interactions between societies and selves.

Where then does this take the concept of role? Towards anthropological studies of the meaningful interactions which at first sight are so strange that they seem beyond understanding, but which yield to the kind of analysis that has been developed to deal with ritual, symbolism and the social construction and use of classification systems. The outstanding recent contribution here comes from Mary Douglas.

She provides another beautiful example of the reflexivity that can be achieved by taking the work of a theorist and applying it rigorously to the theorist's own social activity of producing the theory. Durkheim distinguished the sacred and the profane in societies, attributing the special qualities of the sacred to its 'collective' significance for the social group. Douglas, with acknowledgement to Bloor (1973) and Lukes (1973), shows how Durkheim operated a similar classification system himself, placing scientific knowledge into the specially protected category of the sacred where it could be regarded as beyond doubt: it did not need to be explained as something generated by patterns of social interaction in the way that totemic classifications can be so explained.

As soon as we are prepared to take the bold step of regarding science as a system of categories just like any other, generated by social interaction and capable of being explained in relation to it, the way is open for far-reaching investigation. This is, of course, a version of the strong sociology of knowledge already found to be essential in deep reading of self and role theories. What Douglas gives to it is an amazing richness of evidence from anthropological sources, revealed in such patient and ingenious analysis that it cannot be done justice in a short space. Nevertheless, some major points demand consideration.

Douglas will not accept in advance any limitation on the range of investigation to be undertaken. In a sense it is the very certainty of sacred belief and the certainty attributed to self-evidence in logic and science which constitute the sharpest challenge to explore their social base. Nothing is sacred and certainly not certainty.

Consider then the social activity of forming categories or systems of classification: integral to it is the fixing of boundaries which then have to be maintained. These boundaries may occur at the level of the society where certain border conditions apply, or at many other levels, for example around a kinship group where border conditions are specified by marriage rules and the like. (It may be recalled what significance Wilden attached to flows of information and energy at the boundaries of open systems.) According to Douglas, any boundary or class is part of a whole system of boundaries and classes such that the significance of any boundary-relevant practice, object or symbolisation is best understood when general features of the system are known. And the most boundary-relevant phenomena for any system of classification are *anomalous* entities. Like it or not, these constitute a danger to the classification system itself, and their treatment is therefore crucial for understanding the secular or religious cosmologies which are implicit in any system of classification.

The pig, in Judaism, is abominable. Its anomalous quality is that it cleaves the hoof but does not, like the ungulates, chew the cud. Then a bold hypothesis: the Israelites were a people with physically insecure or non-existent boundaries, surrounded by rapacious enemies. Securing the boundaries of the categories in their cosmology, which is after all the symbolic representation of the society, is a reflection of the dangers of the social situation. Boundary crossing, or its symbolic equivalent, category mediation (anomaly), is abominable. Dietary rules pick up and transmit these 'self-evident' concerns so that the societal symbolism resonates with social and historical experience.

Contrast the Lele experience of their societal boundary as revealed by the extent to which their marriage rules allow strangers to come in.

> . . . everything in the Lele working of their rules turns them to hope for sons-in-law or brides from distant places or along half-forgotten genealogical links going several generations back. [20]

Douglas then finds it possible to place in the scheme of things her earlier fieldwork on the pangolin: a small four-legged, tree-dwelling animal, scaly and fish-like in the body; an anomalous creature. The pangolin is like a human being in that it does not run away when met in the forest but bows its head like a man who meets his mother-in-law; it also bears its young singly. The Lele use the pangolin as part of a fertility cult where its anomalous status mediates between human and animal categories. In a sense it brings the fertility of the animal world into the human world in a form which matches the typical single-birth characteristics of the human. There are other aspects of Lele symbolism and practice, too numerous to detail, which reinforce this interpretation.

As an intermediate case, the Karam allow exchange and boundary crossing but with a due caution dictated by their social experience. Such crossing is safeguarded by a system of rules which seek to neutralise dangers and direct beneficial effects. The general thesis holds: that the treatment of anomalies allows precise, seemingly self-evident, boundary maintenance operations to be instituted at various levels of social activity. Relatively secure boundary conditions in which advantageous exchange can be managed tend to produce cosmologies of mediation; relatively insecure, dangerous boundary conditions tend to produce cosmologies with pure categories together with excluded subsets of anomalies marked by dirt, pollution or abomination.

I am immediately struck by the importance given here to boundary conditions and my earlier analysis of what happens to knowledge when it passes over societal boundaries. It now seems that the same material could be reworked in the light of new hypotheses so that the intuitive and hermeneutic analysis of texts could be linked more productively to anthropological data. To take what is probably the clearest example, the passage of knowledge from mainly European sources into the United States what new insights emerge?

American society has relatively secure and open boundaries: it encouraged immigration until 1924 and continues to allow it in a controlled way. In fact, as long as the frontier existed either in actuality or in myth it was a dreamlike boundary which could be pushed back to include even more beautiful territories and riches. People were needed to open up and develop the country. At the same time, pioneering a frontier was a rough and dangerous activity demanding a simple faith that God would guide the settlers, as well as a frugal and practical attitude. Larzer Ziff, reviewing *The Puritan Origins of the American Self*, says

> Only democratic idealism and the frontier compare in force with the shaping effect Puritanism has had on American culture. Democratic idealism generated institutions and although one may, of course, study changing ideas of democracy in the abstract, a record of their continuity resides in the history of the constitutions and governments now existing in the United States. The frontier closed in 1893 (presumably; there is some debate about this resulting from the ways in which 'frontier' may be defined), recently enough for its influence still to be read in American habits as well as American books.[21]

In the early dangerous days of settlement the Puritans saw themselves as the Israelites, wandering in a new land, spreading the light of the gospel as they travelled westwards. It then seems not too fanciful to see the gradual erosion of pure categories of Puritanism, brought about by the very success of settlement and development of the new land. The frontier, secured, takes on the mythological status of a place where rugged, individual enterprise can realise its cacapities; there is opportunity for all comers. From purity to mediation; from Puritanism to a highly secular religiosity.[22]

The fundamental assumptions built into American personality theories now seem to relate quite strikingly to this interpretation of the cultural background. The cosmology *invites all comers*. Not, of course, revolutionaries and radicals who might try to challenge the democratic idealism which has been used to deport and persecute communists through into the days of McCarthyist 'witch-hunts'.

But, revolutionaries apart, any kind of knowledge and philosophy including the European may come in.

All the theorists operate cosmologies of integration, which is also to say cosmologies of mediation. The assumption seems to be that given good will (and the bad will of 'nay-saying' existentialism or the 'aggression' of Freud must not interfere with this), all these foreign ideas can live together or form parts of an integrated whole. Thus, for example, Mead sponsored the immigrant Hegel and married him to behaviourism; the neo-Freudians imported Freud and 'socialised' him; Allport imported nearly everybody and left them milling around getting to know each other; Maslow and Rogers found Freud and existentialism in their baggage and tried not to let it show too much, both using the most transcendent and omnipotent fantasies to mediate wo/man and nature. Erikson, grateful for honoured refuge, gave America its 'stages of life', ending with integrity, containing its identity crisis by the integrative powers of the ego. Kelly, not knowing existentialism, rolled up his sleeves and with an intellectual frontiersman's practicality simply improvised it. Even where not explicitly religious the religiosity of all these theories, their cosmological quality, is clearly apparent.

In addition to explaining why theorists produce certain forms of knowledge, such an analysis deals at the same time with the related question of why societies take up and institutionalise certain forms of knowledge. All the personality theorists whose work was examined had gained at least moderate, and some very widespread, acceptance.

A very interesting case for comparison lies to hand in the migration of the Frankfurt School to the United States in the 1930s. Martin Jay's history of this group shows that in spite of their generally unorthodox stance they were, *in intellectual terms*, surprisingly literal inheritors of the Jewish predicament. Marginal in their own country, Germany; radical intellectuals with a sense of a special mission to safeguard critical reason against fascism; in flight to a country which on their belief about the political function of liberalism could turn fascist, they closed their boundaries against American society and its pragmatic philosophy. Financial independence allowed them to form only tenuous links with American academies; they wrote in German and kept their categories pure until they could return to Germany.

Seeing this isolation as having its costs in lack of academic contact as well as the benefit of being able to preserve a unique critical position, Jay says

> Although often in some contact with the regular faculty at Columbia, the Frankfurt School remained generally outside the main stream of American academic life. This allowed it to make assumptions, such as the equation of pragmatism with positivism, that lacked complete validity. It also cut the Institut off from potential allies in the American intellectual tradition, such as George Herbert Mead.[23]

The incredible persistence of a cosmology of integration and mediation leads again to matchmaking with Mead! Yet is it clear from the earlier analysis that Mead would be disgusted with any suitor who came bearing the gift of Freud. Nor is it certain that the critical theorists would have been able to communicate with a man who had 'integrated' Hegel and behaviourism: in terms of intellectual kinship rules this must surely have seemed to them an unholy and possibly 'abominable' alliance. For this reason it is not in the least surprising that Jay could find only one passing reference to Mead in critical theory.

There is further evidence from Jay's fine and scholarly account that knowledge is subjected to effective selection processes. When the critical theorists first began to seek a refuge

> Pollock made a trip to London in February, 1934, to appraise the possibility of establishing the Institut in England; but intensive negotiations with Sir William Beveridge, director of the London School of Economics, and Farquharson and his colleagues at the Institute of Sociology convinced him of its unlikelihood. The limited opportunities in England for the refugee scholars who began to stream out of Germany in 1933 have been frequently noted.[24]

It must be obvious that the present study shares some concerns of the Frankfurt School; it proceeds at times in a similar critical spirit seeking both to expose and avoid those premature resolutions of conflict that are so damaging to serious exploration. The fact that they tried to take the full import of Marx and Freud brings them into close relevance. Unfortunately, the unavailability of critical theory in English kept most parts other than Marcuse's out of my sight until a very late stage of this work, so I can only note some points of correspondence and difference that come to me as independent checks on common problems. A separate study and thorough comparison are indicated but my general feeling is that I should be unwilling to follow them back into the Mannheim-like stance they have adopted as a result of acceptance and fame.[25]

In respect of the broader problem of constructing a more effective human science, one or two particular lessons can be learned from critical theory. That Marx and Freud are indispensable although nobody has successfully 'integrated' them. That there are systematic relationships between knowledge, ideology, mass communication, political power and economic determination which still defy our understanding and for which no unidisciplinary theory is adequate. That we may be in danger of losing our capacities as well as our opportunities to understand the totality of which we form a part.[26]

At this point I shall leave aside the project of criticism and reconstruction which must clearly go on for a very long time in the new territory opened up by a reflexive and transdisciplinary approach and try to assess rather directly and briefly whether there is now some strong foundation for a role theory capable of dealing with class conflict and women's roles.

Reviewing the critical exposition undertaken in Chapter 5 it is possible to reject immediately that stereotype of role which sees it as simply a socially prescribed dialogue (Bannister and Fransella, following Kelly). On the psychological side we can learn something from Kelly's concept of role. His individualism is so intense in its innocence that it leads to a disguised diatribe against social constraints and social forces of all kinds. (That is why he was never able to 'develop' his central concept.) So the fantasy of an autonomous individual may be discarded and with it the abstraction in psychology of roles from social contexts. Noticing the tendency to polarise self and society evident throughout role theory we register this as a pitfall to be avoided.

It has been argued that choices made in respect of any one role are conditioned by the requirements of other actual or potential roles (Goffman's 'role-distance', modified by Coser's 'role-ambivalence'). This kind of social determinism was qualified by the occurrence of new situations in changing societies, for which no role prescriptions could exist (Emmet). Possibly Java and Bali (Trilling, following Geertz) come close to being perfectly stable—a socially prescribed scenario if not dialogue—but I believe closer study would show this stability to be only relative. There can be few environments or open systems so stable as to call out no new choices. These new social actions may then turn out to be merely adaptive or radically subversive in their consequences; commitment either way in advance is unnecessary and cases must be examined in their context.

At this point, where the issue is creativity in human interaction, we need only note from the symposium that the literary critic's interest is understandably in those aspects of human choice and action which escape role-determination, or which invest role performance with such particularity of expression or style that it takes on artistic significance. It was seen that the professional sociologist, committed to scientific generalisations, was forced to retreat from these unmanageable aspects of role but in the light of new understanding of the relations between disciplines it can be seen as an unproductive splitting of the subject matter. A human science must give full weight to the human capacity to create significance, even though this does not occur routinely. Merleau-Ponty's phenomenology is exemplary in this.

The differentiation of society into various institutions and conflicting groups opens out role theory so that it covers a wider range of situations than the merely consensual, or those involving what Goode calls 'role-strain'.[27] It is necessary to recognise the forced imposition of some roles upon their incumbents and thus allow roles to be seen as alienating. The concept of 'reference group' tends to imply voluntary choice of the group to which one refers one's identity and does not make prominent the involuntary or coerced identifications. In other words, the concept of society as both/and (Wilden) a framework of self-realisation and a system of oppression frees role from its monopoly by 'integrative' theorists. Esterson, Laing and Cooper, and particularly Esterson in his study of the Danzig family, work strongly over this alienative dimension of the concept. It can therefore be seen that when allowed to retain its transdisciplinary power the concept of role can deal with major elements of class conflict.

As to women's roles the new position would require sociologists to apply the principle of reflexivity and study *their own roles* in relation to those they regard as subject matter. The first question to arise on this new foundation of the strong sociology of knowledge would be, 'Who produces, from the basis of what interests, "knowledge" of sex-roles?' As it is, the predominantly male sociologists and anthropologists have been caught with inadequate or non-existent resources in the face of an explosion of interest in women's studies.

Perhaps the most enlightening part of the Committee's investigation was the discovery that many able sociologists . . . abandon the empirical stance and rely upon folk myth and stereotype.[28]

The anthropological literature tells us relatively little about women, and provides almost no theoretical apparatus for understanding, or describing culture from a woman's point of view.[29]

It seems also that the very language of these disciplines is corrupted by biased terminology.[30]

Applying the second principle, transdisciplinarity, if psychologists had paid attention to sex roles as socially constructed phenomena, rather than as simply 'given' either by nature or evolution, they would have seen a problem area to be elucidated rather than a set of individual or sex differences to be mapped. This would have opened out categories of sexuality for exploration rather than freezing the differences by cataloguing them. Even relatively good work in psychology, which knows the problem, can propose solutions which bring female achievement motivation up to the level of males. Apparently the oppression is to be seen as fortuitous and resting upon undesirably 'arbitrary' socialisation.[31]

The new anthopological evidence may serve as a reminder that sex roles are probably the most fundamental categories to be dealt with in any society after the problem of societal boundaries (which they may anyway reflect). Recognition of this heavy weight of ritual, symbolisation and mythology will assist understanding both of the invisibility of the problem in the social and behavioural sciences and of the resistance to change, or even examination, of the deep structure of sex roles.

The historical evidence from Marcus on sexuality and pornography in mid-nineteenth century England shows how the *science* of sexuality, written by men, not only rested on male phantasy but on a projection of the mirror-image of this phantasy onto women. The 'splitting' of virtuous wife and prostitute, the 'double standard' of morality imposed to safeguard inheritance and the exploitation of working-class women and servants, were a crude manifestation of scientifically rationalised oppression. The relation between pornography and science of the day is of some interest.

At all points they touch either by analogy or by analogy through opposition, and sometimes both at once. In both there is a similar split or divided consciousness; both are dominated by the logic of fantasy and association rather than by the logic of events or of consecutive thought. Both are also worlds without psychology; they are worlds of organs and physiology in which everything is convertible into matter. That is to say, both represent a primitive form of materialism. In pornography, this fantasy purports to be subversive and liberating. In Acton's work it represents itself as grimly scientific and ineluctably tragic. What is of largest interest, however, is that at this moment in history a human science—the investigation of sexuality—had attained approximately the same stage of intellectual development as pornography itself.[32]

In short, the science in this sensitive area was profoundly ideological, fantastic and phantastic, and the tragedy is that the social and behavioural sciences have not yet fully cleared themselves of these distortions. Even if we now see a little more clearly, there is work still to be done.

If the domination of women and of social classes has been sustained and facilitated by false knowledge, though created by deeper forces we can hardly articulate, let alone control, then the gain in knowledge which results from letting reflexive light into the dark places in and between impoverished disciplines will not of itself bring liberation. But given the weight of social forces which, as we may now see, inhibit discovery in the human sciences, any movement at all is, in terms of knowledge, a revolutionary step.

9.5 POSTSCRIPT

As I close this beginning stage of what may turn out to be a long journey through the areas opened up by reflexive, transdisciplinary analysis I am struck by two metaphors in the very recent literature. Peter Archibald discusses the relation between psychology, sociology and social psychology under the subtitle 'bad fences make bad neighbours',[33] and Claude Fischer proposes a redefinition of 'alienation' aimed at 'bridging the chasm' between its theoretical and empirical uses.[34] Both contributions are symptomatic of the present concern about the condition of knowledge in the human sciences. Fischer's idea of a chasm corresponds to what I have called 'the interdisciplinary void'. Archibald sees the specialisation and separation of the disciplines as increasing over the past two decades and gives examples of yet further institutional separation. He recognises ideological processes in the split, suggesting a critique which is both sociological and psychological.

> ... whatever psychologists or sociologists were supposed to uniquely do, methodologically, conceptually, theoretically or ideologically, the characterization fitted poorly at best. ... When we couple this questionable empirical status with the logical contradictions among the arguments within the two disciplines' paradigms, I think we are justified in calling both the paradigms and the various combinations of them ideologies in the more restricted Marxist sense; that is, they are justifications, mainly unjustified, that privileged groups use to justify their privileges. The privileges, and certainly not rights in this case (property or otherwise), are the profitable and prestigeful titles of Psychologist and Sociologist. The desirable course of action is clear: both the disciplinary boundaries and the paradigms within them should be torn down and the latter reconstructed. [35]

I am delighted to see an independent analysis that agrees in some respects with my own although I notice that Archibald's interpretation of the situation is both more and less radical than mine. He seems to see the split as affecting more of the subject matter of the separate disciplines than I do, with the implication that the fences separating them should be torn down—the disciplines should be put together completely; I suggest, rather, the identification of mediation phenomena (such as role) and radically reflexive work in these areas. On the other hand, it seems to me that Archibald underestimates both the extent to which the disciplines are *professionalised*, making it necessary to draw boundaries which locate a monopoly of certain kinds of research and practice, and the extent to which these *professional property* rights are deeply and historically institutionalised. I see no reason to hope that Archibald's exhortation to tear down the fences (an integration fantasy resting on the cosmology of neighbourly good will) should be heeded by the very 'interested' people to whom it is addressed. Tear down the fence but the 'chasm' remains. And to push this point to its limits, if the bodies of knowledge we construct are ideological in the fully Marxian sense, does he think the deeper interests we serve will allow us to relinquish professional property rights which are the privilege we enjoy in return for the production of separate, manageable, exchangeable units of knowledge: our intellectual commodities?

REFERENCES

1 F. Dainton. *Enquiry into the Flow of Candidates in Science and Technology into Higher Education*, Cmnd 3541, HMSO, London (1968)
2 G. E. R. Lloyd. *Polarity and Analogy: two types of argumentation in early Greek thought*, Cambridge University Press, London (1966), p. 67
3 A. Salomon. German sociology. In *Twentieth Century Sociology* (eds G. Gurvitch and W. E. Moore), McLeod, Toronto (1945), p. 596
4 L. D. Easton and K. H. Guddat. *Writings of the Young Marx on Philosophy and Society*, Anchor, New York (1967), p. 402
5 J. R. Ravetz. *Scientific Knowledge and its Social Problems*, Clarendon, Oxford (1971), p. 94
6 D. Martindale. *The Nature and Types of Sociological Theory*, Routledge, London (1961), p. 529
7 R. Nisbet. *The Sociological Tradition*, Heinemann, London (1967), p. viii
8 T. Bottomore. *Sociology*, Allen & Unwin, London (1971), p. 19
9 D. Bloor. *Knowledge and Social Imagery*, Routledge, London (1976)
10 L. Wittgenstein. *Remarks on the Foundations of Mathematics*, Blackwell, Oxford (1956)
11 M. Douglas, *Natural Symbols*, Penguin, Harmondsworth, Middx (Barrie & Rockliff, London, 1970)
12 A. MacIntyre. Breaking the chains of reason. In *Out of Apathy* (ed. E. P. Thompson), New Left Books, London (1960), p. 209
13 ibid., p. 227
14 P. Worsley. The distribution of power in industrial society. In *The Development of Industrial Societies*, Sociological Review Monograph No. 8, University of Keele Press, Keele, Staffs (1964), p. 15
15 H. Popitz. Role as an element of sociological theory. In *Role* (ed. J. A. Jackson), Cambridge University Press, London (1972), p. 35
16 L. Trilling. Why we read Jane Austen, *Times Lit. Suppl.*, 3860, 5 March (1976), p. 252

17 C. Geertz. In L. Trilling, Why we read Jane Austen, *Times Lit. Suppl.*, 3860, 5 March (1976), p. 252
18 L. Trilling. ibid., p. 252
19 B. Bernstein. *Class, Codes and Control*, Routledge, London (1971)
20 M. Douglas. *Implicit Meanings*, Routledge, London (1975), p. 297
21 L Ziff. Founding fathers and sons, *Times Lit. Suppl.*, 16 July (1976), p. 869. Review of S. Bercovitch, *The Puritan Origins of the American Self*, Yale University Press, New Haven, Conn., and London (1975)
22 A. MacIntyre. *Secularization and Moral Change*, Oxford University Press, Oxford (1967), p. 32
23 M. Jay. *The Dialectical Imagination*, Heinemann, London (1973), p. 289
24 ibid., p. 37
25 ibid., p. 292
26 R. Jacoby. *Social Amnesia*, Beacon Press, Boston, Mass. (1975)
27 W. J. Goode. A theory of role strain, *Am. Sociol. Rev.*, 25 (1960), 483–96
28 A. Oakley. *The Sociology of Housework*, Martin Robertson, London (1974), p. 24
29 M. Z. Rosaldo and L. Lamphere. *Woman, Culture and Society*, Stanford University Press, Stanford, Calif. (1974), p. vi
30 C. Ehrlich. The male sociologist's burden: the place of women in marriage and family texts, *J. Marriage & Fam.*, 33, 3 (1971), 421–30
31 E. E. Maccoby and C. N. Jacklin. *The Psychology of Sex Differences*, Oxford University Press, Oxford (1975), p. 1
   I am grateful to Esther Saraga for this observation
32 S. Marcus. *The Other Victorians*, Wiedenfeld & Nicolson, London (1966), p. 32
33 W. P. Archibald. Psychology, sociology and social psychology: bad fences make bad neighbours, *Br. J. Sociol.*, 27, 2 (1976)
34 C. S. Fischer. Alienation: trying to bridge the chasm, *Br. J. Sociol.*, 27, 1 (1976)
35 W. P. Archibald. Psychology, sociology and social psychology: bad fences make bad neighbours, *Br. J. Sociol.*, 27, 2 (1976), 124

Bibliography

Works cited by name in addition to numbered chapter references.

Adorno, T. W. *et al.* (1950). *The Authoritarian Personality*, Harper & Row, New York and London

Aristotle (1955). *The Ethics* (trans. J. A. K. Thompson), Penguin, Harmondsworth, Middx

Ayer, A. J. (1971). *Language, Truth and Logic*, Penguin, Harmondsworth, Middx (Gollancz, London, 1936)

Bateson, G. (1973). *Steps to an Ecology of Mind*, Paladin, St Albans (Chandler, Aylesbury, 1972)

Bloor, D. (1973). Wittgenstein and Mannheim on the sociology of mathematics, *Studies Hist. Philos. Sci.*, **4**, 2

Blumer, H. (1962). Society as symbolic interaction. In *Human Behaviour and Social Processes* (ed. A. Rose), Routledge, London (Houghton Mifflin, Boston, Mass., 1962)

Chomsky, N. (1957). *Syntactic Structures*, Mouton, The Hague

Comte, A. (1875). *The Positive Philosophy of Auguste Comte* (trans. H. Martineau), Kegan Paul, Trench & Trubner, London (Paris, 1830–42)

Cooper, D. G. (1971). *The Death of the Family*, Penguin, Harmondsworth, Middx

Coser, R. L. (1966). Role distance, sociological ambivalence, and transitional status systems, *Am. J. Sociol.*, **72**, 2, 173–187

Coser, L. and Rosenberg, B. (1969). *Sociological Theory: a Book of Readings*, Collier-Macmillan, New York and London

Dahrendorf, R. (1968). *Essays in the Theory of Society*, Routledge, London

Dahrendorf, R. (1958). Out of utopia, *Am. J. Sociol.*, **64**, 2, 115–127

Department of Health and Social Security (1972). *National Health Service Reorganisation: England*, Cmnd 5055, HMSO, London

Duncan, H. D. (1968). *Communication and Social Order*, Oxford University Press, Oxford and New York (Bedminster, 1962)

Emmet, D. (1958). *Function, Purpose and Powers*, Macmillan, London and Basingstoke (2nd edn, 1972)

Esterson, A. (1972). *The Leaves of Spring*, Penguin, Harmonds-worth, Middx (Tavistock, London, 1970)

Gerth, H. and Mills, C. W. (1954). *Character and Social Structure*, Routledge, London

Goffman, E. (1961). *Asylums: essays on the social situation of mental patients and other inmates*, Doubleday, New York

Gouldner, A. (1971). *The Coming Crisis of Western Sociology*, Heinemann, London

Inkles, A. (1959). Personality and social structure. In *Sociology Today* (ed. R. K. Merton *et al.*), Basic Books, New York

Janowitz, M. (1972). Professionalization of sociology, *Am. J. Sociol.*, **78**, July

Kant, I. (1971). *On the Foundation of Morality* (trans. B. E. A. Liddell), Indiana University Press, Bloomington, Ind.

Laing, R. D. (1961). *The Self and Others*, Tavistock, London (Penguin, Harmondsworth, Middx, 1971)

Laing, R. D. (1960). *The Divided Self*, Tavistock, London (Penguin, Harmondsworth, Middx, 1965)

Laing, R. D. (1967). *The Politics of Experience and the Bird of Paradise*, Penguin, Harmondsworth, Middx

Laing, R. D. (1976). *The Politics of the Family*, Penguin, Harmonds-worth, Middx (Tavistock, London, 1971 and Canadian Broad-casting Corporation, 1969)

Laing, R. D. and Cooper, D. G. (1964). *Reason and Violence*, Tavistock, London

Laing, R. D. and Esterson, A. (1964). *Sanity, Madness and the Family*, Penguin, Harmondsworth, Middx (Tavistock, London, 1964)

Levinson, D. J. (1959). Role, personality, and social structure, *J. abnorm. Soc. Psychol.* **58**, 170–180

Linton, R. (1936). *The Study of Man*, Appleton–Century–Croft, New York

Lukes, S. (1973). *Émile Durkheim*, Allen Lane, London

Marcuse, H. (1969). *Eros and Civilisation*, Sphere, London (Beacon Press, Boston, Mass., 1955)

Marx, K. (1970). *Economic and Philosophical Manuscripts of 1884* (trans. M. Milligan), Lawrence & Wishart, London (Inter-national, New York, 1964)

Marx, K. (1971). *The Grundrisse* (trans. D. McLellan), Macmillan, London and Basingstoke

Mead, G. H. (1934). *Mind, Self and Society*, University of Chicago Press, Chicago and London

Merton, R. K. (1957). The role-set: problems in sociological theory, *Br. J. Sociol.*, **8**, 106–120

Merton, R. K. and Kitt, A. S. (1950). *Continuities in Social Research, studies in the scope and method of 'The American Soldier'* (ed. R. K. Merton and P. F. Lazarsfeld), Free Press, New York

Mills, C. W. (1939). Language, logic and culture, *Am. Sociol. Rev.*, **4**, 672

Park, R. E. and Burgess, E. W. (1921). *Introduction to the Science of Sociology*, University of Chicago Press, Chicago and London

Parsons, T. (1951). *The Social System*, Routledge, London

Parsons, T. (1954). *Essays in Sociological Theory* (rev. edn), Free Press, New York (Free Press, 1949)

Royal Commission on the Law Relating to Mental Illness and Mental Deficiency (1954–57). *Report*, Cmnd 169, HMSO, London

Sartre, J-P. (1965). *Nausea*, Penguin, Harmondsworth, Middx (Gallinard, Paris, 1938)

Scheff, T. (1964). Social conditions for rationality, *Am. Behav. Sci.*, **7**, March, 21–27

Sherif, M. (1953). Reference groups in human relations. In *Group Relations at the Crossroads* (ed. M. Sherif and M. O. Wilson), Harper & Row, New York

Shils, E. (1965). The calling of sociology. In *Theories of Society* (ed. T. Parsons *et al.*), Collier-Macmillan, New York and London (Free Press, Glencoe, 1961)

Sills, D. (ed.) (1968). *International Encyclopedia of the Social Sciences*, Collier-Macmillan, New York and London

Sumner, W. G. (1906). *Folkways*, William Graham Sumner, Ginn & Co., Boston, Mass.

Szasz, T. (1962). *The Myth of Mental Illness*, Secker & Warburg, London

Todd, Rt Hon. Lord (1968). *Report of the Royal Commission on Medical Education*, Cmnd 3569, HMSO, London

Wrong, D. (1961). The oversocialized conception of man in modern sociology, *Am. Sociol. Rev.*, **26**, 183–193

Znaniecki, F. (1940). *The Social Role of the Man of Knowledge*, Columbia University Press, New York

Index